HISTORY
AND
HISTORIANS
OF
POLITICAL
ECONOMY

HISTORY
AND
HISTORIANS
OF
POLITICAL
ECONOMY

Werner Stark
Edited by Charles M. A. Clark

Transaction Publishers
New Brunswick (U.S.A.) and London (U.K.)

Library of Congress Catalog Number: 93-18092
ISBN: 1-56000-108-9
Printed in the United States of America

Library of Congress Cataloging-in-Publication Data

Stark, Werner, 1909-
    History and historians of political economy/Werner Stark;
edited by Charles Michael Andres Clark.
    p.   cm.
    Includes bibliographical references and index.
    ISBN 1-56000-108-9
    1. Economics—Historiography. 2. Economic
history—Historiography. I. Clark, Charles Michael Andres. II.
Title.
    HB75.S6898   1994
    330'.09—dc20   93-18092
                                                                     CIP

Non ridere non lugere neque detestari sed intelligere
Spinoza, *Tractatus Politicus* I, 4.

Contents

Preface

Werner Stark was just a few months short of his thirtieth birthday when he began work on the book that is only now, five decades later, being offered to the public. By some strange coincidence, I was the same age when Doyle McCarthy first showed me the original manuscript which formed part of Werner Stark's papers, donated to Fordham University in 1989 by Kate Stark, Werner's widow. The manuscript was 200 single-spaced pages in length, with the ambiguous title *History and Historians of Political Economy*. With much assistance, the process of turning this frail manuscript into a "finished" monograph has finally come to an end.

The process started with the transfer of the text from a photocopy of Stark's manuscript into a user-friendly format—word processing. This arduous task was skillfully accomplished by Doris Berritto of St. John's University's word processing center. This work would still be a long way in the future had St. John's University, especially the good offices of Dean Laurence Mauer, not provided Berritto's great abilities to this project.

The next task was the editing of the manuscript. My overall editorial policy was to interfere as little as possible with Stark's original text—this is his book and not mine. I thus resisted as much as possible any temptation to augment or delete. However, Stark's translation from the original German (of which no copy could be

found) was often awkward and required some fixing, mostly in the
form of breaking-up overly complex sentences. The next step was the
checking of citations and quotations for accuracy. This task was quite
difficult for a number of reasons. First, I had to find the editions of
the works that Stark quoted. In finding these works I had the
assistance of Roberta Pessah, Eileen Kennedy, Eugene Orlowski, and
Marilyn Heidenfelder of St. John's University Library's Interlibrary
Loan Department. Unfortunately there were a few works that either
Stark had not left enough information in the text for us to find or that
we could not find a copy at a library willing to interlibrary loan it.
Quotations from English and French were checked for accuracy.
Quotations from other languages were checked for the accuracy of the
citation. No effort was made to check the compatibility of Stark's
translations with other now existing English translations. In the case
of quotations from Adam Smith and David Ricardo I have added the
citation to the definitive editions of their respective works. Stark's
habit of using foreign phrases, particularly from Latin, required some
translation. This I limited to those words or phrases which would not
be familiar to the average historian of ideas. For the Latin translations
I had the assistance of Eric Plumer of the University of Notre Dame.

The next step in the process was to modernize the method of citation
and to transfer Stark's endnotes into footnotes. Parenthetical citations
are now standard, at least in the history of economic thought, and it
was the method Stark had employed in the manuscript, however
incomplete his citations tended to be. The text was then put into the
style requirements of Transaction Publishers, with some adjustments
in the manuscript to increase the readability of the text. In this task
I had the most able assistance of Karen Stuppi my copyeditor at
Transaction.

One of the most time consuming and difficult tasks was the creation
of a bibliography. Stark original manuscript had a hand written list
of the major works in the history of economic thought; this included
eighteen books. Yet Stark quotes from or cites over two hundred
works in the manuscript. Great effort was made to provide the full
bibliographic citation, yet sadly there were a few works listed by Stark
that we could not track down, even with the adroit assistance of my
two graduate assistants; Charles Campbell and Chris Pryce.

Jacqueline Cox, modern archivist at King's College Library,

Cambridge University, provided invaluable assistance in accessing the Keynes-Stark correspondence mentioned in the introduction.

I must also thank my production editor Esther Luckett and Irving Horowitz of Transaction for their support and patience on this project. Madeline Engel of Lehman College, C.U.N.Y., and Robin Das of Fordham University, both provided information on Stark which helped to improve the quality of this work.

Most importantly, I must acknowledge and express my appreciation to E. Doyle McCarthy of Fordham University, who has been instrumental to this project at every stage.

Lastly I must thank Fordham University for their kind permission to publish this manuscript.

Introduction

In August of 1939, Werner Stark (1909-85) fled Czechoslovakia for the safety and intellectual freedom of Cambridge, England. Stark's research in this period (1939-44), while concentrated on the history of economic ideas, laid the foundation of his subsequent important contributions to the sociology of knowledge and social theory. It also won the admiration of many leading Cambridge economists, including Joan Robinson, Maurice Dobb, and, most significantly, John Maynard Keynes, who referred to Stark as "one of the most learned men on these matters [the history of economic thought] that I have ever come across."[1] Although Stark published many of the results of his research while at Cambridge (two books and many journal articles on the history of political economy), the centerpiece of his efforts was a manuscript entitled *History and Historians of Political Economy*, which is here being published in its original and complete form for the first time.

Stark's most significant and lasting contribution to scholarship is certainly his contribution to the sociology of knowledge, and it is in

---

1. Letter from John Maynard Keynes to Maurice Dobb, 24 January 1941, Keynes Collection, King's College Library, Cambridge. Unpublished writings of J.M. Keynes copyright The Provost and Scholars of King's College, Cambridge 1993.

this light that *History and Historians of Political Economy* should be seen. In *History and Historians of Political Economy* we not only have Stark's complete analysis of the history of economic thought, we see how the study of the history of economic ideas suggested to Stark the paramount influence of social and historical factors on the development of social theory. It was in studying the history of economic doctrines that convinced Stark of the fundamental place of the sociology of knowledge in the understanding of social ideas.

The publication of *History and Historians of Political Economy* is an important event in the study of the history of social ideas, particularly economic ideas, and, even though it has been more than fifty years since it was completed, the themes of this book are of surprisingly contemporary. The questions Stark raises: How should past theories be understood and explained? What is the relationship between ideas and events? Do economic theories reflect universal truths or relative ones? are as relevant, and as unsettled, today as they where when Stark undertook his analysis of the history of economic thought. In writing this book Stark became convinced of the relativity of economic doctrines and of the fundamental role played by social and historical context in the creation of social theory.

It is ironic that the history of economic thought should lead Stark to the sociology of knowledge. In the subsequent fifty years historians of economic thought have, for the most part, gone out of their way to separate economic theories from their social and historical context. This formalization of economic theory and historiography are coming under increasing criticism, further adding to the significance of *History and Historians of Political Economy*.

Werner Stark's Career

Werner Stark was born on 2 December 1909, in Marienbad, Bohemia to Adolf (a physician) and Jenny Stark. In 1928 he entered the University of Hamburg to study the social sciences where he received his Dr.rer.pol in 1934. Stark also attended the London School of Economics (1930-31), the University of Geneva (1933), and the University of Prague, where he received a Dr.jur. in 1936. Stark's dissertation, *Ursprung und Aufstieg des landwirtschaftlichen Gross betriebs in den bohmischen Landern* [Origin and Development of

Large-scale Agricultural Enterprise in Bohemia and Moravia], was in the field of economic history and reflected the general interest of the time in the question of the origins and essence of capitalism.

With the demise of democracy in Germany in 1934, Werner Stark moved to Prague, working first as a newspaper man and a bank clerk. Oskar Engländer invited him to write a book on social policy, and Stark was appointed to the Prague School of Political Science. Stark taught there until the German invasion of 1939, which prompted his move to England.[2]

After World War II, Stark obtained teaching positions at the University of Edinburgh, Scotland (1945-51), the University of Manchester, England (1951-63), and Fordham University (1963-1975). After his retirement from Fordham, Stark moved to Salzburg, Austria, where he was honorary professor at the University of Salzburg until his death in October 1985.

Stark is most noted for his contributions to sociology, including many works in social theory and the sociology of knowledge: *The Sociology of Knowledge* (1958, 1991), *Social Theory and Christian Thought* (1959), *Montesquieu: A Pioneer of the Sociology of Knowledge* (1960), and *The Fundamental Forms of Social Thought* (1962); in the sociology of religion: *The Sociology of Religion*, five volumes (1966-72); and Stark's six volume magnum opus, *The Social Bond* (1976-87), the last volume of which Stark sadly did not live to complete.

Stark in Cambridge

Almost all of Werner Stark's published works in the history of economic thought derive from his residency at Cambridge.[3] Stark lived at Cambridge from 1939 to 1944, yet his only official connection

---

2. In the correspondence between Keynes and Dobb it is suggested that Stark's fleeing the Nazis was prompted not only by his being Jewish, but also in his being wanted for harboring others who were hiding from the SS.

3. Stark did continue to publish articles in the field of the history of economic thought (Stark 1947, 1950, 1954, 1955, 1956, 1958, and 1959) yet these were mainly the result of ideas first developed, and often written, in this period.

to the university was as a guest lecture in economics in 1941-42. During this period, Stark was supported by a grant from the Society for the Protection of Science and Learning, an organization that helped many refugee scholars, supplemented by occasional income from writing and his work on the Bentham papers.

At Cambridge Stark found two essential ingredients that were to prove crucial for the continuation of his efforts: Cambridge's excellent library and John Maynard Keynes. The breath and depth of Stark's research in this period, which will be evident to all who read this volume, indicate the necessity of the former; knowledge of the hardships of the time tells us of the importance of the latter.

In "A Survey of My Scholarly Work" Stark (Engel 1975: 5) writes of how he became acquainted with Keynes.

> In order to prove as quickly as possible that I had a contribution to make to the culture into the midst of which my fate had propelled me, I decided to produce next an article rather than a book, and I chose as my topic "Jeremy Bentham as an Economist." I had always been interested in the history of economic thought for its own sake, and I had wondered for a long time why the great utilitarian philosopher, who was close to such outstanding economists as David Ricardo and John Stuart Mill and no mean economist himself had never been made the subject of a monograph. I submitted my paper to the prestigious *Economic Journal*, and it was immediately accepted. I was invited to visit the editor, J.M. Keynes, presently to become Lord Keynes, and was kindly and cordially received. Indeed, I gained in this great thinker a true friend.

Keynes not only had the University of Cambridge give Stark the opportunity to teach, he induced the Royal Economic Society to commission Stark to prepare a critical edition of Bentham's economic writings. Furthermore, when the Society for the Protection of Science and Learning wanted to cut Stark's grant (they wanted him to obtain work as a German or History teacher at a secondary school, which Stark, with no success, attempted to obtain) Keynes intervened, offering to fund half of the grant with his own money.[4]   Keynes

---

4. Keynes paid for half the grant (£14) until 1944, when Stark was drafted into the army. When the society wanted to terminate the grant completely, Keynes again intervened, offering to fully fund it. The society backed down and soon after Stark was employed in military intelligence. It is clear that Stark never knew of Keynes's

argued to the society that Stark was busy at work on many important scholarly projects, stating that Stark is "one of the half dozen most learned people going on his own subject, namely, the history and valuation of economic thought"[5] and suggesting that Stark could best contribute to society by pursuing his research. A true friend indeed!

The most significant published results of Stark's research at Cambridge are two books on the history of economic thought: *The Ideal Foundations of Economic Thought* (1943, 1975) and *The History of Economics in its Relation to Social Development* (1944). *The Ideal Foundations of Economic Thought* examines the influence of philosophical realism and philosophical nominalism, and the trend towards individualism and social atomism. These are issues that dominate Stark's later writings, not only in the sociology of knowledge, particularly in *The Fundamental Forms of Social Thought*, but also in his *The Social Bond*, where Stark's central concern is the conflict between individualism and community.

Just as *The Ideal Foundations of Economic Thought* emphasizes the importance of the theorist's vision of the ideal order in their formulating theories of the existing order, *The History of Economics in Relation to Social Development* underscores the important role of the existing material conditions on our creation of social theory. Together they represent the two areas of interest for the sociology of knowledge.

The History of Economics in Relation to Social Development is a revised version of the last chapter of *History and Historians of Political Economy*, which Stark had originally entitled "Economic History and Economic Theory" and which was finally given the title "The Material Contents of the History of Political Economy." In the preface to *The History of Economics*, Stark states that his essay is based on a much larger work.

> The form in which I present this essay to the public is not the one in which I first put it to paper. When I came to this country in August 1939, I began a critical investigation of all the books which have been written on the

---

extraordinary generosity (Keynes supported many other refugee scholars as well).

5. Letter from Keynes to the Society for the Protection of Science and Learning.

history of economic thought, in the order of their publication. . . . The result was a rather lengthy book in which the reader had to make his way through long disquisitions and discussions until the positive thesis of the author was reached. The work might have been very interesting for one who intended to write on the development of economics, but it would have heavily taxed the patience of those who only want to read about it.

Thus I came to the conclusion that it would be better for the propagation of my idea to put it forward in a positive and direct way, without carrying on a war of words with those who have cultivated the same field before me. If I have succeeded in proving my thesis, I have also succeeded in disproving theirs.

The reception of *The History of Economics* was generally favorable —it went through four editions and was translated into Italian, Japanese (four editions), German, and Spanish (two editions)—yet Stark did not have much of an impact on the study of the history of economic thought. This is so for a number of reasons. First, his book was released during the war, which limited the amount of attention it received from scholars. (Stark and Keynes in February of 1941 discussed delaying the release of Stark's book on the history of economics. It is likely that they were discussing *History and Historians of Political Economy* and not the revised and much shorter *History of Economics*. Keynes's argument was that since the subject matter was not of pressing interest, it would have a greater impact after the war, when scholars would not be so preoccupied.) The translations were much more widely reviewed than was the original.

Second, Stark was too optimistic regarding the belief that merely successfully presenting his thesis was all that was required. To influence historians of ideas, a war of words would be necessary. The most notable comments on *The History of Economics* came from George Stigler in an essay in the *American Economic Review* entitled "The Influence of Events and Policies on Economic Theory" (Stigler 1965). Stigler contended that environment has played no active role in the formation of economic doctrines, and uses Stark as an example of how erroneous this view is. Stigler writes:

An example both contemporary and extreme is afforded by W. Stark, who has said the 'modern economics immediately appears as a simple product of historical development, as a mirroring of the socio-economic reality within which it took its origin, not unlike the various theories which have preceded it.' Literally read, Stark seems to assert even that the growth of mechanization between 1817 and 1820 forced Ricardo to qualify the labor theory of value published in the former year (1965: 17).

Most subsequent historians of economic thought who mention Stark merely reiterate Stigler's comments (see Blaug 1962). By not publishing the full version of his work, which includes a penetrating critique of the approach to economic historiography advocated by Stigler and Blaug (and which came to dominate the field), Stark allows their critique to go unchallenged.

Third, and most significantly, the study of the history of economic thought has come under the influence (domination) of the philosophy of science and its religion of logical positivism. Historians of economics seem to suffer from the same physics envy that has driven economic theorists toward mathematical formalism and the imitation of the natural sciences. The emulation of the natural sciences by economic theorists required emptying economic theory of all historical and social context (Clark 1992); the influence of Karl Popper and the philosophy of science on economic historiography required the same separation of theory and reality. Yet, just as the exclusion of historical and social context from economic theory has lead to the "crisis in economic theory," historians are increasingly questioning the benefits of the application of the philosophy of science to the historiography of economics.

History and Historians of Political Economy

History and Historians of Political Economy is divided into two sections: "The Literature on the History of Political Economy" and "The Fundamental Problem: Reality and Ideas." The first section is an attempt to explain the beginnings of the history of economic thought and the two dominant approaches to the subject: the theoretical and the historical. Section two examines the relationship between phenomena and the explanation of phenomena—theory. Here Stark finds three approaches: the critical, the descriptive, and the explanatory. In the last chapter, Stark applies the explanatory method to various developments in the history of economic thought.

In the opening sentence Stark states his relativistic perspective:

The historiography of political economy, as a distinct study, is about a century old. It developed in France in opposition to the predominance of the rationalistic and liberal theories emanating from England that laid claim to unrestricted validity although they corresponded only to the capitalistic conditions of the rich island and were inapplicable to the still semifeudal continent. Thus, it sprang from the same root as all modern historiography: the overcoming of the absolute system of reason by the relativistic idea of development, the conquest of the Enlightenment by Romanticism. (3)

We see from the very start Stark's attention to historical and social context. In the first section Stark's analysis centers on the three central problems in the historiography of economic thought: the origins of economics as a science; the development of economic theory by stages in schools or by historical epochs; and the character of economics as a science, the separation of valid theorists from hacks. Starting with Eugen Dühring and Wilhelm Roscher, Stark finds two approaches to these questions: the historical approach and the theoretical approach.

The historical approach includes such historians as Roscher, Eisenhart, Ingram, Espinas, Spann, Haney, Gonnard, and Salin. After examining each of their respective analyses of the history of political economy from the perspective of the three central questions, Stark concludes:

[H]istoricism had hardly altered its character at all in the fifty years between Wilhelm Roscher and Edgar Salin. Its followers, with very few exceptions, gave the same answer to the three basic problems of the history of economic thought. The origin of political economy they are inclined to find in antiquity—in spite of the ever-present knowledge of the change of economic life they rarely perceived its entire change of character; the basis for the division of development they are inclined to seek in the great periods of cultural history, not in the small alterations in abstract theory, because the science of economics means to them only a part in the broad stream of evolution; and lastly as regards the delimitation of the field of investigation proper to economic science, they wish to comprehend and describe the whole reflection of the economic system in the human mind—for they are reluctant to divide what really belonged together. Behind all these ideas, however, is the great creed of the spirit born of romanticism that all life, however manifold its variety in space and time may appear, must be understood as a grand and indivisible unity. (57)

The theoretical approach is followed by Dühring, Cossa, Gide and

Rist, Schumpeter, Boucke, Bousquet, and Roll. In contrast to the historical approach, the theoretical approach dates the origins of economic science in the eighteenth century, either with Cantillon, Quesnay, or Smith, because, as Stark states, "the conception is dominant that economic theory is a systematic science and cannot therefore be conceived before the appearance of a system of ideas, before the breakthrough of the idea of system" (111-12). The development of political economy is divided by schools "because the theoreticians direct all their attention to the doctrines and therefore the diversity in particulars impresses their minds more strongly than the unity in general" (112). As to the character of economic science, the theoretical approach is based on the view that true economics emulates the natural sciences, and thus they concentrate on a narrow range of phenomena in search for eternal truths.

Stark concludes the first section of *History and Historians of Political Economy* with his own answers to the three basic questions of the historiography of political economy. Stark states, "*Viewed historically, political economy is the doctrine of the order dominant in exchange economy*" (115 emphasis in the original). To this statement Stark adds this footnote:

The theoreticians who stand in the Lausanne tradition will probably reject this description. They base their deductions as a rule on two concepts that seem to be timeless: scarcity and choice between alternative uses of scarce means. In this sense Robbins says in his *Essay on the Nature and Significance of Economic Science* (1937: 16): "Economics is the science which studies human behaviour as a relationship between ends and scarce means which have alternative uses." This definition seems to exclude the restriction of the science to a certain economic order. . . . Now, man is of course always confronted with the scarcity of provision. Without it there would be not only no economy but also no culture. Human behavior in this situation and toward this situation, however, is totally different in different social systems. The *homo oeconomicus* studied by the classicists and neoclassicists is only one form of the *homo rationalis* typical of modern times. (Even the famous Robinson Crusoe is only the man of modern society in isolation, not some isolated man—such a one cannot exist and least of all as a being capable of reasonable choice.) In the organized or natural economy of the past the *homo traditionalis* was the dominant type. To him the same rules cannot be applicable as to his much younger brother. The view of the theoreticians of the Lausanne tradition is itself characteristic of the mentality of modern man: he is so imbued with rationalism that he cannot understand how homo sapiens can possibly have acted in the struggle

for existence otherwise than reasonably. Yet there were thousands of years
between Totem and Tabu. (115, note 2)

Thus, for Stark the origins of political economy can only be found
with the appearance of the market economy, something that starts to
happen in the sixteenth century. As for stages of development, Stark
finds four, with each stage being linked to another branch of
knowledge. The first stage comprises the mercantilists and is linked
to jurisprudence. The second stage consists of Quesnay, Smith, and
the early classical economists. This stage is linked to deism and
natural law philosophy. The third stage comes as a reaction to the
second; it reflects on history and evolution, and includes Müller,
Sismondi, and Marx. The fourth stage is the emulation of the exact
sciences and comprises neoclassical economic theory.   After
establishing the stages of development, Stark sets out to investigate the
internal dynamics that brought such a history about. This is the
material for the second section.

The central problem for the historiography of any discipline is the
relationship between reality and theory, between that which is to be
explained and the explanation. This problem is further complicated in
the social sciences because both the reality and the theories that try to
explain that reality are social creations. According to Stark there have
been three approaches to the historiography of political economy: the
critical, the descriptive, and the explanatory.

The Critical Approach

The critical approach rejects any notions of causality between
economic phenomena and economic ideas. This approach takes as its
basic premise that the history of ideas should be judged from the
perspective of what is the currently accepted dogma, the view of the
development of the discipline being that of the progressive realization
of absolute truths. For Stark this is the approach of Dühring, Ferrara,
Marx (although Marx occasionally breaks from this perspective into
the sociology of knowledge), Rambaud, Spann, Gide and Rist, and
most importantly Schumpeter. Stark's analysis is from 1939-41 and
thus is based on Schumpeter's *Epochen der Dogmen - und
Methodengeschichte* [Economic Doctrine and Method] and not the
more famous and extensive *History of Economic Analysis*. Stark

wrote a lengthy review of *History of Economic Analysis* (Stark 1955), in which he notes that Schumpeter has in essence not deviated from his original position, for the *History of Economic Analysis* is very much the history of the discovery and development of the concept of general equilibrium, which for Schumpeter is the most fundamental problem for the economic theorist. Schumpeter (1954: 969) writes:

> [F]rom the standpoint of any exact science, the existence of a "uniquely determined equilibrium (set of values)" is . . . of utmost importance, even if proof has to be purchased at the price of very restrictive assumptions; without any possibility of proving the existence of uniquely determined equilibrium . . . at however high a level of abstraction, a field of phenomena is really a chaos that is not under analytic control.

Thus, the development of economic analysis is, for Schumpeter, the development of tools for the purpose of explicating general equilibrium. The fallacy of Schumpeter's approach, which is the dominant one in current history of economic thought scholarship, is summed up succinctly by Stark in the following passage (149):

> In the final paragraph of his historical investigation Schumpeter openly asserted the essential equality of all theories heretofore propounded. "Fundamentally the physiocrats already aimed at what we aim at today, and if we concentrate on the matter and not on the form given to it, it is often difficult to find in a vehemently worded contest a correspondingly sharp expression of the objective differences" (1914: 124). Certainly Quesnay wished to fathom the character of national economy in the same way as did Marshall—just as Ptolemy and Copernicus were united in the endeavor to penetrate the laws of the universe. But nature is immutable, and society is constantly changing; so a scientific history of theoretical economics can only be built on the idea of evolution, on the idea of historical relativism, which is foreign to Schumpeter's rationalist thought.

The critical approach typically notes the mistakes and improvements in the development of political economy, with the measuring rod being contemporary theory. Thus, the development of economic theory is seen as a mere intellectual exercise, independent of the developments in the actual economy, the rationalist pursuit of absolute truths. As Stark so clearly shows, followers of the critical approach are more often interested in demonstrating the validity of their theoretical perspective than in understanding the ideas of the past, a point which is as true of Marx as it is for Schumpeter.

The Descriptive Approach

The descriptive approach also eschews causality, yet unlike the critical approach, they reframe from judging past theories from the perspective of the present. Their aim is to depict the views of the past as honestly and faithfully as possible. This could be done by relating the development of political economy to the history of ideas or to social and economic history, but no attempt is made to explain any causality between them. The historians who fall into this category are: Espinas, Gonnard, Salin, Boucke, Bousquet, and Cossa. Stark concludes that this approach typically conveys "more an idea of the atmosphere in which the theories have formed themselves than of the roots from which they have sprung" (197).

The Explanatory Approach

The underlying question for the historian of the explanatory approach is how and why particular theories arise. This approach is based on "the conviction that the economic ideas must be understood as the natural products of the real and ideal order of society and economy of their time" (137), and their efforts are an attempt to "try to explain all ideas with reference to the period of their origin" (199). Representatives of this approach are Ingram, Haney, Scott, and Roll. The approach is nicely summarized by Ingram:

> The history of Political Economy must be distinguished from the economic history of mankind. . . . But these two branches of research, though distinct, yet stand in the closest relation to each other; the rise and the form of economic doctrines have been largely conditioned by the practical situation, needs and tendencies of the corresponding epochs. (1915: 2)

It is in the explanatory approach that we find the seeds of Stark's *Sociology of Knowledge* (1958b, 1991).

Following Richard Rorty (1984) we can distinguish four genres of the historiography of ideas: rational reconstruction, the attempt to understand past theorists as contemporaries; historical reconstruction, which attempts to understand theories and theorists on their own terms; *Geistesgeschichte* "(literally, 'history of the spirit'), which tries to identify the central question that past thinkers have posed and to show how they came to be central to their systems of thought" (Blaug 1990: 27); and doxography, which views the theoretical development from the perspective of current theories, reformulating their ideas so that they agree with ours. Stark's bearing on contemporary issues in the historiography of ideas becomes apparent once the connections between the critical approach and rational reconstruction and doxography and the descriptive approach and historical reconstruction are made.

Rorty's argument was that what was needed is "better contextualist historical reconstructions on the one hand, and more self-confident *Geistesgeschichte* on the other" (Rorty 1984: 63). Rorty notes that *Geistesgeschichte* is a synthesis of aspects of rational reconstruction and historical reconstruction. This approach to the history of philosophical ideas is advocated by Rorty because of the essential differences between philosophy and the natural sciences. This difference between the natural and social sciences, between a reality man finds and a reality man creates, is at the heart of Stark's work in the history of ideas. Stark's explanatory approach, which is fully developed in his *Sociology of Knowledge*, is very similar to Rorty's *Geistesgeschichte* in its attempted synthesis of the critical and descriptive approaches, its being based on the claim that the social sciences are different in essence from the natural, and most importantly, in its position that social theories are social phenomena, to be explained and understood in their social and historical context.

References

Blaug, Marc. 1962. *Economic Theory in Retrospect*. Homewood, Ill.: Richard D. Irwin, Inc.

———. 1990. On the Historiography of Economics. *Journal of the History of Economic Thought* 12:27-37.

Clark, Charles M. A. 1992. *Economic Theory and Natural Philosophy*. Aldershot: Edward Elgar.

Engel, Madeline H. Ed. 1975. *The Sociological Writings of Werner Stark: Bibliography and Selected Annotations*. Privately printed.

Rorty, Richard. 1984. The Historiography of Philosophy: Four Genres. In *Philosophy in History*. Edited by Richard Rorty, J. B. Schneewind and Quentin Skinner. Cambridge: Cambridge University Press.

Schumpeter, Joseph. 1914. *Epochen der Dogmen - und Methodengeschichte.* Tübingen, Germany: J.C.B. Mohr.

——. 1954. *History of Economic Analysis.* New York: Oxford University Press.

Stark, Werner. 1943. *The Ideal Foundations of Economic Thought.* London: Kegan Paul, Trench, Trubner & Co.; Clifton, N.J.: Kelley, 1975.

——. 1944. *The History of Economics in its Relation to Social Development.* London: Kegan Paul, Trench, Trubner & Co.

——. 1947. Diminishing Utility Reconsidered. *Kyklos* 1:321-44.

——. 1950. Stable Equilibrium Re-examined. *Kyklos* 4:218-32.

——. 1955. Joseph Schumpeters Umwertung der Werte. *Kyklos* 9:225-47.

——. 1956. *The Contained Economy: An Interpretation of Medieval Economic Thought.* Aquinas Paper no. 26.

——. 1958a. die Dogmengeschichte der Volkswirtschaftslehre im Lichte des Pragmatismus (The History of Economic Doctrines in the Light of Pragmatism). *Kyklos* 11:425-30.

——. 1958b. *The Sociology of Knowledge. An Essay in Aid of a Deeper Understanding of the History of Ideas.* London: Routledge & Kegan Paul; New Brunswick, N.J.: Transaction Publishers 1991.

——. 1959. 'The Classical Situation' in Political Economy. *Kyklos* 12:57-65.

——. 1960. *Montesquieu: Pioneer of the Sociology of Knowledge.* London: Routledge & Kegan Paul.

——. 1962. *The Fundamental Forms of Social Thought.* London: Routledge & Kegan Paul; New York: Fordham University Press.

——. 1966-1972. *The Sociology of Religion.* 5 vol. London: Routledge & Kegan Paul; New York: Fordham University Press.

——. 1976-87. *The Social Bond.* 6 vol. New York: Fordham University Press.

Stigler, George. 1965. The Influence of Events and Policies on Economic Theory. In *Essays in the History of Economics.* Chicago: The University of Chicago Press.

I

The Literature on the History of Political Economy

1

The Beginnings

The historiography of political economy, as a distinct study, is about a century old. It developed in France in opposition to the predominance of the rationalistic and liberal theories emanating from England that laid claim to unrestricted validity although they corresponded only to the capitalistic conditions of the rich island and were inapplicable to the still semifeudal continent. Thus, it sprang from the same root as all modern historiography: the overcoming of the absolutistic system of reason by the relativistic idea of development, the conquest of the Enlightenment by romanticism.

The originally antirationalistic,[1] romantic, character of the historiography of political economy is manifest in the first two works devoted to it: Jérôme-Adolphe Blanqui's *Histoire de l'Economie Politique en Europe* (1837-38) and Albert de Villeneuve-Bargemont's

---

1. What the rationalists thought of the value of a historical treatment of the development of political economy is shown by a remark of J. B. Say in his *Cours complet d'economie politique pratique* (1840: 561): "What could we gain by recollecting absurd opinions, doctrines that are discredited and deserve to be so? It would be at the same time useless and irksome to exhume them." This is a point of view that can only be adopted by a man who is convinced that there is an eternal truth, and that he holds it!

Histoire de l'Economie Politique (1841). Both Blanqui and Villeneuve considered it their task to oppose the school of Adam Smith. What Blanqui envisaged was a French political economy in contrast to the English one, a doctrine to which the heart and not the reason should have given birth. Villeneuve wished to confront the areligious economic theory across the Channel with a Christian doctrine. Consequently the aim of both books is dogmatic, not historical; their purpose was less to show how political economy had developed in the past than how it was to be developed in the future.

Important progress beyond this stage of thought was made by the next two works: Travers Twiss's *View of the Progress of Political Economy in Europe* (1847) and Julius Kautz's *Geschichtliche Entwicklung der National-Oekonomik und ihrer Literatur* (1860), whose approach to the development of economic science was purely historical. Their authors, however, failed to find a suitable viewpoint from which to impartially survey the field they were trying to describe; they lacked the necessary sense of proportion for us to acclaim them as the founders of our science. It was Eugen Dühring and Wilhelm Roscher who laid the foundations on which all subsequent students of this subject have built.

Eugen Dühring and Wilhelm Roscher! The contrast between these two men symbolizes, as it were, the inner contradiction of the nineteenth century. Roscher was a child of German romanticism and idealism; his learning was based on philology and history. Dühring was a representative of international positivism and materialism; his thought centered on philosophy and mechanics. Roscher wished to study the past in order to understand the present; Dühring wished to understand the present in order to mould the future. Roscher strove to perceive the laws of development by observing the changing life; Dühring endeavored to understand the essence of their nature through spiritual penetration of the lasting phenomena. Roscher was endowed with a keen appreciation of all the trivialities of life; Dühring was concerned with the ultimate problems of existence. Consequently, Roscher's works are characterized by the exhausting breadth of their description, Dühring's writings by the concentrated sharpness of their thought.[2] Even the characters of the two men formed a striking

---

2. It is impossible to dismiss Dühring simply as "muddleheaded," as Roll does (1938: 12). Schumpeter's favorable judgement is not unjustified (1914: 20). Even Schmoller

contrast.   Roscher was a modest scholar, conservative, full of understanding for all developments and ideas, aloof from public strife, but fond of social intercourse; Dühring was an ardent controversialist, a reformer, full of hatred and scorn toward all opposed views, involved in innumerable polemics, a thorough individualist.   Roscher died, highly honored, the master of three generations of scholars; Dühring ended his life rejected and despised, a forgotten relic of times long past.   Yet he had not deserved such a fate.   If Schmoller could call Roscher the universally educated historian of culture among political economists (Schmoller 1888: 152), Dühring might with equal aptness be described as the scientifically educated natural scientist in their ranks.

Wilhelm Roscher (1817-1894) set out to transform the deductive and abstract economics of Ricardo and Rau into an inductive and concrete science.   Coming from the famous school of the historians of culture at Goettingen, he was not satisfied with the rationalistic and mechanistic view of economic life that the English classics had sketched, and aimed at an organic and sociological treatment.   In his *System der Volkswirtschaft* (1854-94) he tried to fulfill the program that, at the age of twenty-six, he had outlined in his *Grundriss zu Vorlesungen über die Staatswirthschaft nach geschichtlicher Methode* (1843).   In the preface to this manifesto of historicism in political economy, he declared four considerations to be essential:

1. The sociological consideration.   The subject matter of investigation should be not only economic wealth, but also political man.   For this it is necessary to outline what the people thought about economic life and what they willed in it, what ends they set for themselves and what results they achieved, and what reasons lay behind their aims as well as their achievements.   This can be accomplished only in close collaboration with all the other sciences of national life, above all with those of law, politics, and culture.
2. The historical consideration.   A nation is more than the sum total of the individuals alive at one time.   It has roots in the past and lives on into the future.   Anyone, therefore, who desires to study national economy as the economy of a nation must not be content with a knowledge of the present.

---

who did not appreciate Dühring, and whom Dühring hated, said: "Dühring is a highly gifted philosopher . . . originally perhaps more profound and of greater talents than Roscher," and this is saying much (Schmoller 1888: 162 et seq.).

3. The comparative consideration. In order to single out from the mass of facts what is essential and regularly recurring, all peoples must be compared with one another, and at the various stages of their development.
4. The relativistic consideration. The leading string of the child is as improper for the man as the crutch of the old. Science is not simply to praise or to blame the phenomena of economic life, but to understand their *raison d'être*.

With this "historico-physiological method" conceived in the vein of Savigny and Eichhorn and reminiscent of Comte, Ranke, Gervinus, and Hegel, Roscher wished to create an anatomy and physiology of national economy. But what he envisaged as his final aim was a kind of idealistic philosophy of history, based on economics. He saw the development of man over the centuries as a sequence of necessary stages, through which he has passed according to definite laws. It is not without reason therefore that Schmoller compares him with Montesquieu, Herder, Buckle, and Ritter.

While in this way Roscher sought to bring political economy as a descriptive study into the sphere of history, Dühring endeavored to relate it as a theoretical subject to the natural sciences. He, too, approached economic theory with solid philosophical convictions, but he was a philosopher of nature, not of history. This blind thinker tried during his long life (1833-1921) not only to solve the problems of society, but also the problems of the universe. His first publications, the *Natürliche Dialektik* and the *Der Werth des Lebens* (1865), brought Comte's positivism to Germany. The *Kritische Geschichte der Philosophie* (1869) and the *Kritische Geschichte der allgemeinen Principien der Mechanik* (1873) discussed and refuted the views of his predecessors. Finally, his monistic and materialistic interpretation of life, which considers the task of philosophy to be solely the increase of our knowledge of reality, is fully developed in the three works of his maturity, the names of which indicate their character: *Kursus der Philosophie als streng wissenschaftlicher Weltanschauung* (1875), *Der Ersatz der Religion durch Vollkommeneres* (1882), and *Wirklichkeitsphilosophie* (1895). A whole world lies between this rationalistic sobriety and the metaphysical enthusiasm of romanticism.

Dühring's position in the history of economic thought may best be defined by calling him the last disciple of Adam Smith. His direct inspiration, indeed, was Henry Carey whom he revered as his master; but what he advocated was a return to the fundamental tenets of the great Scotsman, and in particular to his desire for a causal explanation of the economic phenomena, which had been neglected by historicism with its purely documentary erudition. His *Kritische Grundlegung der Volkswirtschaftslehre* (1866), and later his *Cursus der National-und Sozialökonomie* (1873), which show his theoretical leanings, closed the broad gap between the work of Mill and the work of Jevons and Menger, and served as a bridge from the classical to the neoclassical doctrine.

What Dühring had in mind was a sound synthesis between inductive preparation and rational analysis of the matter of science, an equilibrium between descriptive representation and theoretical explanation of the economic phenomena and processes. The observation of facts, however, he regarded only as a necessary preliminary, and not as an end in itself, and his view of it was nearer to that of Quetelet than to that of Schmoller: on the basis of a theoretical formulation of the question, exact information should be obtained, information on the relative importance and magnitude of the essential phenomena, capable of forming the foundation for further deduction. It should lead up to the theory explaining the variety of life in the section under observation, to the real task of the economic theoretician. Dühring, as he himself puts it, aimed at "the connection of the exact means of quantitative statements with the speculation on the possible reasons of the phenomena" (Albrecht 1925: 755)—a methodological aim, rare in the age of historicism.

In opposition to the dominant ideas of his time, Eugen Dühring believed in the existence of economic laws in the sense of generally valid regularities for the economic activities of men, and hence in the possibility of scientific truths valid "not only for a certain region and for a certain period, but for the historical and geographical connex in its broadest extent." This is a consequence of the persuasion that human nature is unchangeable. Dühring indeed neatly distinguishes between "natural economic laws" (production), which have their basis in necessities of the constitution of nature, and "social norms" (distribution), which originate in interhuman relations. But even the social norms he does not regard as subject to historical relativity. Characteristic are his remarks on the "social law of free competition," which may be considered as the prototype of a social norm.

> A certain competition is a typical feature of all human endeavor. . . . Man
> in society . . . always represents a force which presses on the collateral
> forces or is pressed by them. . . . In social struggle the atoms repel one
> another in one respect, while in another regard they strive together towards
> the same aim. (Dühring 1900: 759)

In this sense Dühring associates self-interest as the instinct of self-promotion with the instinct of self-preservation and represents it as natural to man: everywhere the language and spirit of the natural sciences, nowhere a trace of historicism!

It was only natural that men so fundamentally different as Roscher and Dühring should have produced fundamentally different works on the development of political economy. As Schmoller strikingly remarked (1888: 163), Dühring wrote as a philosopher, Roscher as a philologist. But better still the contrast is described by the assertion that Roscher approached the past as a historian, Dühring as a theoretician. The history of any thought can obviously be treated either from the historical or from the dogmatic point of view: each dogma, put into words, is an expression of a time and an embodiment of a science. Roscher saw more the one, Dühring more the other side of the coin, the ideal description of which is only attained by a full account of both.

But Roscher and Dühring not only show us the two different approaches to the problem—they represent, at the same time, the two possibilities of its solution, which have hitherto been offered by literature: Roscher the relativistic and descriptive representation of the historical school, Dühring the absolutistic and critical conception of classicism and postclassicism. As the political economy of the twentieth century arose from a synthesis of the inductively investigating and deductively theorizing tendencies, the whole historiography of economic science may be divided into two great groups: that which is predominantly historical and that which is predominantly theoretical. The one originates with Roscher, the other with Dühring.

Now three problems are of outstanding importance in the historiography of political economy and may serve as a test for the judgment and classification of every single work: the problems of the origin, the development, and the character of the science.

The problem of the origin arises in the development of any science, but it is especially intricate in political economy. Never was a paternity more hotly contested than this: Socrates and Aristotle, Bodinus and Serra, Monchretien and Petty, Cantillon and Carl, Quesnay, Smith, and Ricardo have been named as the founders of our science, and if it is but a matter of opinion whether Serra was more important than Monchretien or Quesnay than Cantillon, a basic decision must at least be reached as to whether economic science arose in ancient or modern times. That even on this elementary matter no unity has hitherto been established indicates a difficult question of principle.

The problem of the development of political economy arises from the fact that history is not simply a sequence in time of essentially independent arbitrary acts, but a process penetrated by strict regularity, which takes place in definite stages or phases. It is the perception of these phases—we call them sections or periods—that is the issue. The rhythm of development is hidden behind the manifold complexities of life, and it is not easy to discern its outlines. Here a second fundamental decision must be made: is it the rise and fall of a few general ideas or the change of many individual systems of thought that constitutes the essence of evolution? In other words: should we group the thinkers of the past according to ages or according to schools? Only when this question has been answered can we proceed to the further problem of how the different general ideas or individual systems of thought are to be distinguished.

Last but not least there arises the problem of the character of political economy. In every period there is a wide range of ideas on economic life, from the primitive concepts of the man in the street to the overrefined theories of the Paretos and Edgeworths. Where is the line of division between science and popular ideas? Even he who does not answer this question explicitly must implicitly make up his mind how the answer should run if he wishes to write a history of political economy. And here also one is confronted with a decision in principle: is the scope of the historian's investigation to be wide or narrow? Looking at the present it may be easy enough to separate the corn from the chaff, but looking at the past all seems closely connected; abstract thinkers and primitive talkers, however much we may divide them, are still bound together because they have drawn from a common source—the age in which they lived.

The whole contrast between Roscher and Dühring, and that is between the historical and the theoretical concept of the history of political economy, will be clear only when we examine their works with reference to these three problems. On each point the views of these two men were diametrically opposed, and between those who have carried on their task the old combat has not, to this day, been fought to an end.

On the problem of the origin of political economy Roscher expressed himself in the preface to his main work, *Geschichte der NationalÖkonomik in Deutschland* (1874). For him "the beginnings of the Political Economy of a people lie where its scientific minds first begin to reflect seriously and zealously on economic problems" (1874: vi). Now Roscher is not the man to give the words "problems of political economy" an exact meaning. To him political economy means simply economy and so it is not surprising that (after a short discussion of the canon and Germanic law of the Middle Ages) he begins his considerations with humanists and reformers. In view of this procedure it will be allowable and even necessary to inquire whether the humanists and reformers were in fact the first who "seriously and zealously" reflected on economic problems (in the indistinct sense in which Roscher uses this expression). If Roscher takes the elector August I of Saxony into his *Geschichte der NationalÖkonomik*, why not also Charlemagne or Charles IV who—as every one knows—were more important as "public economists" than that territorial prince? The reason is—and we do no wrong to Roscher by suggesting it—that he wished to treat only modern times (or rather, the time after 1492, because to the critical mind the notion of modernity means something different in economic development than in political history). His work forms part of a collection entitled "Geschichte der Wissenschaften in Deutschland; Neuere Zeit." So it is not internal, but only an external reason that determined Roscher to open his considerations with humanists and reformers, who in our science cannot claim any epoch-making importance.

Where Roscher looked for the first origin of political economy is manifest in his study *Über das Verhältnis der National-Oekonomik zum klassischen Alterthume*, written in 1849. In it he discusses Say's opinion that the ancients possessed no clear ideas of the essence, formation, distribution, and consumption of wealth, and, repudiating this view, he follows Blanqui, who believed that the beginnings of economic science could be found with the Greeks. "I mention first of all the sublime name of Thukydides," he says[3] "and confess in reverence and gratitude that, even on economic matters, I have not learnt more from any later man than from him." And he speaks of a "Hellenic Science of National Economy" without noticing that this expression contains a contradiction in terms, for beyond the domestic economies of Greek antiquity only single-town economies were formed, not an all-Hellenic national economy. Such a concept of the ancient origin of political economy may rest on a double error. First, there is a mistaken idea of the character and task of our science. Not every utterance on economic matters is political economy. The proper object is the study of the hidden laws that govern the (capitalistic) market economy based on a fully developed division of labor, as it has arisen in modern times. On the other hand, the wrong conception may prevail, that—in spite of some differences—the ancient economy was on the whole of the same nature as the modern, so that both represent an identical object of cognition, while in reality the old domestic economy is distinct from modern national economy in its most essential characteristics.

Both these errors dominated Roscher's train of thought. Not only was his notion of economic science very vague but he lacked also a clear understanding of the contrast between the ancient and modern economic systems. He enumerates, it is true, some distinguishing features: the institution of slavery, the small importance of capital in production as compared with nature and labor, the low development of industry, the almost complete absence of credit in ancient times, and so forth. But he does not perceive that the economic orders in question are different types of essence: the one natural economy, the other market economy; the one domestic economy, the other national economy. The greatest weakness of historicism comes to light here: the inability to advance from the variety of experience to the unity of concept, a weakness that has not only marred their theoretical work,

---

3. I quote from *Ansichten der Volkswirtschaft aus dem geschichtlichen Standpunkte*, 3d. ed (1878: 7).

but also impeded their historical studies, and has only been overcome by Max Weber's historico-sociological typology.

That Roscher decided in favor of the ancient origin of political economy is to be explained by his adherence to Hegel and romanticism. He who conceives all as an emanation of a continually changing national spirit must look for an economic science wherever the national spirit manifests itself, in the remotest past as well as in the immediate present. That the ideas vary so greatly in their substance through the centuries cannot prevent him from regarding them as *one* science, for each perception is to his mind valid only relatively to the time and space of its birth.

As the national spirit permeates and dominates all the cultural phenomena of a period, it is necessary to conceive and represent each epoch as a unity. The doctrinal discussions of the past, however loudly and passionately the struggle may have been waged, must not conceal the fact that all contemporaries were in the last analysis subject to one idea. It is these unifying ideas that must be found. Their mutual delimitation—of the visible forms of the absolute spirit following one another—helps identify the periodization of the development of economic thought.

Starting from such considerations Roscher divided his material, comprising five centuries, into three sections, each covering a different age of German economics:[4] theologico-humanistic, politico-cameralistic, and scientific. Roscher does not disclose what basic idea

---

4. It seems, however, that Roscher regarded this division of the subject matter correct only for a work treating solely German thinkers and thoughts. A general history of political economy he would perhaps have formed differently. "Even today one will not be fundamentally in error," he says (Roscher 1874: 593 et seq.), "in dividing the whole history of economic thought into two main parts: before and since Adam Smith; so that all the earlier ideas appear as a preparation for his work, all the later as a continuation of, or opposition to, his work." It may be surprising to find this view expressed by a man who founded a school, which, as exemplified by Bruno Hildebrand, made the attack on Smithianism its main task; but it is understandable if we take into consideration that Smith was the most realistic of all the theoreticians of liberalism, Roscher the most liberal of all the followers of realism, that a certain sympathy between them was founded in their very characters; moreover it must be remembered that Roscher was much too much a child of his time to escape from the influence of Smith whose "industrial system" was almost as applicable to the Germany of 1854 as to the England of 1776.

is behind this division, but in the denomination of the three periods his leading motive may be discerned. In the theologico-humanistic age, reaching from the renaissance to the end of the Thirty Years War, the "spiritual leaders of German national economy," whose ideas Roscher wishes to represent (1874: v), approached "the object of their mission" either from the theological or from the ethical side. In doing so, however, they were, as we may critically observe, theologians or philosophers rather than economists for whom there can be but one point of view: the immanent one. Even Roscher seems to have dimly realized this, for, with a flash of true insight, he quotes Lorenz von Stein's conviction with approval that "Political Economy proper starts only where national economy becomes an object of public activities . . . and serves to provide arguments and aims for these public activities" (1874: 231)—in mercantilism. This marks the second period of development. The economic science of the "politico-cameralistic age," which, according to Roscher, extends from the end of the Thirty Years War to the age of Frederic the Great, is characterized by its habit of regarding its problems from the political point of view and solving them in the interests of the state. In the "scientific age of German economics," however, the aim is neither to teach economic ethics nor to motivate economic politics, but simply to seek the truth. Its basis is neither moral theology nor political ideology, but solely the thirst for knowledge, the will to scientific penetration.

That the idea just described led to the threefold division adopted by Roscher is shown by his account of the position of mercantilism in the development of thought. He says:

> While the scholastic doctrine of economics considered properly only the economically active individual and that in regard of his conscience, while the newer cosmopolitan economics again has a great inclination to consider only the individuals and that in regard to their interest; the mercantilistic system is the origin of the economic treatment of the people. According to it, each nation, or more exactly each state, must fully unfold its economic forces. (1874: 232)

A secondary motive for Roscher's adoption of this scheme was probably his conception that the development of economic thought is essentially a progress that is accomplished in three stages. In his little treatise *Zur Geschichte der englischen Volkswirthschaftslehre* (1851) he compares the growth of science with the growth of man. Characteristic of the romantic interpretation of the world and life, he says,

> During the Middle Ages proper the English came no nearer than any other of the newer nations to developing a system of political science. Obviously for the same reason for which the Greeks achieved it only after Pericles. To perform great deeds, to create beautiful works of art, even youth is able,—but for systematic reflection thereon a maturity of spirit is indispensable which in peoples as well as in individuals is formed only in later life. And the systems of political economy are usually still younger than those of . . . higher politics, just as scientific research explored the movement of the heavenly bodies much earlier than the simple processes of cooking.

No great advance was made in this respect in early modern times, that is, the period between 1492 and 1648. Only the politico-cameralistic age made, in contrast to the theologico-humanistic, definite progress toward the independence of the ideas concerned with national economy: "The childish dependence of Political Economy on theology or jurisprudence diminishes, the science of national economy is studied for itself and by men who see in it their life-work, and therefore it becomes more and more systematic" (1874: 235). And in the same direction lies the progress that led later to the "scientific epoch." Turgot was to Roscher's mind the pioneer who first succeeded in separating political economy "from its informal fusion with natural law, politics etc." (1874: 481), and this fact combined with the labors of Quesnay "to direct the science to the investigation of the unchangeable physico-moral laws of nature which are at the base of all social life" is for him the reason for regarding the physiocrats as the initiators of a new era in the development of economic science.

If this last utterance clearly shows that Roscher stood partly under the influence of the eighteenth century—an influence from which even Hegel, who admired Say and Ricardo, not Müller and Gentz, did not escape—his view of the scope of political economy proves him a genuine romanticist. If the national spirit lives in and behind all social ideas, why draw an artificial line of demarcation between science and the general opinions of the time? The historian must regard all phenomena of life in the same way, be they high or low, and his task is fulfilled only if he has sketched an exhaustive picture of the past. So thought such men as Roscher.

To an age, however, in which this view no longer survives, the breadth of Roscher's description must appear as a great defect. Does not the decisive mistake of Roscher's work (and of historicism in general) lie in the lack of clear concepts that is manifested at every step? Roscher wishes to write a history of political economy, but in reality he gives a medley of the most varied utterances on economic matters, which often cannot be brought within the confines of science, and still less into the frame of political economy. He starts with "great economic authorities" (1874: 18), which we are amazed to see treated as such: Heinrich von Langenstein and Heinrich von Hoyta, whose scattered remarks on economic questions are perhaps not without interest but which are moral reasonings or at best moral theology rather than social science. And in this way he proceeds, bringing in Celtes and Wimpheling, Erasmus and Luther, Thomasius and Wolff, Wieland and Hegel, Joseph II and Frederic II! If Roscher accused Marperger of "having acted senselessly" in "including in the essay 'Erstes Hundert gelehrter Kaufleute' (1717) even men like Solon, Thales, Socrates, Platon, Mohamed" (1874: 569), this reproach may with greater justice be made against him than against the old Marperger, who had not, like him, undertaken to write a scientific history of political economy.

Roscher knows only one principle of selection and limitation: the national one, and this principle—as Roscher himself realized—is not justified in itself. His book was published in a series entitled "Geschichte der Wissenschaften in Deutschland" and it was probably for that reason that he confined his study to Germany. For the man who wished to derive his principles from the observation of reality, however, it was clear that the internationality of modern development and therewith of modern economics demanded a comprehensive treatment.

> The Germanic and Romance nations are bound together in a thousand ways so that most of their evolutions are common and are only executed earlier, more strongly, more happily, with one people than with the other. . . . We must therefore, in order really to understand our subject-matter, always take into account the literature of that foreign nation which at the time is the center of gravity: that is to say now the Italian, now the French, especially however the English. (Roscher 1874: vi)

Yet, in spite of this point of view—correct on the whole—the concentration on Germany is the only limitation to which Roscher submits. No wonder that his work extends to almost 1100 pages! One has to agree with Ingram that it is a "marvelous monument of erudition and industry" (Ingram 1915: 201). It is in a certain sense the principal work of Wilhelm Roscher who spent fifteen years, a quarter of his active life, on it. But one must not fail to note the critical implication of that praise: erudition and industry, learning and diligence, are not yet science, and without clearness as to the basic concepts of political economy no history of this science can possibly be written.

It is evidence of the fact that Roscher had no clear idea of the true essence and tasks of economic theory, that he speaks of a "price theory" of Luther, that in his view utterances of Zwingli concerning the moral worth of labor "remind us of the new over-estimation of the labor factor since Locke and Ricardo" (1874: 74), and that he thinks it fit to call the trite observation of Agricola that "the damage which mines may do to fields, forests, and rivers, may [!] be greater than the gain" (50) an "idea of Political Economy." And similarly it must appear strange that Roscher regards the historian Moeser as the greatest German economist of the eighteenth century, a century that includes Becher, Hoernigk, Buesch, and Sonnenfels. Indeed Moeser is a man of great merit in his field but his scattered utterances on economic doctrine and policy—laboriously collected by Roscher from his vast works—are merely the fancies of an idealist who believed himself to have found in the departed greatness of the Middle Ages a guiding star toward a better future.

As Roscher regarded all eminent German politicians, philosophers, historians, lawyers, and even poets as important economists, he also included an exact account of Goethe; the grotesqueness of Roscher's work from which all critical judgment seems to be absent becomes in this connection particularly obvious.

> In golden sentences [he suggests (1874: 479)] Goethe . . . has enriched Political Economy. Besides what is offered in that regard in Hermann und Dorothea, I merely mention the sayings of Theresa: that only the spiritual union with men makes the empty earth into an inhabited garden; that everybody is well-to-do who knows how to administer what he has; to be overrich, however, is a burdensome thing, if one lacks this capacity. Or the

beautiful words of the old man in the Wanderjahre, that loving attention to what a man has makes him rich in accumulating a treasure of memory in small things.

It is indeed a miserable "political economy" in which ideas like these represent "golden sentences"! But still more grotesque than Roscher's praise of Goethe the economist is his censure of him: "The description of some branches of economy such as horse-breeding, industry, arts, etc. from the point of view of human education in the Wanderjahre is rather poor." As if Goethe had been a man of science and not an artist! As if he had pursued economics and not poetry!

Roscher once expressed the opinion that "the economist should combine the systematic profundity of the philosopher and the clearness of thought and concepts of the mathematician and lawyer with the broad fullness and vivacity of the historian" (1874: 330). It is a splendid program that he proclaimed in these words. His own work, however, entirely fails to achieve this high aim. It creates at best the impression that political economy consists of a medley of philosophic, juristic, and historic ideas; with this criticism we may leave Wilhelm Roscher's *Geschichte der NationalÖkonomik*.

Eugen Dühring was indeed a different man. For him not all was sacred that life brings forth; he acknowledged as valuable only what was in accordance with his own views. If Roscher's leading motive was understanding, Dühring's watchword was criticism. But criticism means judgment, and judgment presupposes clear and firm convictions. These Dühring had in abundance.

Dühring's clarity of thought is apparent in his investigation of the question of when political economy proper appeared for the first time. An opponent of historicism, Dühring contends in his *Kritische Geschichte der Nationalökonomie und des Sozialismus* (1900, first edition 1871) that only he who gives to the term economic doctrine a wholly indefinite meaning might date its origin far back through the centuries, while he who does not treat it superficially must regard it as essentially modern. "People have talked voluminously about the poorest moralizings and passed off the inevitable reflections which must take place in any sound brain in view of certain external facts of the economic situation as proof of the existence of scientific insight" (1900: 178). The allusion to Roscher is evident. Such "scientific hodge-podge" (819) Dühring rejected. He assigned the economic conceptions and ideas brought forth by the ancient world and the Middle Ages to the historian of culture. In an ingenious digression he suggests what purpose their analysis might serve in connection with historical studies: to find out "how far economic consciousness reached and what conditions in economic life remained, so to speak, unconscious facts of nature" (19). Political economy and its history, as Dühring sees it, cannot possibly gain anything by their contemplation. "The sciences of Political Economy and Society are elements of the most modern kind and are neither consistent with ancient romanticism which was directed towards the deification of the state, nor with medieval romanticism which looked towards the magic transcendentality of religion" (588). Even the system of knowledge of early modern times, mercantilism, he does not acknowledge as science, because the center of gravity of that doctrine was to be looked for in practice. The physiocrats are the first representatives of a merely theoretical speculation, and for Dühring the history of political economy only begins with them.

Dühring in this way solved the problem of the origin of the science not through the consideration of the mystical national spirit of the past, but from the point of view of the rational intellect of the present. Science and physical science are one to him—what lies beyond should be on the rubbish heap. Here lives the spirit of the supermaterialism of the 1860s and 1870s that made the history of the world begin with Galileo and despised the Middle Ages as a period of the darkest superstition—superstition that did not seem to him to differ from the brightest faith.

It is in accordance with this fundamental attitude of stressing the intellectual side that Dühring divided the thinkers of the past into schools according to their theoretical controversies. He did not wish to group them according to vague general ideas but according to clear doctrinal principles—both in different ages and in each age.

There are two historical processes that Dühring follows: the development of "scientific economics" and the development of what he calls "socialistics." He is well aware that the two are distinct in character and must be distinguished both in thought and history. His very definitions make that clear. "Scientific economics" is for him the science of material interests and consists mainly in the discovery of the natural laws according to which these interests act and interact.

"Socialistics," however, cultivate the idea of conscious collective interference in the economic process without regard to the natural laws of individual behavior. Dühring treats both types of thought in one work—the pure theory together with the practical art—because he believes that both streams flow toward one end: to the system of Dühring himself in which they are—as he claims—harmoniously united. So to him the history of political economy and socialism becomes the understructure of his own doctrine of "personalism," which appears as the crowning achievement of a hundred years of mental effort.

As Dühring conceives the history of political economy in principle as the previous history of his own view, he considers, above all, the thinkers who might be regarded as his predecessors. He collects them into groups, each of which leads one step nearer to his "personalism," and now and then inserts chapters treating the deviations from this way toward the "only possible prospect." Thus, he comes in the end to ten sections that cover and divide the whole.

Dühring first of all deals with the "time before the scientific attempts," that is, practically, mercantilism. As "precursors and evidence of a more rational economics" he values Petty, Locke, Boisguillebert, and Vauban. Law, however, he regards as the true, if unconscious, initiator of a new epoch because he replaced the precious metals (not only in practice but also in theory) by paper and so destroyed the basic concept of the old school. The second chapter is devoted to the "physiocrats and the contemporary Scottish pioneers." Quesnay marked an epoch because he was the first to follow a purely theoretical speculation. Hume represents the transition to Adam Smith who is studied in the third section entitled "The Theoretical System of Industry." To Dühring, Adam Smith is beyond question the founder of economic theory. It is characteristic of Dühring's strictly theoretical way of thinking that the main progressive step he attributes to Adam Smith is the fact that he was the first to make economic relations, without the intervention of money, the object of his analysis, while the physiocrats still calculated in monetary magnitudes.

According to Dühring, two lines of thought originate in Smith. The one, a scientific progress, leads by way of Carey to Dühring himself. The second, which he rejects, is represented by Ricardo and Malthus.

These two men are treated in the fourth chapter. However, the Malthus-Ricardian theory is for Dühring not more than "an occasional deviation in the development of economic insight" (1900: 18) and only Ricardo is credited with "some intelligence." So classicism is not further followed up, and the fifth section is devoted to the "older socialism," which is sharply distinguished from political fiction (Plato, Morus, Harrington).

Rather abruptly Dühring now turns to Thuenen and List ("German Economics," sixth chapter). Thuenen, we are told, by his method, by the abstractions with which he worked and by the schemata that he reached in a speculative way, advanced the science (i.e., in the direction toward Dühring); List, "the German economist par excellence" (1900: 351), discovered "the economic principle of nationality," the contrast of productive forces and (static) values that played an important part in Dühring's own thinking and is therefore at this juncture praised as an "idea fundamental for the science" (364). As Dühring sees the intellectual work of List in very close connection with the achievement of Carey, there follows a seventh chapter "American Economics and Its Relation to the Contemporaneous European Developments." Carey's formula of the theory of value, suggesting value to be the measure of resistance put up by nature to the acquisition of the objects desired by men, was the immediate basis of Dühring's own doctrine, and thus, so far as theory is concerned, the necessary historical ground has been covered. Only the development of socialism remains to be studied.

The eighth chapter—built up as an antithesis—consequently deals with "newer socialism." Dühring contrasts the "French representatives," among whom he highly appreciates Louis Blanc, and "Germano-judaic formations" (Karl Marx and Ferdinand Lassalle), which he most passionately rejects. The ninth section bears the title "The Ideas of the Commune and the Last Third of the Nineteenth Century." Finally, the tenth and last chapter is called: "Last Elements in Destruction and Construction." It is a piece of propaganda for Dühring's economic and social theory, "personalism," and so is a suitable finish to the whole work, which the author intended should present his own system in its historical significance (or rather, in the historical significance that he ascribed to it).

In the delimitation of the range and proportions of his work, Dühring again shows his critical mind. His principle is to value and to select, and so he proceeds from valuation to valuation. The conviction of his time that there are absolute standards by which we are able to decide— and decide with final validity—what is good and what is bad is apparent here. Dühring wished to produce a history of political economy and socialism and he therefore consistently excluded all other studies however closely akin: the sciences of finance and statistics, economic morals, and even economic policy. In his description of Law's ideas he leaves the practical experiment of the Scotsman out of the picture. Similarly only a small number of authors is selected for analysis and discussion. "For the history of Political Economy as well as for its present state the presentation of those ideas which either belong originally and personally to a scientific individual or else strikingly express the common course of thought is alone of real value" (1900: 131). Many an important economist is passed over in Dühring's book. In vain we look for Mun or Steuart who apparently failed to interest him either as individuals or as children of their age.

If its secure theoretical foundation is the peculiar value and charm of Dühring's work, it is also the cause of its regrettable narrowness. For while in Roscher's mind history was too much in the foreground, Dühring was too exclusively interested in theory. To put it differently, while Roscher lacked understanding of economic theory, Dühring failed in the comprehension of economic history; he had indeed no historical sense at all. He did not contemplate the development of thought, as did later Schumpeter or Gide and Rist, from the point of view of theory in general. The theoretical discussion of the ideas of the past is not in itself opposed to their historical interpretation; it should, in fact, go hand in hand with it—but from the point of view of one theory, his own. And it is this that represents the "critical" element in Dühring's *Critical History of Political Economy and Socialism* and that must provoke criticism and countercriticism from others.

2

The Historical Approach

Roscher and Dühring aroused deep and lasting interest in the development of political economy and, at the same time, gave the treatment of the subject a scientific basis. But Roscher's work was much too broad and Dühring's book much too egocentric to permit the clear outlines of the progress of thought to appear. It was Hugo Eisenhart who first undertook the important task of presenting a short and lucid sketch of the past of economics; in 1888 he published a small book entitled *Geschichte der Nationaloekonomik.*

Hugo Eisenhart (1811-1893), like Wilhelm Roscher, had his roots in the ideal world of German romanticism, but it was not so much the historical as the sociological and organic aspect of this doctrine that dominated his labors. This is manifest in both the main works that he has left, the *Philosophie des Staats oder Allgemeine Socialtheorie* (1843), the second volume of which bears the subtitle: "Positives System der Volkswirthschaft oder Oekonomische Socialtheorie," and *Die gegenwaertige Staatenwelt in ihrer natuerlichen Gliederung* (1856). His basic concept—later to be most fully developed in Albert Schaffle's *Bau und Leben des sozialen Koerpers* (1875)—was the thesis that society must be regarded as an organism: political science he defined as "knowledge of the social body" (Eisenhart 1843: vii), and he wished to make it the "great and comprehensive doctrine of the

23

totality of human relations" (xx). He envisaged economic theory as part of this superimposed sociology—it is the spirit of Comte that animates this view!

Eisenhart considered it to be the task of the economic thought of his age to oppose a modern system of positive welfare policy to the outworn teachings of Adam Smith, which he calls the negative system of purely liberating welfare economics. He did not reject the causal analysis of reality pursued by Smith,[1] but sought to connect it with a teleological doctrine of social reform. In this endeavor to place beside the observing science of the "Is" an ethical and Christian doctrine of the "Ought," Eisenhart reminds us of Sismondi who was so much more successful than he. He says: "National economy ought not . . . simply to distribute the goods produced by division of labor nor the science of it simply teach the laws of this distribution—but rather in such a way that everybody who is part of this system of life obtains as great a quantity of goods of all kind, material as well as immaterial, for his one proper product or object of exchange as is necessary to make him that perfect man which is the common and ultimate end of the community dominating all systems" (1843: chap. 2, 8 et seq.). It is the great movement of romanticism from narrow catallactics to a broader economics and from economics to a broad sociology that determines Eisenhart's basic concepts.

Already this short description of Eisenhart's mentality leads us to expect that he did not treat the history of political economy as an uncritical historian, but as a critical sociologist. The great contrast between the social constitutions of the ancient and the new world was plain to him, and he therefore decided, unlike Roscher, to assume the modern origin of our science. According to his view, antiquity and the Middle Ages could not create a political economy in the exact sense of the word for three reasons: 1. because all scientific endeavor was and remained purely abstract; 2. because the real state of economy did not develop beyond the primitive forms of the manor and

---

1. Indeed, even from the point of view of pure theory Hugo Eisenhart belongs to the forgotten who should be rediscovered. His attitude to Smith and Malthus, Ricardo and McMulloch, is not uninteresting. Cf. *Positives System der Volkswirtschaft* (1844), especially Chapter 2 ("On the Purpose of National Economy" in concreto) and Chapter 3 ("The Mechanism for the Realization of the Natural Price").

natural economy, or rather because there existed, strictly speaking, only an "aggregate of private economies" but no "real national economy" (1843: 3, 7); and 3. because a moral stigma seemed to cling to economic activities, which impeded the formation of a higher economic doctrine. Of these three arguments Eisenhart, in accordance with his pronounced ethical attitude, regards the ethical and psychological argument as the most striking and decisive (1843: 3); but however we distribute the weight (on examination, the second point, the reference to the character of the older times as a natural economy, will appear the argument *kat' exochen* [*par excellence*]): it is certain that Eisenhart affirmed an important truth that should never be lost sight of in our studies.

Eisenhart, however,—and here-in lies his special merit—also endeavored on the basis of his fundamental views to fix more exactly the time of the origin of economic thought in the strict sense of the word, and he reached the conclusion that we have to regard the rise of money economy as the internal and external cause of the genesis of political economy. Political economy is the science of the national exchange economy of modern times. Money, however, was the first sign and similarly the most important promotor of modern exchange economy. Thus, it is easy to understand how it became the first object of scientific discussion in the modern sense. "No doubt," says Eisenhart (1881: 8) "the first investigations of an economic nature were evoked by the appearance of a stronger demand for money as it was caused by the transition of society to a general system of exchange and commerce." This process of transformation took place "on the verge of modern times" (9). And the passing from natural to exchange and money economy offered not only the internal reason but also the external occasion for the rise of political economy. This was given by the "vast increase of the means of payment in Europe, with which the discovery of America met the increased needs as in a providential disposition" (10), the price revolution of the sixteenth and seventeenth centuries. If one considers the importance of the change in the literature on monetary theory and monetary policy from the critique of governmental mint policy to the investigation of economic market phenomena—it led, to put it shortly, from normative and moralizing treatment to causal and understanding analysis, from Buridanus to Bodinus—one must acknowledge Eisenhart's view as fully justified.

As Eisenhart conceives political economy as a union of economic theory and welfare policy, as a synthesis of the analysis of the "Is" and the doctrine of the "Ought," he takes his principle of division from the borderland between these realms of ideas. He distinguishes a naive period (mercantilism), a critical and liberal period (physiocracy, industrial system, and the Manchester School), and last of all an organic period (socialism, historicism, and the like). He sees the essential difference between the three ages in the character and principles of their political programs. "On poor theoretical suppositions," he says (1881: 27 et seq.);

> mercantilism had immediately built a practical system of welfare work. Just as our old physicians gathered their knowledge of medicine at the sickbed without needing the weight of scientific understanding either of their object or their means, so they (the mercantilists) formed their principles from case to case. . . . With the liberal systems, however, begins the critical and purely scientific work . . . with the aim of testing, guided by the knowledge of the object, the necessities of government and developing its rules . . . and in the end there results (the discovery of) a natural order of things which makes it doubtful whether there is any need at all for public interference except to free society . . . from . . . chains.

Thus, Eisenhart opposes the empiricism of mercantilistic welfare politics to the doctrinairism of the liberal dogma. Lastly the organic period subordinates the activity of the state less to the principle of experience or doctrine than to ethical considerations. It comprises a number of systems that aim at "making the unfettered economy subservient to the proclaimed object of the state . . . to find for all questions a solution in harmony with the moral ends of the whole" (101). The liberal and organic periods are therefore opposed to each other as are individualism and—to use a modern term—universalism. Of List, Eisenhart says:

> Applying the critical standard with which Sismondi had judged the internal economic policy of common liberalism to its external economic policy he arrives at the same result, to wit that it rests on an utterly wrong, individualistic, principle which deranges life. So he moves in the same direction towards a renewal of economic ideas with the aim of a harmonious community of life. (162)

From Eisenhart's point of view, this periodization is quite consistent: he founded it on the changing principle of welfare policy, and, as this represented the kernel of his investigation, he was justified in doing so. However, as soon as his wide conception of political economy is no longer accepted—and since 1860 there has been a tendency to free it from all ethical accessories—the fundamental idea of his division will appear no longer to be based on the central concepts of the science and therefore will be wrong. Then indeed, Eisenhart's whole book will shrink to a mere relic of the past.

In England interest in the history of political economy had been awakened by Cliffe Leslie, who in 1875 published a thorough discussion of Roscher's work in the widely read Fortnightly Review.[2] But it was not until ten years later that there appeared a description of the development of economic science capable of replacing the old and unsatisfactory sketch of Travers Twiss: *History of Political Economy* by the Irishman John Kells Ingram (1823-1907), which was first published as a contribution to the Encyclopaedia Britannica (1885) and then expanded into a book (1888).

Ingram described Eisenhart's treatise as a "vigorous and original sketch," and this valuation shows the inner similarity of the two investigations, a similarity derived from the fact that both men were of the romantic school. But while Eisenhart's teachers were Schelling, Stahl, Savigny, and Eiselen, Ingram's great master was Auguste Comte. His whole life was dominated by the great Frenchman: "Instead of taking Auguste Comte's sociology as a beginning from which to develop independently," says Ely in his preface to the posthumous edition of Ingram's *History* (1915: xiv), "he made Auguste Comte his goal." That is in general true, even outside Ingram's sociological work; his *Outlines of the History of Religion* (1900) and *Practical Morals* (1904) confirm Ely's verdict in the same way as his economic program, published in *The Present Position and Prospects of Political Economy* (1878).

Ingram's views on the tasks of political economy, which held only a modest place in his wide circle of interests reaching from mathematics to philology, found their clearest expression in his preface to Ely's *Introduction to the Study of Political Economy* (1891).

---

2. [Reprinted in Leslie 1969].

Here he puts forward four postulates:

1. A sociological postulate. "The study of wealth cannot be isolated . . . from other social phenomena . . . There is but one great Science of Sociology, of which Economics forms a single chapter."
2. A historical postulate. "Economic Science . . . must be not statical only, but also dynamical. It must not assume one fixed state of society and suppose that it has to deal solely with laws of coexistence, ignoring those of succession."
3. A methodological postulate. "Whilst recognizing the real, and not inconsiderable, place which belongs to deduction in economics ... inductive research must preponderate." Comparison is especially important in method.
4. An ethical postulate. Ingram wished that a "more humane and genial" attitude should replace the old "dryness and hardness," above all that the social problem should be treated and solved in the spirit of social responsibility.

The similarity of this program to that drawn up by Roscher, nearly fifty years before, is evident at a glance. And yet—what a difference between their two works! While Roscher's aim is broadness, Ingram's is profundity. While Roscher seems to confirm the hard saying of d'Alembert quoted with approval by Say (1840: 561) that the search for the ideas of others has its cause in the searcher's lack of solid and clear concepts of his own, Ingram exposes its error. He does not bring together without distinction the doctrines of earlier thinkers,[3] but, convinced of the truth of his point of view, founded on Comte's evolutionist philosophy and sociology, he propounds a really historical and scientific description of the development of thought, in so far as economy was its subject. He treats however, only those ideas and systems that may be regarded as political economy in a strict sense of the word. He never loses sight of his two working concepts: historical development and economic theory, and their simultaneous application to the past of political economy makes his book one of the best that has ever been written on this subject.

Ingram, like almost all supporters of historical relativism, knows no

---

3. What he says on Jevons is significant: "His name will survive in connection, not with new theoretical constructions, but with his treatment of practical problems . . . and . . . his energetic tendency to a renovation of economic method" (1915: 229).

fixed starting point for the development of the science of economic life. He, too, opens his work with a discussion of antiquity, with a description of the ancient oriental theocracies. But as a disciple of Comte he is convinced that the period before roughly 1300 A.D. is economically and ideologically so different from modern times that it is quite useless to treat them in the same manner. The first two chapters of his study: "Ancient Times" and "The Middle Ages," are therefore only intended to describe the general character of economic thought in those periods and to interpret it in the light of its factual conditions—not least clearly to establish its essential difference from the economic science of later times. "[T]he science," Ingram says shortly and distinctly of Political Economy (1915: 21), "is essentially a modern one."

To support this judgement Ingram stresses two points: a realistic and an ideal one. "It is evident," he points out,

> that for any considerable development of social theory two conditions must be fulfilled. First, the phenomena must have exhibited themselves on a sufficiently extended scale to supply adequate matter for observation and afford a satisfactory basis for scientific generalisations; and secondly . . . there must have been such a previous cultivation of the simpler sciences as will have both furnished the necessary data of doctrine and prepared the proper methods of investigation. (1915: 5)

Viewed outside Comte's magic circle, only the first of these two arguments seems decisive. It sounds almost commonplace, although it is of the highest importance in view of the many attempts to discover a science of national economy before the rise of the national economies themselves. The second argument leads us to ask what sciences there are that form a condition for the development of a sociology comprising in itself political economy. Ingram, always following Comte, thinks of mathematics, astronomy, physics, chemistry, and biology, without which—according to Comte's "law of decreasing generality and increasing complexity"—a positive social science is, as he believes, impossible. But this supposed law is only an a priori construction. It is indeed true that the sciences build systematically on one another—it is the task of philosophy to investigate their system, and Comte's efforts in that direction are certainly deserving of attention—but it is wrong to construct a historical sequence from a systematic order: on that point the historian Ingram thought somewhat unhistorically.

On the division of the development of political economy into periods Ingram expressed himself as follows: "The history of economic inquiry is most naturally divided into the three great periods of 1. the ancient, 2. the mediaeval, and 3. the modern worlds" (1915: 5). Thus, it may seem as if Ingram had uncritically accepted the traditional conceptions. But this is not so. Not only does Ingram (like Comte) close the Middle Ages with the thirteenth century, but he also suggests an ingenious periodization of the last six hundred years that is again reminiscent of Auguste Comte (cf. 1876: 461, 488, 508).

In modern times he once more distinguished three phases prior to the present, the age of the historical school. The first phase reaches from the end of the thirteenth century to the end of the fifteenth century. It was incapable of definite achievement in political economy, as the system of medieval economy had not yet entirely disappeared and that of modern economy was still only partially developed. The second phase covers the sixteenth and seventeenth centuries, a period, as Ingram stresses, in which industrial life was subservient to the aims of the state, especially its lust for power. The third phase runs roughly from 1700 to 1840. Ingram entitles the chapter devoted to this epoch "The System of Natural Liberty." More often, however, and more aptly from his point of view, he speaks of a "Negative School" —negative in so far as their principle of policy, the laissez faire, was purely negative. To this Negative School, which in Ingram's time was also called the Old School, he opposes in the end a New School, the school of historicism characterized by a new and, in essence, humanitarian demand for public intervention in economic life.

If we examine Ingram's scheme critically two things must be kept apart: the periodization in itself and its motivation. As regards the latter it is hard to understand why economic policy should have been made decisive, why the relation of economy and the state should have been made the basis. Each historical process bears the principle of its periodization in itself and the task of the historian can only be to recognize where what we may call the natural periods begin and end. The standard by which Ingram measures the history of economic theory is, however, not innate but exogenous.

The motivation of Ingram's attempt at periodization is, however, of only secondary importance, since he, as a genuine historian, has instinctively, as it were, come upon the truth in spite of his questionable argument. Indeed the correct boundary lines lie where Ingram has placed them: with the physiocrats and later, around 1840, in the rise of historicism which Ingram, biased as he is in favor of his master, begins with Auguste Comte. Comte's positivism, which founded all science on induction, observation, and comparison, was indeed of outstanding importance for historicism; but it does not originate with him. When his *Cours de philosophie positive* began to appear in 1830, Sismondi's *Nouveaux Principes* had already been in existence for more than a decade.

Political economy is to Ingram "the theory of social wealth" (1915: 2) and with Say he also calls it the science of production, distribution, and consumption. Only what falls within this framework is historically investigated; everything else—especially socialism—remains outside the survey. Indeed, Ingram goes so far as to mention Marx only in passing without describing his work, although Marx was not only a socialist but also a representative of pure theory (and moreover a representative of the sociological and historical method that Ingram regarded as the only correct one). Such a blemish, however, does not outweigh the great advantage that Ingram's work draws from its author's strict self-limitation, and it is in a true sense a history of political economy as might be expected from the clear definition of its subject matter.

In France as in England there was after 1880 a general conviction that the literature on the development of political economy written about half a century previously was both inadequate in itself and obsolete, and should be replaced by something better. But only in the year 1891 did Alfred Espinas publish his small *Histoire des Doctrines Economiques* presenting a short survey of the wide field that is to be considered.

Like Roscher, Dühring, Ingram, and Eisenhart, Espinas (1844-1922) was a man of vast erudition. His literary activities began with the translation of Herbert Spencer's *Principles of Psychology* and this work introduced him to Comte's world of thought in its English development (toward a strictly rationalistic and mechanical view of life). Espinas' whole achievement has its roots in Spencer. It comprises publications on philosophy (*La Philosophie Sociale du*

XVIIIe siècle et la révolution, 1898; *Etudes su l'Histoire de la philosophie de l'Action. Descartes et la Morale* ed. 1925 and others) and psychology, sociology, and pedagogy (*Idee Générale de la Pédagogie*, 1884).

Espinas's ideas on social science are laid down in his widely read thesis *Des sociétés animales* (1877) in which—as in Spencer— organistic and mechanistic, romantic and positive, sociological and physical influences are curiously intermingled and connected. Espinas, rejecting individualism in all its forms, saw society biologically as an organism, and that characterizes the romantic and sociological element; but he believed it to be subject to strict physical laws, such as the law of the natural division and concentration of labor, and that brings him near the materialistic philosophers of 1870, Haeckel and Carneri. This union of the two great tendencies of the nineteenth century, of older romanticism and newer rationalism, he took for the ideal basis of all social sciences. This is manifest in his essay in the *Revue philosophique* of 1901; "Être ou ne pas être, ou du Postulat de la Sociologie."

In this article Espinas discusses in a typical manner the relation of biology and sociology. He first stresses the difference between the aggregate of cells in the human body and the aggregate of men in the body social: "The link which unites the cells in the blastoderme is as material as the mutual coherence of the cells or their fixation by the intercellular substance. . . . All these links are biological, that is to say physico-chemical. . . . On the contrary the link uniting the blastodermes among themselves in society is psychological." (1901: 465). But this difference is in fact bridged over:

> The uniting feature is the family. The family is a society. The living many-celled beings which compose it are connected by interpsychic links. It is not the family which nourishes itself. . . . Nutrition, growth, sleep etc. remain for the individual. The work which prepares and secures these individual functions, [however], is collective: here we have the social phenomenon. But it is necessary to acknowledge at the same time that the biological functions, however subordinated to social ends, are in their turn the *conditio sine qua non*. . . . All society is composed of families. In consequence *all society has an organic basis*, and this universal fact, *this law of nature*, cannot fail to exercise a deep influence on the whole of social life which science should not neglect. (1901: 466 et seq.)

It is obvious from these words that, of the two main ideas of romanticism, the organic and the historical, here only the first is followed out to its ultimate conclusion. The latter is almost totally neglected. Espinas's view of history is purely rationalistic. Already the treatment of the problem of the origin of our science proves that he possessed no critical ability in historical matters.

For Espinas the founders of political economy were Socrates, Plato, and Aristotle. "Socrates is the first whose reflections on that subject have been handed down to us . . . Plato has contributed . . . towards the foundation of the science of wealth. . . . Aristotle . . . if he is not the founder . . . has more clearly perceived its object" (1891: 20, 35, 38). In the introduction to the book he expresses the conviction that political economy is neither older nor younger than the other sciences: "Economics has followed the destiny common to all branches of knowledge. It was born at Athens in the fifth century" (6). Espinas, indeed, says in a later connection discussing the dark period between the fifth and the tenth centuries A.D.: "Economic reflection . . . can only begin where there is a sufficiently developed economic life" (72); the primitive state of economy in the time under consideration, however, did not offer a suitable scientific subject. But this sentence is hardly more than a superficiality for Espinas. Not a developed economic system (which existed also in Charlemagne's times), but a developed system of national economy is the condition and object of political economy, a truth alien to Espinas's physical and therefore unhistorical way of thinking. For that reason Espinas's description of economic development after the opening of the second millennium is without great value. He sees in it merely the unfolding of commerce and industry without noticing that, what is really important, is the rise of a new economic system, of exchange economy, and thus the realistic investigation teaches him little or nothing.

Since Espinas is blind to the essential change in the object of the science of economic life, his attempt at periodization is not very successful. He distinguishes between ancient times, the Middle Ages, the Renaissance, and modern times. The chapter on the ancient thinkers bears the title "Conflit du point de vue utilitaire et du point de vue moral." The Middle Ages seem in his view to bring this conflict to an end, but at the same time to raise a new point in the discussion: "Triomphe du point de vue moral et religieux.

Commencement du naturalisme." The Renaissance shows (besides the "Restauration des doctrines antiques") a strong development of this new principle, a "Progrès du naturalisme." This naturalism (the terminology is very unfortunate; it springs from the rationalistic contrast between theological and metaphysical philosophy on the one hand, and natural and positivistic philosophy on the other) consists of the view that the pursuit of material wealth is not to be conceived and judged under the aspect of divinity or morals, but regarded without prejudice and acknowledged as legitimate. Espinas even believes himself capable of determining the exact point of change; the year 1615.

> Eventually, in 1615, appeared a work that dared to acknowledge in its very title the legitimacy of the pursuit of wealth and the high importance of economic functions in the life of states; economics which had been domestic turn political and openly propose as their aim the indefinite extension of public riches. This audacious move was due to a Frenchman, Antoine de Monchrétien. (1891: 8)

Espinas divided the period of the "Prépondérance du naturalisme," that is the history of doctrines since Monchrétien, into four sections that he describes in two ways: according to their supposed theoretical principles, and according to their political nature. The first epoch is that of mercantilism. Espinas speaks of a "theory of artificial wealth." The second epoch coincides with physiocracy. It develops the "theory of natural wealth." Then, liberalism as the third epoch gives birth to the watchword "development of wealth for its own sake by labor." It extends into the fourth epoch, the present. "Adam Smith," Espinas says (1891: 10) "proved that wealth is derived neither from the decrees of princes nor from the produce of the earth alone, but from the labor of man." Thus, he is of the opinion that it was the basic idea of mercantilism to produce welfare artificially (by public measures), that of physiocracy was that only nature creates it (by the collaboration of her forces in agriculture), and finally that of liberalism was that labor is its proper source—and this difference in the doctrines provides his principle for the periodization of development.

Espinas believes this periodization to be justified also from the political side. Spencer's interpretation of political history as a progress of the state from absolute and militaristic coercion to pacific and industrial freedom is the basis of his thought here. Mercantilism is a "policy of royal interests." The theory of natural wealth is different. It is a "humanitarian policy of the rulers." It is so to speak morally on a higher level. The school originated by Adam Smith, however, stands for the idea of humanity. It follows the vision of a "universal economic republic."

Espinas's endeavor to differentiate the four schools not only by their theoretical ideas, but also by their practical and political principles is certainly sound. But his concept suffers from one fundamental defect: it is not genuinely historical, it does not deduce its periodization from the past but rather interprets it into the past. Espinas believes a progressive movement to be traceable throughout history. This is significant of the man who was imbued with the doctrines of the French and English apostles of progress, with the ideas of Condorcet, Blanc, and Comte as well as of Spencer, without freeing them from their artificiality by a deeper knowledge of the past. The intellectual progressive movement can be found in the overcoming of the one-sided views of mercantilists and physiocrats by Adam Smith's doctrine of labor as the source of value, whereas the political progressive movement is seen in the replacement of monarchical and national egotism by the humanitarian ideal of liberalism. This second concept especially shows what Espinas's periodization really is: a construction a priori and nothing more.

Espinas refers to "Political Economy as a social science in the modern democracies." But it is for him theoretically as well as practically only a continuation of the previous stage, in spite of historicism, socialism, organicism, and all the slogans of those days. In wishing theoretically to build traditional economics into sociology, the science of the future, and practically to assist in forming out of the historical nations the coming "United States of Europe," Espinas proves once more his teleological philosophy of history, his belief in progress that is preconceived and not learned from reality.

To this unhistorical and aprioristic attitude of Espinas his definition of economic science corresponds. It is for him simply the "science that studies wealth"—indifferent as to whether this wealth consists in slaves, estates, or capital, whether it conforms to the conceptions of antiquity, the Middle Ages, or modern times. This indefinite notion does not, of course, provide Espinas with any principle of selection, so that his investigation constantly transgresses its proper limits. Christ's words that it is easier for a camel to go through the eye of a needle than for a rich man to enter into the kingdom of God, and those concerning the fowls of the air who neither sow nor reap and are yet fed by the heavenly Father, he feels, should not be omitted from his *Histoire des Doctrines Économiques*, because they contain a view on the "fundamental questions of economic science, property or riches and labor" (1891: 64 et seq.)! He includes in his book not only socialism, but also political fiction; Campanella, Rousseau, and Mably appear side by side with Mun, Quesnay, and Turgot as if they had been men of the same kind. Thus, Espinas combines the lack of clear concepts of historicism with the lack of historical understanding of rationalism; and, indeed, in spite of his leaning towards the organic theory of society, a dull rationalism represents the dominating feature of his whole investigation.

By the beginning of the present century the great impulse that romanticism had given to the intellectual life of Europe had almost passed away. Even the narrow field of knowledge to which this study is devoted proves how it decreased from decade to decade; Roscher and Eisenhart were genuine representatives of the romantical spirit, one of its historical, the other of its organic doctrine. Ingram was not equally so. The positivism of Comte to which he conformed was, indeed, a product of romanticism, but it contained—as an aftereffect of the eighteenth century—many elements of rationalism that developed afresh after 1860 and were led by Herbert Spencer from the sociological and idealistic into the physical and materialistic channel. Espinas's sociology affords a striking proof of this fact.

In the development of dogma that took a parallel course, the first decade of the twentieth century marks the culmination of the doctrine of Jevons, Menger, and Walras. The spirit of the exact sciences governed political economy. Yet, by 1910, there arose in the midst of the citadel of the new theory, in Austria, a countermovement that called for a return to romanticism. It was an apostate of Menger's school, Othmar Spann (born 1878), who fought for this demand with much spirit, and not without success.

Spann's doctrine, which has become known by the name of universalism, is to be understood in all its parts as an opposition to classical and neoclassical teachings. It opposes to the materialism of the natural sciences an idealism of the social sciences (1924, 1928); to the cosmopolitan individualism a national collectivism (1930); to the atomistic equalitarian state a totalitarian state of estates (1931); to the causal analysis of economy a teleological interpretation of economy (1918); to the theory of market prices a theory of productive contributions (1918). In a word: Spann wished to give a comprehensive counterdoctrine in contrast to the economic doctrine of Menger, which he regarded as a new classicism, in the same way as Adam Müller had contrasted his counterdoctrine to Smith's doctrine a century before. This similarity between Müller and Spann applies also to their position within romanticism and neoromanticism, for both follow more the organic theory of society than the historical view of life. Spann's basic idea is the predominance of the social element over the individual: society is not simply a sum of single individuals, but the single individuals are merely members of society. Yet this view is for Spann an absolute dogma unconnected with any relativistic theory of development, and this also determines his attitude, often lacking in understanding, toward the past of political economy as it is manifest in his widely read book *Die Haupttheorien der Volkswirtschaftslehre* (1932 [1911]). In his history of doctrines, too, Spann shows himself a romanticist, but a romantic doctrinaire, not a romantic historian, and so his whole description comes seriously near to the concept prevailing in the hostile camp, the camp of individualism and rationalism.

The question whether political economy is a modern science or whether its origin is to be sought in antiquity Spann leaves (like many other points) in obscurity. On the one hand he says (1932: 1): "Neither in classical Antiquity nor yet in the Middle Ages did there arise any finished systems of politico-economic thought." Shortly afterward, however, he observes (2): "Nevertheless the beginnings of our science[4] go back into ancient times to Plato and Aristotle." Now this ambiguity is not confined to Spann alone: we find it in Gonnard and Haney, Salin and Roll, Schumpeter and Cossa. What distinguishes him, however, is the following sentence: "Even in those

---

4. The text is "Wirtschaft." But here a misprint must have crept into the original; the English translation rightly says "science" (1932: 26).

earlier times (Antiquity and the Middle Ages) politico-economic thought (volkswirtschaftliches Denken) may well have been grounded on economic evolution" (1932: 1). For, Spann continues, society has not, as Bücher thinks, risen from domestic economy to feudal and town economy and hence to exchange economy. Even in the stone age there was an all-European commerce; in the Bronze Age export trade; and in Babylon, a fully developed monetary system. He regards Bücher's doctrine of the stages of economic development as historically and theoretically wrong. Why then did mankind not develop a systematic science of economics before the sixteenth century? Spann advances a half-spiritual half-economic reason: "The mind, directed in those epochs towards the heroic and transcendental, regarded the economic sphere of activity in life with but little esteem—as always in periods with an organized economy." For Spann cannot help admitting that "generally the economy of ancient times was more organized . . . and, because predominantly agricultural, simpler."

What induced Spann to reject Bücher's doctrine of economic stages is the consideration that it does not do justice to the many-sidedness of life. Certainly there never was anywhere a pure "closed domestic economy"; this conception is not an exact picture of reality, but only a simplifying ideal type. Even the most self-sufficient manor in the early Middle Ages was now and then visited by a wandering merchant; but was the merchant and not the manor the symbol of the economy of the early Middle Ages?[5] Certainly Bücher's doctrine of economic stages has all the defects of a pale abstraction. But does it not strikingly characterize the preponderating element of each age? And can we reach a characterization of an epoch if we do not stress the typical and neglect the exceptional? Spann who attacks Bücher seems not to notice that he proceeds in exactly the same way; he distinguishes between "the economy of ancient times" as "more organized, and because predominantly agricultural, simpler," and the unorganized "totally free, individualistic exchange economy"—only he puts in the place of the clear, if somewhat abstract, notions of Bücher

---

5. Certainly there was "genuine capitalism" in antiquity, as Spann says (1932: 128)—but should we call Iran a capitalistic country because there are some capitalistic enterprises?

his own unclear and certainly not more realistic conceptions. For if one contrasts organized and individualistic economy, domestic or town economy and national economy, natural economy and money economy—in the last resort one always means the same: the contrast of the ancient and medieval[6] to the modern system. And only the modern system gave political economy (in the true sense of the word) its basis: "At the beginning of the modern ages for the first time a whole series of interdependent investigations on . . . questions of national economy makes its appearance in what is called mercantilism or the mercantile system" (1932: 3) writes Spann. That is just at the time that organized economy began to give way to individualistic economy, or—in Bücher's words—town and feudal economy to national and exchange economy.

A closed modern system of political economy does not exist for Spann. He sees *two* trends of development side by side; at the beginning of one stand, Quesnay and Smith, and at the beginning of the other, Adam Müller (1932: vi, 34):

> It simply cannot be denied that a red thread runs through economic teaching from Adam Müller to the new historical school; that the names of Adam Müller, Fichte, Baader, Freiherr vom Stein, List, Thuenen, Roscher, Hildebrand, Knies, Bernhardi, Schmoller (and even those of Carlyle, Ruskin, Carey) form, as it were, a single line of descent; and that they embody a universalist-organic and idealist doctrine contrasting with the atomist-individualist and materialist doctrine of Smith, Ricardo, Say, Rau, Menger, Jevons, (1932: v)

In view of this fundamental division of the whole spiritual heritage of

---

6. Spann is partially justified in emphasizing that the view of Rodbertus and Bücher is wrong, according to which antiquity on the whole did not outgrow the stage of *oikos* economy. But on the other hand antiquity never fully developed exchange economy; it appeared always only as a superstructure on a natural basis, however rich it may have been in itself. Thus, Spann must admit of the time of the Roman emperors that "the spread of huge latifundia undoubtedly resulted in a certain reversion from a capitalist exchange economy towards a more natural domestic economy" (1932: 2). In other words; although in the old world the formation of an exchange economy began, it did not become the dominant form of economic life; therefore, (as we see in Plato and Aristotle, Cato and Cicero) its aspect was never positive, but always only negative and destructive and so could not give rise to a "political economy."

economic science one would expect Spann to construct a clear periodization of development on the basis of the two great tendencies. But it is not so. He distinguishes twelve chapters that, loosely following each other according to the progress of time, are not distinctly separated from one another: the days before the mercantile system, individualist natural right, introduction to the basic problem of sociology (individualism vs. universalism), transition to the physiocratic system, the physiocratic doctrinal system, the fully developed individualist or classical teachings, German economics (this eighth chapter occupies the center), Carey's optimism and its counterparts on the continent of Europe, a short account of the evolution of socialism, the historical school (including social reform and the theory of marginal utility), and lastly present-day economic science—a scheme that leaves much to be desired. To the sentence *qui bene distinguit, bene docet* [the one who is good at drawing distinctions, teaches well], Spann did not conform.

But in not keeping consistently to one point of view, in not opposing the individualistic doctrine to the universalist one, or the English theoreticians to the German, but in contrasting instead individualist and German teaching, Spann conveys the false impression that the way for his theories was prepared by as famous a man as Johann Heinrich von Thuenen. "In spite of Thuenen's obvious dependence upon Ricardo" he says (1932: 109-10) "in spite of unparalleled abstractness, the most specialized everyday reality is fully mastered, a truly Shakespearean insight into the actual world is presented." In opposition to Ricardo's method, which is atomistic and mechanistic, he claims that the universalist spirit is at work. Thuenen, we are told, would be impossible without Adam Müller.[7]   But that is to give

---

7. Spann does not indicate that Müller, in a passage that seems so far to have escaped notice, in fact foreshadows Thuenen's basic idea. We read in the *Elemente der Staatskunst* (ed. 1936: 298 et seq., 325):

> Land, capital, and labor are not . . . sources of wealth in themselves, but only elements of it: their active reciprocal effect is the only source of wealth. . . . When these effects have lasted for some time on the surface of the earth, they portray themselves almost mathematically, I should say: on the map. There arise on the surface of the earth manifold circles which restrict and delimit one another in the way of the bee cells; there arise

Thuenen an entirely wrong interpretation: he was in every respect a dutiful son of English classicism; he was indeed (with Hermann) the German classicist par excellence. He was as abstract as Ricardo, but Ricardo was as universalist (for that can only mean in this connection: concerned with the whole of national economy) as he. If classicism is characterized by a leaning toward isolation and the belief in physical laws of economy, Thuenen might justly be regarded as its prototype. The preface to the second edition of his work, published in 1842, says with perfect clarity that simplifying suppositions that differ from reality are

> necessary in order to describe in isolation and bring to perception the influence of a certain factor of which we obtain in reality but an indistinct picture because it appears there always in conflict with other factors effective at the same time. This form of investigation gave me light and clarity on so many points and seems to me to be capable of such extended use that I regard it as the *most important* point in this whole publication.

So Thuenen belongs in his method to Ricardo, and not to Müller. He even rejected Adam Smith as too empirical and descriptive! The broad outlook of romanticism comprising all society as well as its deep understanding of history were foreign to this man of figures.

Although Spann according to his basic thesis endeavored to widen the scope of his description in the direction of romanticism, although he included men like Franz von Baader, Bernhardi, Carlyle, and Ruskin, he still concentrated his attention on economic theory in the strict sense of the word. He rightly excluded socialism, which he

---

> certain districts of agricultural property in the centres of which the workmen settle. . . . This tendency of economic activities to centre according to actual mathematical laws shows itself in still greater dimensions in the present time. . . . Each economic object has a certain circuit of life. Let us imagine for example the absence of waterways, a bushel of corn has on land a certain district within which it can be sold. As soon as the distance becomes so great that the cost of freight surpasses the local price of wheat, the sphere of life of that particular corn ceases.

But that does not prove that Thuenen was a romanticist, rather inversely that Müller was very deeply influenced by rationalism, a point that is also to be observed in other connections. Cf. note.

regarded not as a theory of economy, but as a moral idea. And even if he put into relief the philosophic and sociological conceptions of the great thinkers, he never transgressed the right measure: for he represents only the connections without the knowledge of which a full understanding of economic doctrines cannot be reached, and so he shows in the delimitation of his field of work the superiority of a dogmatic as he allows his drawbacks to be perceived in the division of development.

In the United States also a protest against the mechanistic and abstract conception of economic science and life as it had been accepted all over the world since about 1870 began to be raised by 1910. The new movement is connected with the name of Thorstein Veblen whose *Theory of the Leisure Class* (1899) and *Instinct of Workmanship* (1914) exerted a deep influence on the general discussion. In connection with it there arose a strong revival of interest in the development of political economy, which was but scantily provided for by Ingram's *History*. This book had in the twenty-five years after its first publication gained high renown in all Anglo-Saxon countries. But it was too short to present the intellectual world of the past in all its fullness. So it was the task of the day to write a comprehensive sketch of the history of economic thought that, although building upon the foundations laid by Ingram, avoided his obvious faults: the too great dependence upon Comte's philosophy and sociology, which had by this time become somewhat obsolete, and the too summary treatment of the subject that left more questions open than it answered. This work was undertaken by Lewis H. Haney.

Lewis H. Haney (born 1882) claims to belong to no school. "My first study of economics" he says, "was Ingram's *History*. I was then exposed successively to Welfare Economics, Neo-Classicism, Austrian School, and Historical School doctrines. I find some truth in all. I find complete truth in none" (1936: vi). But Haney acknowledges Richard T. Ely as his master, and Ely in his turn, regarded himself as the disciple of Karl Knies, so that the descent from historicism is after all beyond doubt (1936: viii; Ely 1938). It is also manifest in Haney's work: he is interested in the sociological aspect of economic theory (1914); he wrote a careful historical monograph from which his historical inclinations may be perceived (1908-10); and in the treatment of actual problems he prefers the inductive method that characterizes him and his realistic and sociological approach (1913, 1931). Haney vigorously upholds the concept proper to so-called historicism (in the wider sense of the word) that the great questions of political economy cannot be mastered in isolation from their setting in real life.

> Starting from an eclectic set of principles, derived in part from organic, in part from individualistic sociology, he considers a social point of view the only correct one for judging economic phenomena. He endeavors to prove that the concept of economic value as well as the phenomena of price and distribution form essentially social categories and that a study of these will produce satisfactory results only when it is attempted from the outset from a social point of view. (Suranyi-Unger 1931: 225-26)

This breadth of view comes to light also in Haney's *History of Economic Thought* (1936). He is aware of the fact that theoreticians and theories of the past must be interpreted in relation to their basis and background in life, and this basis and background he understands in a material as well as an intellectual sense, as social environment and as philosophic creed. Nobody conceived his mission as a historian of political economy in a more comprehensive way than Haney.

Haney tried to evade the intricate problem of the origin of our science by distinguishing—as had Cossa before him—between "history of economics" and "history of economic thought," between a narrower and a broader concept. "The History of Economics," he says (1936: 3), "deals with a science. . . . It is limited to times in which economic ideas have become distinct, unified, and organized; it is a history of *systems* of economic thought." This is not the case with the history of economic thought. It has a broader field in view, for it is concerned with the development of economic ideas in general, that is, with those ideas that also appear before the rise of a systematic science of economics or go side by side with it. While the history of economic thought must go back to the "unrelated primitive ideas of the earliest times," the history of economics can start only with the physiocrats. Before their time "economic thoughts have been gleaned mostly from books on religion, politics, or jurisprudence. . . . They formed no separate science, but lay inchoate within other bodies of doctrine" (169). Haney considers the achievement of the physiocrats and of Adam Smith to have been a building constructed from bricks given to them. "To found the science of economics . . . it was necessary to sever these scattered economic ideas and bring them together in a separate system of thought" (169). Thus, Haney does not represent the older ideas as unscientific and oppose to them the newer as scientific. So far he is right. He sees the progress effected by the middle of the eighteenth century only as the construction of a system of thought instead of hitherto unconnected single ideas. Yet the formation of a system by 1750 is but the external sign of an internal change that actually marks the epoch: the transition to modern exchange and national economy, to the form of society resting on the division and concentration of labor on a national scale. The physiocrats combined isolated observations into a comprehensive picture, after development had combined isolated economies in a comprehensive body. We must understand the idea of a system—more deeply than Haney—in its historical root in order really to grasp its full significance.

Haney—this must be emphasized—was indeed clearly aware of the connection between the rise of national and the rise of political economy, although he seems to push the more formal point of systematics into the foreground. "With the rise of nations and the growth of money economy" he says (1936: 755) "came the Mercantilist period, which is transitional and marks the dawn of Economics as a science." He understood and stated that in ancient and medieval times the objective conditions for the formation of an economic science were lacking:

> The subject-matter of Economics, as a social science, is human relations. . . . An independent domestic economy means a large degree of economic isolation, and this characterizes the states of antiquity. . . . [D]uring the period of the Middle Ages . . . the situation was not dissimilar. . . . Only with the growth of division of labor and exchange could economic relations grow in number and significance, and develop that volume, complexity, and intensity which are required to stimulate economic thought. (1936: 32, 34, 32)

In these words the true solution of the problem of the origin of political economy is propounded—not only, as Haney's book suggests, a reason for the tardy development of economic theory. For only modern times gave rise to the interdependence of all members of society that is, as Haney himself emphasizes, essential for the origin of our science.

The history of economic thought is in this way degraded to a mere introduction to the history of economics. "[O]ne must understand 'Mercantilism,' if one is to understand the Classical Economics of Adam Smith and his followers" Haney says (1936: 37). "But no thorough understanding of Mercantilism is possible without knowing something of medieval conditions and thought which preceded it." So his investigation leads him away from the eighteenth century toward earlier times, rather than from previous times towards the eighteenth century.

Haney divides the description of the development of scientific economics since 1750 into the following chapters: 1. "The Founders" (Physiocracy and Adam Smith); 2. "The Early Followers" (Bentham, Malthus, Ricardo, Carey, Bastiat, Senior, Say, Thuenen); 3. "Opponents and Leading Critics" (Lauderdale, Rae, Sismondi, Müller, List, Saint-Simon); 4. "The Restatement" (J. St. Mill); 5. "Opponents and Leading Critics" (Marx, R. Jones, Leslie, Ingram, Roscher, Hildebrand, Schmoller, and others); 6. "Attempts at Reconstruction" (Gossen, Jevons, Walras, Menger, and Marshall). This division is based on the conviction that there is a standard theory represented by Adam Smith, Stuart Mill, and Alfred Marshall, and that the theoreticians of the past in the last analysis split into two groups: into followers and opponents of the ruling doctrine. Haney sees in the history of dogmas a conflict between the two systems. He says,

> Beginning with Divine law and authority there came, in the sixteenth century, the reaction of the Renaissance and Humanism. Then naturalism became predominant in the Classicism of the eighteenth and early nineteenth century only to be followed by the double reaction of Romanticism and Historicism. Finally, the evolutionary-equilibrium school of Neo-Classicism emerged about 1890; and this in turn has brought on the 'Institutional' and the 'Universalist' or Neo-Romantic reactions. (1936: 784)

For the future Haney expects a new victory of the classical ideas. Obviously the permanent opposition of orthodoxy and criticism is his leading thought.

It is evident that this point of view is systematic rather than historical; this is shown especially by the inner grouping of the subject matter that Haney adopted. If his concept seems to demand it, Haney does not hesitate to separate what was united in life. Thus, for example, F.B.W. Hermann appears only after Schmoller, although the latter died in 1917, the former as early as 1868; thus, Bastiat comes before Say, so that the relation of predecessor to follower, teacher and disciple, seems inverted.

But this critical and systematic attitude does not tempt Haney into following an easy absolutism. He sees in all doctrines the connection of changing and lasting elements, and can everywhere find the contribution that a theory has made to the mass of knowledge that is today common property. To find the roots of the *communis opinio* of our days in the past was apparently the leading motive of his work. He therefore confines himself to economic theory in the proper sense of the word; fancy-mongers like Fourier he mentions only in passing, and he treats the whole of socialism as it should be treated in any history of political economy: "merely to indicate some aspects of its significance as a criticism of economic theory" (1936: 425, footnote 1). On the other hand, he looks for neglected theoreticians who have helped to shape modern thought, however small their contribution may have been: Lauderdale, Rae, Mc Leod, Richard Jones are to be named in this connection. And this concentration and consistency that governs his plan of selection is equally manifest in his analysis. Haney not only describes the main theories that he finds propounded by each thinker, but searches in each work for the basic concepts of the science. Thus, for instance, he looks for the rudiments of the theory of value with mercantilists and physiocrats and demonstrates them to the reader—a practice which greatly enriches his work. If from the fusion of the historical and the theoretical methods of approach we may expect the most enlightening study of the past of economic thought, Haney has certainly chosen the right course.

After the great shock that international scientific life suffered between 1914 and 1918, the necessity of surveying and valuing afresh the old heritage of culture became apparent. The historical point of view seemed best for the spirit of the time; the revolutions that afflicted Europe after the end of the war proved that even seemingly eternal values are only of limited duration, that even they, as all things human, rise and fall, and from the turmoil of the present mankind sought refuge in the past, where all difficulties seemed conquered, all problems solved, and all wounds healed. From these sentiments historicism, at least on the European continent, gained a new impulse.

The historiography of political economy was above all enriched by one great achievement: René Gonnard's three-volume *Histoire des Doctrines Economiques* (1930 [1921-22]). This work reflects the spirit of its epoch: the disinclination toward the old liberalism, which was rightly or wrongly made responsible for the disaster of the Great War; the refutation of the new socialism, which, adding social convulsions to the existing political problems, threatened the world with fresh catastrophes; and lastly, the hope of an organic solution lying between liberalism and socialism that would on the one hand overcome the struggle of all against all, and on the other avoid the immolation of the individual on the altar of mass dictatorship—in short a philosophy springing from the same roots as European romanticism after the French Revolution and the Napoleonic wars a century earlier.

Charles René Gonnard (born 1874) is one of the leading representatives of the historical movement in French economics. His lifework consists of numerous separate investigations based on the inductive method, the topics of which are derived from the problems of history, geography, and sociology. His publications on the problem of population are the most important (1898, 1907, 1923, 1927a); he also wrote some interesting papers on the economic and political problems of southeastern Europe (1908, 1911, 1927b); and lastly he is the author of valuable monographs on the history of political economy which prepared him for his comprehensive survey (1904a, 1904b, 1923). Recently he published a *Histoire des Doctrines Monétaires dans ses Rapports avec l'Histoire des Monnaies* in two volumes (1935-36).

Gonnard's *Histoire des Doctrines Économiques* is the most mature achievement in this realm that international historicism has yet produced. The merits and demerits of this great intellectual movement to which the social sciences owe so much are equally embodied in this work.

Without discussing the problem of the origin of political economy and its character, Gonnard opens his investigations with antiquity. He raises, however, the question concerning why economic science did not reach a high stage of development with the Greeks, and offers two explanations: "In the first place the very fact of the Greeks' extreme preoccupation with the state and its theory tended to turn their eyes away from economic phenomena . . . and, moreover, we must notice that these economic phenomena were definitely less apparent and striking than today" (1930: 4). And Gonnard does not stop at this superficial statement, but advances to the kernel of the problem: "For a long time there was no national economy proper, but only a collection of little private economies; the transition hardly made itself felt in the classical age." But he does not deduce the consequence of this perception that seems to force itself upon us: that the ancients, because they had no developed national economy, could not form a political economy but only—if we can call it so—a domestic economy, a doctrine of the *oikos*.

Gonnard demonstrates better than his predecessors that this science of domestic economy flourished with the Greeks and Romans. He names Jeron, Callicratides, Caretes of Paros, Xenophon, Cato, Varro, Columella, and Palladius, and calls special attention to the economic consideration in the narrower sense that Cato made on the different yields of the single crops, Varro on the productivity of free and forced labor, and Columella on the contrast between large and small agricultural estates. In describing these *scriptores de re rustica* [writers on agriculture] as "theoreticians of the old rural economy" (1930: 16)—they were indeed, *mutatis mutandis* to the ancient domestic and natural economy, what the classics were to modern exchange and national economy—only one small step divides him from the perception of the essential difference between precapitalistic and capitalistic economics, one step, however, that he failed to take. When using a striking simile he says: "In closing the study . . . of the economic concepts of the Middle Ages to embark upon that of the following period, one has the impression of leaving a cathedral of harmonious proportions . . . and of venturing forth into the turmoil of a market-place . . . amongst groups of merchants and packs of merchandize" (41), he rightly grasped the contrast between two worlds. But he did not think out what this contrast means for the history of economic thought.

The transition from mercantilism to physiocracy Gonnard viewed in the traditional manner: as a transition from empiricism to science, as a transition from practical contemplation to theoretical penetration. But this standpoint is open to attack in two ways: historically and in principle. Historically in so far as Quesnay's thought was in the last resort almost as pragmatical as the thought of Petty or Genovesi. Gonnard himself stresses this point in quoting a word of Goblot (1930:

189, cf. especially 202): "The physiocrats proposed to themselves a practical problem: the best means of increasing public riches"—hence, the same problem that the mercantilists had treated, only approached from a different angle. But even as concerns principle one cannot maintain that Quesnay was the first to treat economic life really scientifically; he strove indeed to find physical laws, but were they so superior in their essence and value to the rules of experience that Serra had propounded? Gonnard, who expresses the conviction that "patient observation and induction will probably [forever] remain the basis of the most fruitful economic method" (433), could not well answer this question in the affirmative without incurring the charge of inconsistency.

Gonnard saw the evolution of economic science with deep understanding of its dramatic element. He divided the past into six periods that he characterized poetically and at the same time appropriately as follows: the Doctrine of Moderation (antiquity and the Middle Ages); the Triumph of Plutus (mercantilism); the Revenge of Ceres (physiocracy); Prometheus Unchained (liberalism from Hume and Smith to the Austrians and mathematicians); the Revolt of Vulcanus (socialism); and the Lesson of Experience (Sismondi, List, Roscher, Schmoller, Le Play, syndicalism, and solidarism). Nobody will doubt that here the character of the great groups in the history of theories is ingeniously comprehended and described. For is not the essence of mercantilism the breakthrough of capitalistic thought that centers in material gain? Is not physiocracy the protest of an agrarian society against the predominance of trade and industry decreed from above? And what constitutes the character of liberalism, if not the will to unchain the productive forces? What characterizes the doctrine of socialism better than the reference to the revolt of the working masses against their fate?

One thing, however, is very striking in Gonnard's principle of division, the fact that the nineteenth century is not conceived as a whole with a uniform development from classicism over historicism to neoclassicism, but as a period in which the three great tendencies of thought—liberalism, socialism, and the historico-ethical school—continually coexisted, almost as if they had always developed in isolation side by side. This part of the work has the character of three monographs, all extending from the beginning of the century up to the time of writing, and we may presume that one of the basic concepts of the author lies behind this scheme.

This is indeed the case. While most other historians of political economy, especially Gide and Haney, view the evolution as a steady opposition of classicism and its adversaries, Gonnard believes it to be a struggle between ideological and realistic, abstract and concrete conceptions, or—practically—between the ideals of individualism (which are on the whole identical with those of socialism)[8] and the ideals of the organic doctrine (family, profession, and nation).

> The most comprehensive point of view from which to judge the conflict of economic doctrines is not perhaps the habitually chosen point of view of a contrast between the socialist and the liberal theses, but the point of view of a contest led simultaneously by the two inimical brothers, the liberal and the socialist, in the name of the rationalistic dogmas, against the doctrines of experience and realism. (1930: 261)

His sympathies lie with realism. "The lesson of experience" has a double meaning in Gonnard's mind. They characterize on the one hand the doctrinal essence of the school, the conviction that experience should be the basis of science; on the other they express the belief that history leads from ideology to realism, a realism that is superior in theory and politics to all other doctrines.

The conviction that individualism and socialism are germane and even identical in their nature forms one of the fundamental theses in Gonnard's work. Unlike Dühring or Gide, he views the two doctrines not as connected or fused in the present by a great synthesis, but as springing from a common origin. Already antiquity, as he suggests, developed both ideas side by side, socialism in Greek philosophy, individualism in Roman law. In the Renaissance there appears again a "double current of individualism and socialism" "the waters of which, issued from the same rock, mingle more than once in their parallel course towards the sea" (1930: 67). "In the last resort both are born from the aspiration of the individual to freedom" (260). This

---

8. "The liberal school and socialism developed . . . two parallel ideologies which . . . are inspired by the same individualist concept. One might say that the doctrine of Manchester is the individualism of the strong—and the doctrine of the socialists the individualism of the weak" (1930: 583).

is the decisive idea on which, according to Gonnard, both theories are built. "All . . . are inspired by the same individualist philosophy. . . . All agree in the greatest possible liberation of the individual against the natural intermediary groupings of family, nation, profession" (503). "Modern socialism is the twin brother of Manchester liberalism: their quarrels are family quarrels" (440).

No doubt Gonnard has here put into relief a fact that is too often forgotten. The inner connection between liberalism and socialism, as he sees it, indeed exists. The ideal that both doctrines proclaimed is the perfect conciliation between individual and common interests, a society without tensions and problems in which the welfare of all members represents the highest of all laws. The program of liberalism was originally as social[9] as the program of socialism is individualistic; freedom in the state and freedom in economic life—only that liberalism strove to reach this aim by private property in the means of production, while socialism believes it is to be realized by common property in the means of production.

So far so good. But in observing the ideological affinity of the two systems we must not (like Gonnard) forget their historical contrast. Liberalism was the ideology of the bourgeoisie in their struggle against feudalism, socialism is the ideology of the workers in their struggle against capitalism—a contrast as great as that between the eighteenth and the nineteenth centuries, a contrast that Gonnard does not describe or appreciate.

Between liberalism and socialism there stands the experience of the industrial revolution. The bourgeoisie of the eighteenth century envisaged as ideal a society of independent citizens who—furnished with secure property in their means of production—could, under the system of free competition, promote their well-being only by serving their neighbors with all their might, that is to say, a classless society to which—because of its equality of opportunities—all social problems must necessarily be foreign. It seemed for one fleeting moment as if this dream were to become a reality—the moment in which Adam Smith created his eternal monument of liberalism. But a new factor

---

9. Gonnard one-sidedly puts into relief only the individualist element in socialism, but not the social element in liberalism.

appeared on the field that changed the face of society: the industrial revolution. It divided the industrial producers into capitalists and proletarians, shifting all the means of production into the hands of the capitalists and leaving to the proletarians nothing but their labor-power—and thus the old ideal was destroyed, for equality in economic life was annihilated and only liberty in political life went over into the nineteenth century. At this point, of course, the spirits also parted. Liberalism turned from a revolutionary into a conservative doctrine because the bourgeoisie retained from their old program only the demand for political freedom, flinging overboard the will to economic equality. Socialism changed from a utopian dream into a political movement when the working class proclaimed the will to continue the struggle for the realization of the old ideal of society in a new way, by the abolition of private property in the means of production.

In his splendid appreciation of the two great Frenchmen of the Restoration—J.B. Say and Saint-Simon—Gonnard touches (one would say unconsciously) on the essential point. "According to Saint-Simon" he says (1930: 363), "society must be organized, while, according to Say, it regulates itself spontaneously." Here opens the abyss that yawns between liberalism and socialism. Gonnard himself named three institutions that divide the two doctrines from one another: productive property, free competition, and social inequality. Liberalism advocates their preservation, socialism their removal—a contrast that is much more than a slight difference between otherwise identical ideologies.

Capitalistic society, as it developed after 1790 in England and France, rests on productive property, free competition, and social inequality. Therefore, the theory of liberalism since Smith is an analysis of reality, and hence a genuine science; socialism (in so far as it is not, like that of Marx, social critique that also takes the existing order as its object) is only an ideology, the formation of a day-dream or at best of a program. "There is no science but of what exists. Now, what ought to be, does not exist by its very definition. The society of tomorrow cannot be the object of the investigation of the scientists of today" (Laskine 1920: 63). It follows from this statement that Gonnard's connection of the two doctrines, even their parallel treatment in one work that is after all intended to relate the history of a science, is in the last resort unjustified, not less unjustified than the teleological connection in Dühring and Gide.

Gonnard, however, conceives the decisive antithesis not in the contrast between the analysis of reality and speculation on its transformation, but in the contrast between the a priori or deductive and the a posteriori or inductive view. "Individualism and socialism" he says (1930: 442),

> are better understood if we bear in mind that both depend upon a common ideology, the principal outlines of which have been formulated by the French and English philosophers and economists of the 18th century, on an ideology in its basis above all rational and aprioristic—and the antithesis of which is to be looked for in the whole of the empirical doctrines which have protested in the name of the misunderstood realities—family, nation, profession.

Yet is it possible to suggest that the economic analysis of liberalism and the social critique of socialism were governed by preconceived opinions and that only the historico-ethical thought might call itself genuinely realistic? Precisely a realistic treatment of the history of social economics that (at variance with Gonnard) sees behind all ideas the time and the space that have given them birth will realize that all science, however it may be constituted, is but an attempt to interpret reality—a truth that is nowhere more obvious than in political economy.

The same tendencies that served as a background to Gonnard's great work gave, after 1918, Spann's little book wide circulation in Germany; on both sides of the Rhine the same desire for an organic philosophy of life was dominant with the only difference being that in the country of Descartes it had a more rationalist, in the country of Hegel a more romantic, bias. Nevertheless Spann's book did not everywhere meet with approval, and that is to be explained by the fact that he gives too much prominence to his dogmatic judgment. So there was room for a book of the same type but which treated the past with less prejudice. Such a book was written by Edgar Salin (born 1892).

If we try to assign to Salin a place in the historical tendencies within political economy, we do best to call him a member of the third generation of German historicism. The first generation, represented by Roscher, had indeed in principle embraced a dynamic and realistic interpretation of life, but retained in their economic theory the doctrines of classicism. The second generation, whose leader was Schmoller, casting away the heritage of Ricardo and Thuenen, wished to draw consistent conclusions from their fundamental idea, and, in doing so, lost themselves in positivism and empiricism. Lastly the third generation, which is represented by Max Weber and Werner Sombart, strove by the contemplation of society and history to reach a comprehensive spiritual view that should be in its nature neither aprioristic and aloof from life nor merely descriptive and kaleidoscopic, but should securely grasp the social essence of the phenomena—an endeavor that is also reflected in Salin's work.

Edgar Salin set out not only to grapple with the narrow problems of economic science, but also with the wide questions of culture and history. Evidence of this are his thoughtful and scholarly, but by no means uncriticized, books *Platon und die griechische Utopie* (1921) and *Civitas Dei* (1926). His thought has its roots in the intellectual circle of Stefan George—that aristocratic German poet and prophet who, developing Nietzsche's philosophy of the superman, opposed to the inferior life of reality an ideal counterpart in spirit. The mythical, heroic, and all that is to be comprehended only by intuition, not by reason, are the basis of this superidealistic view of the world, which is derived from Baudelaire, Verlaine, Rossetti, and d'Annunzio, and which had much greater influence on Germany's thought and history than was to be expected from the size of the group that has been called "George-Kreis."

Just as George rejected naturalism in poetry and painting and aimed at a spiritualized art, Salin rejects positivism in sociology and economics and aims at a spiritualized science. He declared, spurning at once the materialism both of Ricardo and of Schmoller—for the rationalistic as well as the empiristic view of the world must appear to this hyperidealism in such a light—that the generation of 1920 must return to the foundations that Müller, List, and Knies had laid in the romantic period, that is, to the foundations on which organic sociology had stood. His view of history is of the same kind: the *Geschichte der Volkswirtschaftslehre* (1923) regards it as its task to depict the development of economic thought in its spiritual connections—a task that is certainly agreeable to a disciple of neoromanticism.

Salin's judgment on the origin of our science runs as follows:

Political Economy as a science is a phenomenon which belongs exclusively
to European and American modernity. Its history opens with the awakening
of the individualist spirit, with the rise of national territories and states, and
with the victory of rationalistic capitalism over the traditional economic
methods of the Middle Ages. (1923: 1)

Now what is unusual in his attitude is not its result—this is natural
enough for a thinker who does not wish to cling to outward
appearances, but seeks to reach the kernel—but its extremely idealistic
motivation. For Salin what is historically decisive is the "change in
the relation of man to economy and science," and he thinks it possible
to disregard the "variation of economic forms and the resulting
variation of doctrine" between the Middle Ages and modern times,
feudalism and capitalism. This extreme view, however, seems to
challenge the contradiction of all historians. For anyone who, like
Salin, would take the historical content of the idea *political* economy
(*Volkswirtschaftslehre*) seriously, must admit the rise of *national*
Economy (*Volkswirtschaft*) (as the modern economy, e.g., in the sense
of Bücher's theory of stages) to be the decisive moment for the origin
of politico-economic science rather than any intellectual developments.
It is the objective element not the subjective that so clearly
distinguishes medieval from modern economic thought; the "Christian
view of the world" hardly changed in its essence. It is characteristic
that in his "Introduction aux oeuvres de Quesnay" Dupont de Nemours
pronounces the great sentence (1923: 21): "The natural order is the
physical constitution which God himself has given to the universe."
The epoch-making change took place not in mind, but in matter, a
truth to which the historically minded economist should not close his
eyes.

The essential element of modern economic science is in Salin's view
its autonomy. It asserts itself externally and internally: externally in
the detachment of its intellectual and doctrinal system from the
theological whole, internally in the acknowledgment of economy as an
end in itself.

Proceeding from this thesis, Salin describes the history of political
economy (i.e., the history of theoretical economics in the proper sense
of the word) as a purely spiritual process. The delineation is clear and
unequivocal; only where he inserts between Mill and Marx a
discussion of the socialistic ideas and ideals—of Joachim of Floris and

Gracchus Babeuf, Saint-Simon and Fourier—a certain deviation is to be perceived. For the socialists before Marx were given to fantasy and not to science; their aim was the vision of an ideal and not the analysis of reality, so that they should not have been included in Salin's work.

Salin divides the history of modern economics into three periods; periods of political, systematic, and evolutionistic science: the first comprises mercantilism, the second physiocracy and classicism, the third historicism and socialism. At the root of this principle of division lies Salin's idealistic philosophy. The reflection that induced him to start an epoch with the appearance of the first mercantilists is his conviction of the "change in general attitude towards the world" between the fourteenth and seventeenth centuries, a change consisting of the fact that whereas the schoolmen had chosen as the goal of their thought the justification of reality, the mercantilists aimed at its investigation; the former had been concerned with apology, the latter with analysis. The mercantilistic period is likewise delimited in a purely intellectual way: to the premercantilistic Middle Ages the aim was the Catholic Cathedral, to the postmercantilistic modern times individual happiness. The mercantilists, however, desired to serve the national state; they pursued a practical and political end, and therefore Salin calls their era the period of "political" science.

The intellectual factor, which, according to Salin's view, led from mercantilism to physiocracy and classicism and replaced the political by the systematic science, was "the union between the philosophy of natural law and economic analysis" as established for some decades after Quesnay. After John Stuart Mill, then, occurs the transition from systematic to evolutionist science. For in that time "the metaphysical leadership" is assumed by the "strangest, deepest, and most mysterious force of the 19th century, the hidden idea which takes the place of the Deity of the Middle Ages and of the Nature of the 18th century: the idea of evolution" (1923: 62).

With the breakthrough of the idea of evolution Salin believes the foundations of present-day economic science to be laid. The chapter entitled "Socialism and Historicism" or "Evolutionistic Science," which closes with a criticism of Schmoller's lifework, is followed only by a short appendix entitled "Successors and Pioneers." Here he discusses the theory of marginal utility that he conceives to be only a "completion of the objective theory," not an epoch-making new achievement (1923: 95). At this juncture historical investigation becomes present-day discussion.

Salin's division of development into three phases is (like Eisenhart's periodization) characteristic of the concept of historicism. He based it not on the narrow dogmatism of the schools, but on the broad philosophy of life of the thinkers of the past, and so a survey of history is presented that shows the parallelism between the progress of economic science and the change of culture in general. For this point was paramount in the thought of all those who professed historicism; it was their highest dogma and deepest conviction that the economic theories of the past, like all intellectual phenomena, are but an expression of social life.

So historicism had hardly altered its character at all in the fifty years between Wilhelm Roscher and Edgar Salin. Its followers, with very few exceptions, gave the same answer to the three basic problems of the history of economic thought. The origin of political economy they are inclined to find in antiquity—in spite of the ever-present knowledge of the change of economic life they rarely perceived its entire change of character; the basis for the division of development they are inclined to seek in the great periods of cultural history, not in the small alterations in abstract theory, because the science of economics means to them only a part in the broad stream of evolution; and lastly as regards the delimitation of the field of investigation proper to economic science, they wish to comprehend and describe the whole reflection of the economic system in the human mind—for they are reluctant to divide what really belonged together. Behind all these ideas, however, is the great creed of the spirit born of romanticism that all life, however manifold its variety in space and time may appear, must be understood as a grand and indivisible unity.

3

The Theoretical Approach

In 1871, the year in which Eugen Dühring first published his *Kritische Geschichte der Nationalökomie und des Sozialismus*, two books appeared that were destined to lead economic thought into entirely new channels: Stanley Jevons's *Theory of Political Economy* and Carl Menger's *Grundsätze der Volkswirthschaftslehre*. To the dominant descriptive economics of the day they opposed an exact economic theory, and the antagonism between these two schools, strikingly expressed in the well-known discussion on method, quickly became so general that it extended to all, even the remotest, branches of economic science. Even on the past of political economy different views were held in the hostile camps, and so it was not long before the historical view of development was confronted by an ideological counterpart.

The first after Dühring, however, to treat the history of doctrines from the point of view of theory, Luigi Cossa (1831-1896), was, in spite of all his understanding of marginal utility, a follower of the old, rather than of the new, classicism. This is manifest in his *Primi elementi di economia politica* (1875) as well as in his *Saggi di economia politica* (1878); and the *Guida allo studio dell'economia politica* (1876), which is of great importance for our discussion, was written in the same spirit. Cossa's position in the development of economic thought is similar to that of John Elliot Cairnes: both belonged to the rear guard of Ricardo's school, which had, for the last time, been so splendidly represented by Mill; and both helped to hand down to a new generation the principles of abstract economic analysis, which, between 1848 and 1871, were almost submerged in the flood of empiricist description of economic reality.

Cossa's attitude toward the central problem of the economic discussion of his time is shown by his own clear words:

> political economy is distinct from all historical and descriptive branches of economics. These branches deal with concrete facts about wealth as they have variously appeared at different times and in different places, while political economy as such is confined to the abstract and unvarying play of typical and assured phenomena. (1893: 11-12)

Pure theory—he speaks aptly of "reasoned economics" (15)—is to him therefore "a science in the strictest sense," and "science . . . is any system of general truth applicable to any given order of facts" (40). He even rejected the fundamental thesis of the historical school, relativism, *expressis verbis*:

> [T]hough the conditions of civilization are variable in their very nature, this does not force us to ignore that the laws of the physical world, the psychical qualities of individuals, together with certain familiar tendencies in social organisations, are now, always were, and will be always, the same. Accordingly those numerous economic facts which spring from them can never undergo any substantial change. Who is so bold . . . as to maintain that the principles of profit and loss, of the influence of scarcity on value, and of the price of merchandise upon output, have purely local and provisional value? (1893: 84-85)

While these considerations are reminiscent of Cherbuliez and Cairnes, Cossa, on the other hand, never wholly escaped from the influence of Roscher whose disciple he had been in his youth. Thus, for example, he did not reject the organic interpretation of society (1893: 10 et seq.), and in his final judgment on the methodological discussion he recognized some measure of truth in the views of both parties: "Social economics," he says (1893: 81), meaning pure theory (cf. 17), "is a science based on observation which employs the deductive and the inductive methods, using them alternately, sometimes in one order, sometimes in another, and assigning to each functions whose relative importance varies according to the requirements of the several parts of which this branch of knowledge consists." He held induction to be more suitable for the theory of production and consumption, and deduction to be suitable for the theory of circulation and distribution—a thesis the first part of which probably no consistent supporter of an economics built upon the principles of natural science would ever accept.

That Cossa was a follower of the last classicists, but had received many ideas from the first historians, is nowhere more apparent than in his *Introduction to the Study of Political Economy* (1893) first published in 1876, the translation of the *Guida* that had been made at the suggestion of Stanley Jevons.[1]

Cossa more than any other author realized the problem involved in the question of the origin of economic science. He believed that the dilemma of the two views, the conflict between the ancient and the modern origin of economics, may be escaped by drawing a clear distinction. We must distinguish, so he thinks, between ideas on the one hand, and systems of ideas on the other:

> [I]t must be allowed as a matter of fact, that no independent economic systems, with a more or less determined field of investigation, and with their own specially adapted methods of research, are to be found before . . . the period of Quesnay and Smith. But on the other hand . . . important economic ideas of a scientific character have been handed down to us either as fragments, or in works treating of applied philosophy, law, and theology, both from ancient and from medieval times, constituting altogether a remarkable portion of our intellectual patrimony. (1893: 127)

So he adopts in the end the opinion that political economy is as old as all the other sciences; critical remarks on Dühring and Eisenhart affirm it (1893: 119). Cossa thus utterly failed to grasp the essential difference between the old and the new ideas, which springs from the fundamental reality that the old ideas had a precapitalistic economy as its object, while the new ideas had a capitalistic *exchange* economy. That no system of economic science was formed before Quesnay is due simply to the fact that the interdependence of all economic

---

1. The first edition bears the title *Guide*, the second, that of 1893, the title *Introduction*. Similarly the Italian editions changed over to the name *Introduzione*.

phenomena did not yet exist, or could not yet be perceived, before the middle of the eighteenth century. It is only modern capitalism that, through the market, draws all producers into one system; only under its aegis could the formation of a system of economic ideas be reached, or rather, only the reflection of the capitalistic order necessarily connects all branches of economic life in theory as it sees them connected in practice. The ideas of precapitalistic times were as isolated as the economic activities of the generally, or at least preponderantly, self-contained social units.

Starting from this viewpoint, Cossa tried to master the problem of the periodization of development. He distinguishes four periods: a fragmentary one (antiquity, the Middle Ages, and some authors of the seventeenth century), an empirical (from the sixteenth to the middle of the eighteenth centuries), a scientific (1750-1850), and lastly a critical one (the present).

In the fragmentary period, the thinkers—mostly divines or philosophers—give us as a rule only fragmentary utterances on economics. "[P]olitical economy as such was parcelled out among and confused with allied branches of knowledge" (1893: 164). The age of empiricism produced numerous special studies on practical problems of production and trade, traffic and taxation. "Polemical writings, defending more or less successfully and exclusively the interest of one set of producers or consumers, gradually took on a definite shape of their own, so as to become empirical systems of political and financial economics" (164). Cantillon and Hume are the immediate forerunners of scientific economics in the strict sense of the word. "The unparalleled merit of having created a scientific system of political economy . . . undoubtedly belongs to a man of genius named François Quesnay" (257). What is the specifically new, the specifically scientific, element in the physiocratic doctrine? "When I speak of theirs as the first scientific system, I intend to convey the fact that they deduced from a few ultimate principles a perfectly homogeneous whole comprising pure economics as well as political and financial economics" (257).

The scientific period in the development of political economy stretches, according to Cossa, from Quesnay through Adam Smith and his immediate followers down to John Stuart Mill. From the middle of the nineteenth century he no longer surveys the literature in its historical sequence, but in its national grouping, including the historical school, the socialist, and the marginal utility theories under the name of criticism (to wit, of the classics). The essence of this criticism he describes as its will to a higher development of the science:

> [B]y comparing the teachings of different schools, and by discussing the foundations of the science, an attempt is in progress which seeks to remove ambiguities, to perfect methods of study, to gather together in greater mass and detail the fruits of observation, to make scientific conclusions more complete and exact, and with the utmost care to frame rules for the practical economist. (1893: 125)

This division of the matter into four parts that Cossa adopts is sound in so far as he, like Eisenhart and Ingram, delimits the periods as they must be delimited according to the nature of the subject. But his description has the further merit of making the character of scientific work in the different ages appear as the principle of periodization. The methodological principle by which Cossa was led, is, no doubt, right. Its realization, however, is less fortunate, for the delineation of the four periods is anything but apt.

First, as regards the fragmentary period, the important characteristic is not that it has produced only isolated utterances on economic questions, but rather that it was concerned more or less with a natural economy, and that not the will to perception prevailed, but a critical attitude based on the standpoint of the "Ought," as is proper to any system of planning. The second period could more aptly be described as fragmentary, because its thinkers in fact discussed only isolated problems, especially problems of population and foreign trade. Cossa calls this age the age of empiricism, but this is not very appropriate. Many thoughts of the mercantilists were the result not of experience but of speculation, just as many thoughts of the classicists sprang not from speculation but from experience. This is also the reason why the mercantile system and classicism cannot be distinguished as empiricism and science: at best they might be compared as fragmentary and synthetic treatment, for (as Cossa has clearly realized) the epoch-making innovation in Quesnay's work is the idea of system, which he was the first (after Cantillon) to conceive. The opposition of classicism to the later schools as science to critique is equally incorrect. We have seen how Cossa describes the aims of scientific work in the period of criticism: the critical point of view is not characteristic of it, but the endeavor of the disciples to perfect the system of the masters—the present is to him indeed, as he says in one place, a "period of revision" (1893: 125) rather than a period of critique. Starting from Cossa's essentially sound foundations one should describe the three successive epochs of the newer development not as fragmentary, scientific, and critical, but as ages of isolated investigations, of the formation of systems, and of the epigones.

Cossa, developing Romagnosi's definition, describes political economy as "an ordered knowledge of the cause, the essence, and the rationale of the social system of wealth" (1893: 10) and assigns to it a twofold task: the finding of the economic laws, and the formulation of the political rules, which govern, or should govern, the economic system. In this way the object of the historical description would seem to be determined. But Cossa exceeds these limits. He follows many side paths: poor relief, public finance, utopias, even research in economic history—without, however, wandering too long from the main course of his investigation. This breadth of view, kept in check by a clear knowledge of the right proportions, gives to Cossa's work its distinctive charm and value. But—like his judgment on the problems of the origin and development of the science—it proves that he did not fully outgrow the conceptions of historicism; in all that he thought and wrote, he was and remained, after all, only an eclectic.

Cossa's book achieved rapid and complete success. Not only did it reach numerous editions in Italy, but it was translated into English, French, Spanish, and German, so that its circulation—*faute de mieux*—became worldwide. But as the deeper classicism sank into the past, the more obsolete Cossa's survey necessarily appeared. Toward the end of the century an attempt was made in France to replace it by something more modern; in 1899 the first edition of Joseph Rambaud's *Histoire des Doctrines Economiques* was published.

Joseph Rambaud's (1845-1919) mentality—expressed in his *Éléments* (1895) and his *Cours d'Economie Politique* (1910)—represents a perfect synthesis between liberalism and Catholicism. "We believe" so runs his creed, "that it is no less easy to draw from the spectacle of the economic world, than from the spectacle of inanimate creation, a hymn in praise of Providence and the infinite wisdom of God"

(Rambaud 1902: 165). He was convinced that there was a uniform and in essence timeless truth offered to man both by revelation, through the medium of theology, and perception, through the medium of science. "If Political Economy" he says (450-51), "is a science, that is to say if it discovers and possesses truths . . . these truths must have their place in the order divine, and . . . the laws which coordinate them must be amongst the innumerable manifestations of the eternal wisdom that has created and governs the world." A confession of relativism seemed to him almost a sacrilege: "In the economic, as in the physical and moral worlds, so long as these two latter do not change, there must exist immutable natural laws imposed upon man who knows them and conforms to them more or less perfectly" (510). History cannot produce a change in the essence: "In the Roman world of the fourth century the economic laws could no less be violated than in the France of 1793" (31). Having this "inexorable fatality of the economic laws" (134) before his eyes, Rambaud defined political economy in the style of Menger and Walras: "Economic science . . . is the knowledge of the relations or laws . . . which connect one phenomenon considered as effect, to another phenomenon which is regarded as its cause" (33).

In spite of this fundamental concept that is put forth with great spirit, Rambaud adopted many ideas ultimately derived from historicism, such as the view that nations represent independent units between man and mankind. "It seems to us that if one will see in the public and civil societies nothing but the sum-total of individuals, one will never be capable of explaining and justifying certain phenomena and certain rights of a social character" (1902: 402-3). And even in the question of methodology he was not uninfluenced by relativism; he speaks of a "barrenness of the mathematical method in political economy" (439) and strongly emphasized the importance of induction: "political economy [should be based]," he says in one place (70), "on the incessant observation of all phenomena of production, exchange, and social life."

The firm belief that the economic system is governed by natural laws and that these natural laws can be discovered by observation led Rambaud to declare political economy to be a modern science.

> The physiocrats, whatsoever errors they have committed, were the first to have the merit of grounding their system on the principle of natural

> economic laws. . . . This is the reason why it is not unjust to begin
> Political Economy proper with the great school of the physiocrats who were
> so thoroughly convinced of the existence and necessity of those laws. (1902:
> 142)

However, if these laws were already working for centuries, why—we
must ask—were they not discovered before 1750? Rambaud gives a
simple answer to this question:

> The long delay which the difficult birth of economic science has undergone,
> had two main reasons: 1) the absence of statistical studies, and 2) contempt
> for the inductive method. Statistics is in fact of entirely recent origin....
> Social phenomena, stated in too fragmentary a manner, did not furnish
> sufficient material to the spirit of observation. . . . The deductive method
> . . . applied to the science of wealth too easily opens the way to aprioristic
> formulae and has never produced anything which has not been promoted
> and sustained by the inductive method. (1902: 9-10)

The argument that Rambaud puts forward here is, however, anything
but consistent. The literature on domestic economy as it developed
after Xenophon and Columella throughout the ages until it reached a
flourishing state in the sixteenth and seventeenth centuries (England's
books on the art of husbandry, Germany's "Haus-Vaeter" literature)
was entirely empirical. Why was national economy not as well treated
empirically? This question Rambaud could at best have answered
from his standpoint by saying: thus it was! But this answer is no
answer.

Rambaud, indeed, like Eisenhart, made an observation that might
have brought him to the proper way: that a special money theory arose
before the general market theory. "In the 13th century," he says
(1902: 75-76), "political economy proper was nowhere to be found
even in germ; it is only in the 14th century that it begins to appear and
on one point of detail alone, i.e., in a theory of money which
perceives or supposes the constancy of certain natural laws of an
economic order." He mentions this in connection with Buridanus,
Oresmius, Biel, Pirkheimer, Copernicus, and the "Gemeine Stymmen
von der Muentze," particularly, however—and this is decidedly a
merit—Bodinus's "Réponse aux paradoxes de M. de Malestroit
touchant l'enchérissement de toutes choses et la monnaie" of 1568.
Rambaud, like Ferrara, understood the importance of Bodinus in the

evolution of economic thought. While Malestroit believed gold to be a stable measure of value (and the rise of prices to be due only to the lowering of the metal contents of the coins), Bodin found that the value of gold declines if its quantity increases (and that the greater amount of precious metals that France now held as compared with previous times, had caused the general dearness)—a perception that, indeed, proves his true insight into economic relations, and his exact observation of facts.

As Rambaud takes the belief in the existence of natural laws in economic life for the criterion of science in political economy, he also bases it on his division. Delimiting the physiocrats from the mercantilists he says:

> A common feature will now approximate the different schools which we shall study: and this common feature is that the economic facts will appear interconnected by relations which arbitrary acts and the fancy of men are unable to change. . . . Such is the doctrine of economic laws characterized by the belief in a certain natural and permanent order of societies. But what is this order? . . . Here opinions may differ. . . . No matter: even if all the writers differ as to the application of the principle they are at least agreed as to its existence and they make it the foundation of their theories leaving to the historical school the illusion that nothing is absolute in this world, leaving to state socialism the error that the state molds and leads the nation as it pleases, leaving finally to absolute socialism the ambition of pretending that man is strong enough to bring paradise to earth, if he only banishes the family, property, or at least individual liberty. (1902: 141-42)

These words make Rambaud's conception obvious and understandable: he first describes the development of the view that he regards as right in its different forms from the physiocrats through Smith, Ricardo, Mill, Carey, Bastiat, Menger, Walras down to LePlay ("Les Théories des Lois Economiques"); then he surveys the first, not too great deviation from truth ("L'Historisme et le Socialisme d'Etat"); and in the end the false and dangerous ideology of socialism ("Le Socialisme").

It might seem for a moment as if this division, in spite of its, one should almost say, moral character, was based on a correct idea, the contrast of the static and dynamic views of life, that is, the contrast of the rationalist economics of Smith and Ricardo and the evolutionist sociology of Knies and Marx. But the appearance is deceptive. For

Rambaud places List and Sismondi with Smith and Ricardo; in grouping he is led by his valuation, not by his knowledge. Because he has some understanding of List's and Sismondi's ideas on economic and social policy, he severs them from Roscher and Comte with whom he is out of sympathy—a procedure that is anything but scientific.

Rambaud conceives as a necessary combination the connection between historicism and state socialism, which was in fact only slight—there was an outspokenly liberal evolutionism, and Darwin's doctrines of the struggle for existence and of the survival of the fittest were very helpful to social (or we should perhaps say a-social) Manchesterism. He says of the group issuing from Hegel and Comte:

> To the principle of the constancy and of the absolute character of the natural laws of economy they oppose the doctrine of the relativity and consequently of the historical changeability of the laws that govern the economic world. To the principle of liberty which the state should leave to the individuals and families they oppose . . . the doctrine of the state as molder and mover of society charged to foresee for the individuals and provide for their needs. The first idea we call *historicism*; the second *state socialism*. In the final analysis they are less two schools than two aspects of the same school. . . . For the historical school, the main idea of which is to reduce the part of the absolute and even to exclude it if possible, easily arrives whichever way it takes, at state socialism . . . because it has abandoned the old formula of intangible and immutable natural laws. (1902: 486, 524-25)

Thus, Rambaud—like Boucke after him—misled by the fact that most (though not all!) followers of historicism were advocates of social reform (by no means of state socialism), has seen the idea of development in political colors. This is fundamentally wrong. For static and evolutionist laws of society may equally appear as subject or not subject to human influence: Rambaud's belief in fixed natural laws of unchanging essence corresponds to Spencer's belief in fixed natural laws of progressing evolution; Owen's conviction that society (conceived as static) may be freely formed corresponds to Lenin's view that the social order, rapidly changing as it is, may be voluntarily turned into a permanent system of communism; the contrasts intersect, and friends as well as enemies of the principle of evolution are divided into followers and adversaries of interventionism, or followers and adversaries of laissez faire.

As Rambaud relegated socialism as it were to a sort of appendix, his investigation gained a certain unity. He follows the development of economic thought fairly closely. Many thinkers who are generally neglected are brought to light, for example Graslin, the antagonist of Quesnay (*Essai analytique sur la richesse et sur l'impôt, où l'on refute la nouvelle doctrine économique*, 1767) and Doubleday, the antagonist of Malthus (*The True Law of Population shown to be connected with the Food of the People*, 1841). If the discussion of these theoreticians is a merit rather than a fault, the opposite is to be said of the inclusion of such men of affairs as Colbert. In this direction Rambaud is not quite sure of his delimitation. Here it becomes manifest that he did not fully overcome the heritage of historicism.

Rambaud's book held the field for only about a decade; then it was quickly, more quickly perhaps than was just, replaced by a work that for neoclassicism had the same importance as Haney's study for historicism: the *Histoire des Doctrines Economiques depuis les Physiocrates* (1909), written by Gide in collaboration with Rist.

Charles Gide (1847-1932), like Cossa, was, at the beginning of his career, subject to historicist influences as they may best be characterized by the names of Auguste Comte and Wilhelm Roscher. But although no doctrinaire by nature, he was still, as Bouglé aptly emphasized, (1932: 1719) no "tempérament d'historien." In the broad synthesis that his economic doctrine represents—it is embodied mainly in his *Principes d'Économie Politique* (1884) and the *Cours d'Économie Politique* (1909)—classicism and neoclassicism form the determining elements, and he has therefore justly been compared to Alfred Marshall with whom he has a common spiritual father: John Stuart Mill.

In his *Cours* Gide rejects the postulate put forward by Comte that political economy must be and must remain part and parcel of a comprehensive sociology, and declares the cultivation of an exact economic theory to be necessary. He describes its scope as follows:

> Political Economy pure . . . studies *the spontaneous relations* that arise between men living together as it might study the relations that arise between any bodies whatsoever, "those necessary relations which derive from the nature of things," as Montesquieu said. . . . Hence it tends to set itself up as a natural science. (Gide 1909: 3)

The term *science* and especially *natural science*, however, is very strictly interpreted by Gide: "When we apply the word 'science' to any branch of human knowledge . . . we mean to say that the facts with which it deals *are connected by certain constant relations which have been discovered and which are called laws*" (5). In this sense Gide definitely affirmed the existence of natural laws in economic life. He is, however, in this respect (as in every other) no extremist, and the method that he follows is so constituted that induction and deduction, abstract thought and concrete observation, are in mutual equilibrium.

Gide's collaborator in his representation of the history of doctrines, Charles Rist (born 1873), is more a practical man than a theoretician. He is one of the leading financial experts of France, and problems of the monetary and banking systems have been the main subjects of his lifework (*Les Finances de guerre de l'Allegmagne* 1921 etc.). His predilection for the history of doctrines is expressed not only in the book written together with Gide, but also in a recently published *Histoire des Doctrines relatives au crédit et à la monnaie depuis John Law* (1938), in which both of Rist's special fields of investigation are most favorably united.

In Gide and Rist historical interest in the past of economics is very light, while the theoretical point of view predominates. Indeed, they do not intend to exclude the representation of ideas that, judged according to the standards of the present, appear erroneous. But it is a pedagogic interest and not a historical one that leads them to adopt this procedure. The discussion of errors, they think, is useful "in showing in what respects certain doctrines are open to criticism either owing to a fault in their logic or through an inexact observation of facts" (Gide and Rist 1909: xii). And they regard the past development of doctrines only as a previous history of the present systems:

> We have endeavored to bring into prominence mainly such doctrines —whether true or false—as have contributed to the formation of ideas generally accepted at the present time, or such as are connected with these in the line of direct descent. In other words, the book is an attempt to give an answer to the following questions: who is responsible for formulating those principles that constitute the framework—provisionary or definitive—of economics as at present taught? (xiii)

In accordance with this dogmatical aim Gide and Rist do not seek the origin of political economy in dark antiquity, but begin with the discussion of the physiocrats. All thinkers before Quesnay were but forerunners; Quesnay was the founder of the science. Gide rightly emphasized the decisive point: the analysis of the *whole* process of national economy that we owe to Quesnay's school. "The physiocrats were the first to grasp the conception of a unified science of society in the full sense of the word, i.e., they were the first to realize that all social facts are linked together by the bonds of inevitable laws" (1909: 3), and this is, indeed, their great contribution to the advancement of learning.

The concentration of interest on modern theories also determined the principle of periodization that Gide and Rist adopted. They group "the doctrines into families according to their descent . . . presenting them in their chronological order" (1909: xiii). Thus, they treat first the founders, then their adversaries; after that the triumph of the liberal school and then the dissidents; lastly, in a fifth chapter, the present. It is easy to perceive in this division the view of the authors: they regard classicism and neoclassicism as the dominant doctrines compared with which all other schools and thinkers, however different they may have been, appear simply as deviations.

This division of the matter shows its strength in the positive and its weakness in the negative definitions. In the sections on the founders and the liberals the evolution of orthodoxy is followed consistently from Smith through Malthus and Ricardo, Say and Bastiat, Nassau Senior and Stuart Mill, down to the hedonists, and thus a comprehensive picture of the character and changes of the classical doctrine is presented. But in those parts of the work that deal with the opposing theories and thoughts there is not the same clarity.[2] Gide and Rist themselves express the conviction that "economic science proper" is the "science that is concerned not with the presentation of

---

2. It is surprising how much space is devoted to the Utopians. Rist indeed discussed the contrast between the realistic and the nonrealistic viewpoints (267 et seq.) but he is not aware how important it is to distinguish in the socialists between the analysis of the present and the hopes of the future. The one—a contribution to science— belongs no doubt to a history of economics; the other, however—a product of imagination—certainly does not. It is absurd to treat Ricardo and Tolstoy in one work.

what ought to be, but simply with the explanation and the understanding of what actually exists" (1909: 777). But their book is a bad illustration of this delimitation of its subject, which certainly conforms to the *communis opinio*. The chapters entitled "The Antagonists" and "The Dissenters" transcend the bounds that the nature of its subject matter has imposed. Here we find Friedrich List inserted between Fourier and Proudhon, Karl Marx between Adolph Wagner and Le Play—in short all the most disparate theories intermingled, which, partly concerned with the analysis of reality, partly aiming at the presentation of an ideal of the state and society, are connected only by the common opposition to liberalism, an opposition, moreover, that is often problematic and by no means uniform. If one wishes, as do Gide and Rist, to choose the doctrines of the schools as the determining factor in periodization, one should regard the positive theses of the single groups as decisive, and not their negative criticisms.

The thoroughgoing comparison of liberal and social or socialistic systems is, however, in line with the logic of the whole investigation in so far as Gide and Rist are of the opinion that a synthesis of the two hostile tendencies constitutes the task of the present. Charles Gide, "the great philosopher of solidarity," as Dandé-Bauell (1932: 1686) calls him, worked all through his life with great devotion for the idea of a cooperation that would put trade and production entirely at the service of the consumers and thus displace the capitalist from his dominant position without infringing upon private property. He regarded himself as a disciple of John Stuart Mill whose work he conceived as a synthesis between Ricardo's liberalism and Saint-Simon's socialism[3] (Gide and Rist 1909: 416); and he confessed that Bastiat's influence on him was as strong as that of Fourier (Miyajima 1934: 101). So Gide sees the ways of liberalism and socialism at the end merge into one, and that explains both the scope and the structure of his *Histoire des Doctrines Economiques*.

The decline of the historicist and organic sociology and the rise of the mechanist and exact economic theory that was manifest in the development from Eisenhart to Espinas is also apparent in the

---

3. Probably not quite rightly; with Mill liberalism was decidedly the dominant note, socialism only a weak undertone.

development from Cossa to Gide and Rist: Cossa was clearly influenced by Roscher; with Rambaud, the theoretical and absolutist element—in spite of his preference for the inductive method—already prevails over all historical relativism; lastly, Gide is a typical representative of the marginal utility school. This school, however, is divided into two branches: a psychological and a mathematical, the latter of which naturally stands in still sharper contrast to the historicistic and organic doctrines than the former. It is represented in the historiography of political economy by Joseph Schumpeter whose study *Epochen der Dogmen—und Methodengeschichte*, published in 1914 in Max Weber's *Grundriss der Sozialokonomik*, marks the complete conquest of the romantic influences on economic thought.

Joseph Schumpeter (1883-1950) is one of the leading pioneers in the theoretical economics of the twentieth century. Starting from Walras and Wieser, he, a keen logician, advanced the analysis of the system of exchange economy in many directions. He was especially successful in the investigation of the dynamics of capitalism (*Theorie der wirtschaftlichen Entwicklung* 1912): he opposed to the inductive presentation of development of the historical school a deductive theory of development of an exact nature. His two volume work *Business Cycles* (1939) analyzes the phenomenon of the trade cycle in all its aspects. His attitude toward the fundamental questions of our science, however, is laid down in his book *Das Wesen und der Hauptinhalt der theoretischen Nationalökonomie,* which was published in 1908.

In the preface to this work Schumpeter states that he had chosen as his field the small "province in the realm of the social sciences which is characterized by the fact that it is capable of exact treatment" (1908: x et seq.). His thought centers on the mechanical notion of equilibrium and the mathematical notion of function, and so he arrives at a mathematical and mechanical conception of the science. "At the root of our discipline" he says (28):

> is . . . the knowledge that all . . . quantities which we shortly describe as economic quantities . . . are mutually interdependent, so that the change of one of them causes the change of all the others. . . . If we find them to be interrelated in such a way that to one given quantity of one or some of them belongs one and only one given quantity of the others, we call the system determined. . . . We call that state, the state of equilibrium. . . . Certain

relations of dependence or functional relations are, therefore, in our view, the subject of our investigations. . . . What is strictly necessary to the determination of the equilibrium of our system of interdependence furnishes the foundation of our theory. (33, 37)

In this sense Schumpeter regards "theoretical economics as having as much the character of an exact science as pure mechanics" (533).

Schumpeter sought to prove that his method was not absolutely contrary to the spirit of historicism. He emphasized that he was clearly aware of the fact that his investigations concern only a single aspect of a single part in the whole of the social sciences. Yet it is just this separation of theoretical economics from the greater connections of life, just this isolating procedure and abstract interpretation, that marks the contrast between theoretical and historicist science, as it is manifest also in the discussions of the history of economic doctrines.

As for the much debated question as to the ancient or modern origin of political economy, Schumpeter decided in favor of the latter alternative. Scientific economics, he says, first appears toward the end of the eighteenth century. But he traces its roots farther back and believes that it arose from the union and mutual permeation of two streams of thought: one derived from classical antiquity was formed by philosophers; the other sprang from interest in practical problems (and is, we may add, modern, for Schumpeter mentions in this connection no writing published before the middle of the sixteenth century). As to the philosophical contribution Schumpeter warns us not to overestimate Aristotle; he believes that, in spite of the predominance of the *oikos*-economy with its autarchy, there were problems of national economy proper. Although that cannot be denied, it must be emphasized against Schumpeter that the environment of Plato and Aristotle, a natural economy just beginning to be dissolved by money economy, presented exchange economy only as a negative decomposing force, not as a positive, fully developed system that alone could have invited analysis. He still declares it to be "wrong to interpret into each chance utterance [of the Greeks on economic matters] all that which later times have connected with sentences of similar wording" (1914: 22). In the philosophy of antiquity Schumpeter sees, not the origin of political economy, but the first source of that empirical and analytical science of mind and society that later appeared under the name of moral philosophy and, by its sociology, prepared the science of economic life; in this respect he is certainly right.

The second stream of thought distinguished by Schumpeter is the popular literature on economic topics that arose between 1550 and 1750, that is, mercantilism, to which he on the whole denies the character of science. He considers this vulgar economics "only in so far as it influenced, or led to, scientific knowledge . . . not as a reflected image of the times" (1914: 29). This artificial separation of the ideas from their basis prevents him from perceiving the essential parallel and mutual connection between the evolution of national economy on the one hand and of political economy on the other. Yet only in the light of this comparison does a satisfactory solution of the problem of the origin of our science and a just appreciation of the importance of the mercantile system seem possible. For the evolution of economic thought from a fragmentary theory of money and foreign trade to a comprehensive analysis is only the reflection of the evolution of exchange economy from its first appearance in the sphere of circulation and commerce to the perfect control of the modern nation.

As political economy is for Schumpeter essentially a science of the whole process of national economy, he describes the physiocrats as the real founders.[4] Their great achievement is "the discovery and intellectual representation of economic circulation," which Schumpeter calls the "central phenomenon of national economy." "Before the physiocrats only local observations on the body economic had been made, they, however, taught us to understand this body in its physiology and anatomy as an organism with a uniform process and uniform conditions of life and gave us the first analysis of this process" (1914: 39, 40). This picture, which, incidentally, dates back to Quesnay, suggests, however, a false analogy: the scientists had always had before them the human body in which the circulation of the blood constitutes the circulation of life so that Harvey's discovery was a new perception in an old object; the economists, on the other hand, had, up to the eighteenth century, always had to study a national

---

4. He does not describe Cantillon's achievement, which he highly appreciates, as epoch-making although he speaks of a "comprehensive analysis on great lines."

economy in which the circulation of goods covered a certainly growing, but still restricted, section so that they could not easily arrive at a comprehensive analysis of it, and Quesnay's discovery must be called a new perception in a new object. Schumpeter's lack of historical sense, the view that the history of doctrines represents a progress from error to truth, not a sequence of equally valuable attempts to understand life in its changes, here clearly comes to light. But we could preserve Schumpeter's simile and say: before the physiocrats the embryo of exchange economy was the object of thought and only those elements were described that resembled the image of perfection; the physiocrats were the first to analyze the new economic order, which, a new being just entering into independent existence, was about to leave the womb of natural economy. Then, we should have explained in a parable the position occupied by mercantilists and physiocrats in the history of knowledge. Yet the work of Quesnay's school is in any case of epoch-making importance, and Schumpeter was right in strongly emphasizing this truth.

So Schumpeter describes first of all the "previous history" as the "development of social economics into a science" and then physiocracy as "the discovery of economic circulation." The later theories are also divided according to schools: after the physiocrats, classicism with its followers up to the eighties; the historical school; and the school of marginal utility.[5] This division of epochs into the history of dogmas and methods is from Schumpeter's standpoint only consistent, as he regards the theories, so to speak, in a historical vacuum, where the unity in dogma and in method may seem more important than the unity in time, where it is therefore better to arrange theoretical schools side by side rather than in historical stages one after the other.

To Schumpeter political economy is simply market analysis with all that belongs to it. When he conducts his investigation, he occasionally represents the abstract economic theories in the light of concrete social facts. His self-limitation is only the result of a consciously adopted method and not the sign of a narrow mind. Behind his words is a

---

5. It is of no consequence that the two latter groups seem to be discussed in one section, because this is distinctly divided into two parts; the first five paragraphs are concerned with the historical doctrine, the next five paragraphs with the marginalist doctrine.

wider knowledge that works in them and through them.

The revival of the historical and dynamic interpretation of life, which made itself felt in international science after 1918, was not without influence on the theory and historiography of political economy. Until about 1920, theoreticians all over the world remained content with the survey of development sketched by Gide and Rist ten years before. Their work had been translated into English, German, Russian, Spanish, Polish, Serbian, and Czech, and had thus achieved a circulation even wider than that of Cossa's book twenty five years earlier. But at the time when Gonnard published his great historicist survey, the conviction was already general that the theoreticians also should produce a broader and deeper study of the evolution of economic thought based both on the principles of theory and the knowledge of history. Progress toward this aim was due especially to two men: the American Fred O. Boucke and the Frenchman G. H. Bousquet. They brought important questions of principle into the debate and communicated a stimulating influence drawn from the study of the great systematic sciences that are so often represented as the models of political economy—philosophy and mathematics.

Fred Oswald Boucke (born 1881) is one of the most independent of the American scholars. His efforts are directed toward a critical examination of the traditional system of economic science (*A Critique of Economics, Doctrinal and Methodological* [1922] and its positive counterpart: *Principles of Economics* [1925]) and this examination was not based on the narrowly economic or social, that is, immanent, standpoint, but constituted an ambitious attempt to test the validity of the teachings of political economy by the standards of other sciences, especially psychology in its most modern form. A rare knowledge of the philosophical, scientific, psychological, and economic literature fitted Boucke for his great enterprise.

The results that Boucke obtained have been summed up as follows:

> [T]he groundwork of orthodox Economics has gradually crumbled because of changes in sciences, basic to the old discipline of catallactics. . . . [T]he recent work of psychologists has shown clearly that intensities of wish or want, such as the economist is interested in, are not ascertainable by any known methods. . . . The derivation of laws of price from a study of human nature must be held impossible. . . . [I]f Economics is to become, more strictly than heretofore, a factual science, reducing abstractions to a minimum and taking the world in substance as it is, the key to an economic

methodology will lie in modern psychology, in the observation of what science actually does to obtain its generalisations, and in a careful examination of law and causation, free from all historical bias. The distinction between causation and law, except as aspects of one and the same situation, the distinction between law and correlation, in the sense that one is causal, but not the other, must be abandoned. Abandoned, too, must be the sharp separation of induction and deduction and the designation of Economics as a deductive science with a purely conceptional basis. Lastly, we must cease to recognize two kinds of economic laws, the static and the dynamic. . . . If we wish to correlate social events as they occur, we cannot count on the restriction of the number of factors that the advocates of statics demand. Statics must be eliminated by studying things exactly as they are, irrespective of their intricacies. (Lemberger 1923: 556-58)

The same independence of view and breadth of concept as in these fundamental considerations is also shown by Boucke in his historical survey of the evolution of our science (*The Development of Economics*):

The study of economic subjects is no doubt almost as old as the history of mankind. . . . If however we wish to find the beginnings of economics *as a science* we need not go back . . . much beyond the middle of the eighteenth century. . . . Only with the appearance of the Physiocrats does economics cease to be a loose bundle of individual facts. Now for the first time a unifying code is sought and proclaimed to exist. (Boucke 1921: 16-17)

In these words Boucke only repeats the *communis doctorum opinio* on the origin of political economy as we find it in Gide-Rist, Haney, and many others. But what distinguishes him is the attempt to justify this thesis (which degrades the mercantilists to mere precursors of the science "because the thought had not yet dominated them that social processes follow laws") from intellectual history and especially from the history of philosophy. The great process of secularization, he holds, which put modern science in the place of the medieval church and substituted the exclusive reliance on research for the unquestioned authority of dogma, has also created the science of economics: "It was the spirit of the Renaissance . . . that gave us a new cosmology and a new philosophy whose by-paths ultimately led to the systematic study of social events" (1921: 24).

This view is part of the heritage that the present age has received from the rationalism of the nineteenth century. In the 1870s the conviction was general that science and natural science were in the last analysis identical, and as modern natural science owes its origin to the Renaissance, the belief prevailed that even modern social science arose from the philosophy of Galileo's period. No one would deny the revolutionary achievement of that epoch in which mankind dethroned tradition and dogma and proclaimed instead criticism and *ratio* [reason] to be the rulers in the realm of knowledge. No one will deny that there is a great truth in the old saying that in the sixteenth century men took the dark spectacles that they had previously worn from their noses and began to see the world as it really was. But what is true for the natural sciences may be untrue for the social sciences. Copernicus regarded the firmament in the new spirit and reached an astronomy different from that of Ptolemy, Vesalius regarded the human body in the new spirit and reached an anatomy different from that of Galen. But between Gabriel Biel and Richard Cantillon, between the last who contemplated economic life from an ethical viewpoint and aimed at formulating norms, and the first who approached the matter without prejudice and sought only knowledge, there were 250 years of slow evolution. In the social sciences, no revolution took place as in the natural sciences, and to this external difference corresponds an internal one: the object of perception proper to the natural sciences is not subject to the human will and appears therefore as eternal; the object of perception of the social sciences, however, is molded by man and his will and therefore changes with the history of humanity. So long as the order of economic life was consciously fashioned, economic science remained normative as it had been in Thomas Aquinas's times. If Boucke says of Justi's work: "Social phenomena are narrowed down to questions of administration in the belief that this is the central theme of economics" (1921: 28), this is easily understood, although the Renaissance was then already three centuries past. Any planned economy asks: what should we do? The new question: what is? could only arise after exchange economy had been developed, that is, when the order of economic life depended no longer on conscious will, but on the unconscious concurrence of isolated individual wills. Only then could economic life be analyzed in the spirit that the Renaissance had given to the world.

Boucke, however, does not content himself with the assertion that the roots of political economy are to be found in the Renaissance; he

also endeavors to demonstrate how in the philosophy of the
seventeenth century, which was a child of the Renaissance spirit as
represented by Bacon, the foundations of the new science slowly
appeared. Three thinkers especially attract his attention: Hobbes,
Locke, and Hume. His conviction is: "[T]he origins of economics lay
in British empiricism and in French mechanism; nowhere else. The
task of sketching the genesis of economics is . . . comparatively easy,
because in noting the ascendancy of Saxon empiricism one has
virtually explained all. . . . [E]conomics . . . was assuredly a by-
product of empiricism" (1921: 30, 103). This assertion contains
implicitly the contention that the great tendency of thought that
developed side by side with empiricism and was opposed to it,
rationalism, was without influence on the origin of political economy.
Boucke in fact says (1921: 31): "Descartes' . . . contributions . . .
need not detain us because they did not as such influence the founders
of economics."

In what then did the contrast between empiricism and rationalism
consist? A short scheme based on Boucke's observations may make
this clear:

Empiricism	Rationalism
Theory of perception	
all the elements of knowledge are post-natally acquired	belief in supersensual sources of knowledge (innate ideas)
Ethics	
common sense standpoint (Hobbes an outspoken opportunist in matters moral)	absolutist view of right and wrong (thinkers like Descartes, Spinoza, Leibniz, and finally Kant grounded their ethical systems on Plato, Aristotle, or the Bible alone).

Boucke endeavors to connect Quesnay and Smith, the founders of
political economy as a science, with the empiricist tradition.

The Physiocrats . . . may justly be considered the founders of economics because they were the first to study social processes from the standpoint of law and causation, exactly as Newton . . . had done in another field. They applied to the body politic what English empiricists had originally tried to discover in individual human nature, namely a principle of regularity in the occurrence of events, according to which they might be connected . . . just as astronomers had explained the varied phenomena of heavens. (1921: 62)

Boucke goes on to say that "Smith's . . . psychology was that of John Locke and Hume. We hear him hint at sensation as the source of ideas. . . . As to the problem of knowledge he no doubt sided with the empiricists" (75).

To discuss first Quesnay as the earlier and older thinker, it is certain that his epistemological views were largely based on the teachings of his contemporary Helvétius who was a materialist of the Lockean type. Adhering to his principles, Quesnay, in his article on "Evidence" published in the *Encyclopédie*, derived all perceptions from experience denying the existence of innate ideas: "The use of our senses is the foundation of all certitude and the basis of all our knowledge" (Quesnay 1888: 774). "The soul cannot arrive at any idea and . . . has no innate ideas. . . . For the sensible objects are the basis of our knowledge . . . and the source of all proof. In fact only by the sensations caused by the sensible objects through our senses, do we reach the perception of the existence of our own sensible being" (1888: 782). These words are a clear confession of empiricism that cannot be questioned. Nevertheless Boucke's thesis is wrong: rationalism, too, was a source of Quesnay's ideas. Besides Helvétius, Malebranche, the follower of Descartes and Spinoza, deeply influenced the metaphysics of the physiocrats. Quesnay refers to him only as a *grand homme*, while of Locke he utters the critical judgment "that the author had on human understanding obscure, imperfect, very vague and very confused conceptions only." But as to philosophy, what divides Quesnay from consistent empiricism and what brings him near to rationalism is the conviction that man is not passive in the reception and formation of knowledge, but actively collaborating, reason constituting the active element. In this sense he criticizes Locke in his "Essai physique sur l'économie animale":

The soul has no . . . ideas by itself. . . . But by its attention it is capable of discovering in the sensations it has many perceptions which it would not

> comprehend without the use of this intellectual faculty; it is by this use that
> it procures the ideas or intellectual concepts and that it is not so limited as
> the sensitive soul of the animals; but Locke often mistook the influence of
> the soul on the body, the action of the soul on the sensations, for the
> influence of the body on the soul. (1888: 745)

Similarly the assumption of two world substances (matter and mind) and the distinction between evident perceptions (*vérités rélles*) and super sensual truths (*vérités révelés*) derive from Malebranche and thus lastly from Descartes.

In ethics too the idealistic and rationalistic influence is manifest. Quesnay knows two motives of human actions, sensual and mental. The latter have their roots in reason (i.e., not in experience) and through them man is connected with God.

> Religion teaches us that the supreme wisdom itself is the light *which lighteth*
> *everyman coming into the world*; that man by his union with the absolute
> spirit is elevated . . . to the knowledge of moral right and wrong, by which
> he is capable of behaving with reason and equity in the use of his liberty;
> by which he discerns the merit and fault of his actions, and by which he
> judges himself in the determinations of his free conscience and in the
> decisions of his will. (1888: 793)

Most apparent is the combination of empiricist and rationalist elements, where Quesnay discusses the moral code to which the soul should conform.

> The legitimate *customs* established between men living in society, the
> prescriptions and comforts of religion, the laws of government . . ., the
> sentiments of humanity; all these motives united with the *natural knowledge*
> *of a first principle* to which we are subject and with the revealed truths,
> form the rules which direct sensible and virtuous men. (1888: 795, emphasis
> added)

The author of *The Theory of Moral Sentiments*, Adam Smith, must, as a friend of the great Hume, no doubt, be regarded as a child of English empiricism. Indeed he says (Smith 1861: 162; [Smith 1976a: 110]):

> Were it possible that a human creature could grow up to manhood in some
> solitary place, without any communication with his own species, he could
> no more think of his own character, of the propriety or demerit of his own

sentiments and conduct, of the beauty or deformity of his own mind, than
of the beauty and deformity of his own face. . . . Bring him into society,
and he is immediately provided with the mirror which he wanted before.
It is placed in the countenance and behaviour of those he lives with, which
always mark when they enter into, and when they disapprove of his
sentiments; and it is here that he first views the propriety and impropriety
of his own passions, the beauty and deformity of his own mind.

And even more clearly (1861: 224 et seq. [1976a: 159]): "[T]he
general rules of morality are formed . . . by finding from experience,
that all actions of a certain kind, or circumstanced in a certain manner,
are approved or disapproved of." In spite of this, one must not simply
represent Adam Smith as an empiricist. He rejected the doctrine of
Locke and Hume, according to which all moral behavior is ultimately
due to the knowledge of the utility of moral actions.[6] On the
contrary, like Shaftesbury and Hutcheson before him, he based his
ethics on the assumption of social and asocial instincts that appear as
original elements of human nature and exist as such before all
experience, even if they make themselves felt only in society. This is
proved in the very first sentence of his work: "How selfish soever
man may be supposed, there are evidently some principles in his
nature, which interest him in the fortune of others . . ." (3). Smith
may conceive the morals of duty as heteronomous, that is, as
impressed upon man from outside—their basis is to him still the
autonomous in man himself, his inclinations, feelings, instincts!
"What is it," he asks (193 et seq. [137]) "which prompts the generous
upon all occasions, and the mean upon many, to sacrifice their own
interests to the greater interests of others?" And his answer is: "It is
reason, principle, conscience, the inhabitant of the breast, the man
within, the great judge and arbiter of our conduct." How far Smith
is from the comfortable morals of utility of Locke, and how near to
the strict morals of principle of Kant, is manifest in these great words:

---

6. Thus, the same development took place in ethics as in the philosophy of religion:
"Deism had called in as the umpire common sense; Wesley fell back upon the truth
that for the vision of God there must be another, higher sense which Christ summed
up as purity of heart" (H.B. Workman in *The History of Christianity in the Light of
Modern Knowledge*, 1929: 687). To identify Smith and Locke would be equivalent
to throwing together Tindal and Wesley.

"As to love our neighbour as we love ourselves is the great law of Christianity, so it is the great precept of nature to love ourselves as we love our neighbour, or what comes to the same thing, as our neighbour is capable of loving us" (27 et seq. [25]). How far is it from here to the grand postulate of Kant: "Act so that the maxime of thy actions might be the law for every man"?

So much for ethics. But even in the theory of perception Smith cannot simply be assigned to the empiricist school. Even here he believes many tendencies of man to be given a priori. Let us only remember that he deduces the division of labor not from the realization of its merits, as they offer themselves in experience, but from an innate bent toward bargaining.

> This division of labor, from which so many advantages are derived, is not originally the effect of any human wisdom, which foresees and intends that general opulence to which it gives occasion. It is the necessary . . . consequence of a certain propensity in human nature which has in view no such extensive utility; the propensity to truck, barter, and exchange one thing for another. (Smith 1904: 75 [Smith 1976b: 25])

Also, "the desire of bettering our condition" is also innate, "comes with us from the womb" (1904: 323 [1976b: 341]).

Hence, neither Quesnay's philosophy nor that of Smith can be understood from empiricism alone; rationalism also contributed to their thought—and thus, contrary to Boucke's thesis, to the formation of political economy. Both men, however, were genuine children of the philosophy of the eighteenth century in that they believed in the existence of a comprehensive order of the universe, which, instituted by the Creator, comprises nature and society alike. Boucke describes this conception as naturalism and, in his view, it marks the first period in the evolution of political economy as a science (for his principle of periodization is the division of the schools according to their philosophical creeds).

> Naturalism was the sequel to dogmatism of the ecclesiastical sort. . . . God was everywhere. The cosmos itself incorporated a divine plan, a product of reason whose replica was the human mind. What evidently accorded most with the achievements of modern science was the depersonalization of God, i.e., the identification of God with nature . . . and the fusion of reason with virtue. (Boucke 1921: 50-51)

In these words Boucke aptly characterized the philosophy of Quesnay and Smith. To them political economy, as Heimann once justly said, was in fact a sort of proof of the existence of God. They endeavored to show that in society as well as in nature there governs a great harmony instituted by the creative spirit of all things, and so they not only followed the program of the empiricist Newton, but also the aim of the rationalist Leibniz. Carey and Bastiat, authors whose activities reached their height between 1840 and 1860, in this respect continued Smith's work. In the fifty years, however, between the death of the master and the appearance of the grand disciples Boucke thinks a different opinion was dominant, an opinion that is to be distinguished from naturalism and which he describes as utilitarianism. Its period extends from Ricardo to John Stuart Mill (and in a certain sense beyond this thinker for whom Boucke has a special regard).

Hence, it appears that Boucke rejects the concept of classicism. He is convinced that Smith and Ricardo, looked upon from the philosophical side, cannot be reckoned as belonging to one school. "*In its beginnings British economics . . . was non-hedonistic. But under Ricardianism a decided change takes place. From there on the hedonistic-utilitarian concept dominates*" (1921: 49). The contrast between the hedonistic and nonhedonistic view coincides with the contrast between a preeminently social and a preeminently individualist attitude—Boucke indeed speaks in this connection of collectivism and individualism (87 et seq., 113 et seq.), but this is an exaggeration, since both Smith and Ricardo envisaged a solution balancing the two principles, "Smith . . . and Ricardo . . . ! Morality for the one basic to all social life, and for the other a personal item that had nothing to do with the problems of science!" (113) Thus, the age of utilitarianism is contrasted with that of naturalism. Boucke describes its characteristic features as follows (117): "A hedonistic psychology, a derivation of group incomes from laws of human nature, the measurement of prices by objective costs or returns, and the assumption of certain human instincts as the basis for individual freedom in production and exchange." The hedonistic psychology is the basis of the most important working concept of the Ricardians, the *homo oeconomicus*. "To obtain the greatest portion of happiness for himself is the object of every rational being," Bentham says in his *Deontology* (cited in Boucke 1921: 124)—it is the exclusive object of that most rational and most rationalistic of all beings, the *homo oeconomicus*. Political economy, says John Stuart Mill (140), "makes entire abstraction of every other human passion or motive except those which may be regarded as perpetually antagonizing principles to the desire of wealth, namely aversion to labor and desire of the present enjoyment of costly indulgences."

That there is a break between Smith and Ricardo that forbids us to connect them too closely has been felt by many historians of political economy. In most cases they divide classicism, as did Gide and Rist, into an optimistic and pessimistic phase. This procedure is, however, rather primitive. Optimism and pessimism are no concepts of science. If Boucke could succeed in proving that Smith and Ricardo in fact followed different philosophical creeds, the argument would indeed be much better founded.

Already external facts, however, give rise to doubts on this point: for example, the fact that the *Manual of Political Economy* (1793) of Jeremy Bentham, the great representative of utilitarian philosophy, keeps entirely in the line of the Smithian doctrine, and that the view of life of Jean B. Say, the great popularizer of Smithian economics, is entirely governed by utilitarian philosophy.[7] And while here the economics of naturalism flows together with that of utilitarianism, it is easy to show in other examples that the philosophy of utilitarianism was not foreign to the age of naturalism. Boucke himself quotes (1921: 121) Hume's words from the *Treatise of Human Nature* of 1739: "The chief springs or actuating principles of the human mind are pleasure and pain" —a thesis that Hartley (*Observations on Man*, 1748), Tucker (*The Light of Nature Persued*, 1768), Paley (*Principles of Moral and Political Philosophy*, 1785), and others have taken up, before Bentham made it the cornerstone of his philosophy. And Bentham himself in the very first sentence of his *Introduction to the Principles of Morals and Legislation* (1789) shows his propinquity to

---

7. In a note to Storch's *Cours d'économie politique* (1823: 6) Say writes about Bentham: "The doctrine of this great man will eventually reign alone, because it is based on the nature of things which does not change, and on the interest of humanity, which will be better understood every day." Boucke did not closely investigate Say's philosophical ideas. They are to be found mainly in the "Petit volume contenant quelques apercus des hommes et de la société," 1817.

the philosophy of naturalism. "Nature," he says, "has placed mankind under the governance of two sovereign masters, pain and pleasure. . . . They govern us in all we do." The difference indeed is this: while Smith believed that an invisible superhuman hand directs all men, Bentham was convinced that the individual will to gain pleasure and to avoid pain is the dominant principle of the social order. But the fundamental idea is in the end the same, whether it appears in a theological guise or without it: that there governs a great law of the universe comprehending nature and men alike, a law to which man must conform whether he finds it good or bad. Is Malthus's dismal doctrine that the instincts implanted in us by nature necessarily produce human poverty due less to this fundamental idea than Smith's or Carey's cheerful belief that all is ordered for the best?

Ricardo and Malthus were—like Quesnay and Smith—still disciples of the philosophy of the eighteenth century. They too admired the great mechanism of social economy that they understood so well yet they were not able to regard it as a testimony of God's goodness.[8] But is goodness a necessary attribute of the divine? By no means! What characterizes God's laws is their inescapability. And Malthus believed not less than Quesnay that the order ruling over economic life is unchangeable and fixed for all times. Only the next generation, which Boucke represents in a third chapter, entitled historicism, adopted a different view.

This next generation, as Boucke himself admits, regarded classicism —rightly—as a uniform doctrine: "To the founders of the Historical School . . . Naturalism and Utilitarian economics were substantially

---

8. Ferrara, one of the most convinced followers of Malthus, indeed interpreted the Malthusian principle of population entirely in the sense of an optimistic deism.

> The instrument which the Creator has used to lead mankind from progress to progress is pain, and for mankind taken as a whole there is no pain the first cause of which is not the excess of population over the means of subsistence. . . . It is evident that in order to conquer the tendency towards idleness man must necessarily feel a pain stronger than the labor requisite to overcome it. . . . It is impossible not to recognize in that pressure, caused by a growing population, an admirable system of means, aimed at the same result, i.e., human progress. (Ferrara 1938: 29)

one. . . . There was no doubt that the two earlier economic systems showed important resemblances, in that both built on individualism" (1921: 185). To it Boucke opposes historicism as its counterpart: "All members of the Historical School were collectivists" (186). This is his basic idea; he does not indeed identify historicism and collectivism. Collectivism is to him the wider, historicism the narrower concept, but this changes nothing in the surprising assertion that the new tendency differed from the old one by its adherence to a nonindividualist, to a collectivist, theory of society: "[Historicism] without collectivism of the socialist sort would have been an odd product, a flesh out of the clear sky that one can imagine but has not seen" (206).

Boucke is in this point far from consistent. After having first compared naturalism and utilitarianism as collectivism and individualism (1921: 114), he now treats them as one concept. But that may be allowed. For anyone who, like Smith, has in mind a society built upon the principle of equality, may without contradiction be at once an individualist and a collectivist.

The assertion, however, that all followers of historicism were collectivists is not acceptable. It is simply wrong. In men like Lujo Brentano in Germany,[9] Thorold Rogers in England, and Louis Wolowski in France, both elements, historicism and individualism, were equally embodied. And there is nothing in that to surprise us. The idea of evolution is philosophically and politically entirely different. Indeed, it comprised, especially in Germany, all intellectual life, and to degrade it to an accessory phenomenon of socialism is to totally misunderstand its historical significance.

The unjustifiable connection of historicism and collectivism causes Boucke to follow the origins of the new tendency back into a time in which there is no trace of the idea of evolution. "[T]his departure from individualism," he says (1921: 189), "Naturalistic or Utilitarian, had its inception in ideals older than the science of economics, or at least just about as old. Not the nineteenth, but the eighteenth century laid the foundations." He mentions at this juncture men like Mably,

---

9. Cf. on this point Stark, *Sozialpolitik*, 1936: 22. That historicism and socialism must not simply be thrown together was already shown by Knies, *Die Politische Okonomie vom Standpunkt der geschichtlichen Methode*, 1853: 24 et seq.

Morelli, Baboeuf, Barnave, Cabet, Fourier, and Godwin!

Of these let us consider only one, the most famous, Charles Fourier! We find in him little of historicism or of collectivism. If we would briefly characterize him, we should term him the Don Quixote of naturalism. His thought started from the conviction that human nature, which he definitely regarded as unchanged throughout the centuries, was so constituted that the free action of its innate tendencies would produce a perfectly harmonious social order. His main idea is exactly the same as that of Adam Smith: the individual following only his own impulses may be sure not only to defend his self-interest, but at the same time to promote the common good, and this blessed fact is a consequence of the work of a benevolent Deity, or as Fourier puts it in a phrase characteristic of his rationalism, of the "Eternal Geometer." No historical development leads toward the system of harmony; man must consciously construct it. Individualism and rationalism govern Fourier's thought, not collectivism and historicism, which were only produced by the age of romanticism.

And as Boucke wrongly transfers the origin of collectivism into the eighteenth century, he also seeks the beginnings of historicism in that age. He is aware that only under Hegel's influence, in Marx and Engels, socialism adopted the idea of evolution, but he believes that the idea in itself is much older. "[T]he outstanding note of [Historicism], namely its historical mindedness . . . goes back to a philosophy of life originally derived from metaphysical questions, and gradually made to converge upon a single field: The history of society" (1921: 207-8). Boucke names in this connection Vico, Montesquieu, Voltaire, Turgot, Condorcet, Condillac, Lessing, Herder and others.

Of these men Condorcet was probably nearest to the idea of evolution that is the basis of modern historiography, and yet an examination of his opinions shows that he was a rationalist and not a historian, a follower of the eighteenth century and not an ancestor of the nineteenth. His *Esquisse d'un tableau historique des progrès de l'esprit humain* (1795) regards the history of mankind as a constant advance toward its ultimate end, a society of absolute legal equality of individuals as well as nations; he endeavored to construct a social mathematics that should reduce evolution to laws, as necessary and constant as the laws of the natural sciences. How differently did such a man as Ranke view history! To him the present was a product of the past and not the past a preparation of the present or future. He rejected all abstract and speculative philosophy of history and aimed at a concrete and inductive investigation of sources. His end was to establish historical facts, not to construct mathematical laws. Condorcet does not resemble the great historian Ranke, but the great rationalist Kant. Kant's works on the philosophy of history, the grand "Idee zu einer allgemeinen Geschichte in weltbuergerlicher Absicht" ["Ideas of a Universal History from a Cosmopolitan Point of View"] (1784) and the splendid essay "Zum ewigen Frieden" ["Perpetual Peace"] (1795) conceive evolution as the progressive fulfillment of a secret plan of nature that leads mankind toward a great end: the realization of the ideal of freedom and peace in the state and between the states. Interpretation of history, not its investigation, is Condorcet's and Kant's endeavor.

Certain passages in Boucke's book, however, suggest that he wished to distinguish the economics of Ricardo and Schmoller not only as individualism and collectivism, but that he also regarded a different philosophical and ethical descent as an element separating and contrasting them. Classicism is to him a child of English empiricism, historicism an offspring of German rationalism.

> The original Utilitarian view that the 'economic man' was at the same time moral, and inevitably so because the pursuit of pleasure is the only test of a love of virtue, was never fully understood on the continent. . . . [Historicism] was essentially an ethical movement descended from German transcendentalism in psychology, logic, and ethics. Empiricism was not supposed to provide an answer to the questions of the Is and Ought. (1921: 217)

In so far as Boucke means by German transcendentalism simply German idealism, as it is embodied in Leibniz, Kant, Schelling, and Hegel, and opposes to it English materialism, the great names of which are Hobbes, Locke, Bentham, and Mill, he has certainly emphasized an important contrast between what he calls utilitarianism and what he calls historicism. In the last resort Smith's philosophy certainly comes from Locke, and that of Schmoller comes from Hegel. But with the comparison of English empiricism or materialism and German transcendentalism or idealism as little is gained for the delimitation of the two phases of political economy as with the comparison of individualism and collectivism. From Hegel a line leads through Fichte to Kant. But what is important for historicism is not that which connects them but that which divides them: rationalism with its static view stands against romanticism with its dynamic outlook (although both may be called idealism), and only the latter stimulated German economic thought. The same is true of ethics. Most members of Schmoller's school brought ethical concepts into economic discussion, and compared with Bentham's disciples they must indeed appear as adherents of strict morals of principle. But they did not conceive the "Ought" as an eternally unchangeable code, exalted over space and time, as did the great man of Koenigsberg, compared with whose categorical imperative they appear almost as opportunists. "The . . . moral systems . . .," Schmoller says (1900: 70), "are rather practical forces of life than results of an exact science." So even here it becomes manifest that there is only one element clearly distinguishing classicism and historicism: the belief in the idea of evolution, in the *panta rhei* [all things change].

Naturalism, utilitarianism, and historicism are followed according to Boucke by a fourth and last period of development, "marginism." It is not difficult to delimit it from historicism. Schmoller and Menger did that quite sufficiently. But it is not easy to distinguish it sharply from utilitarianism; Boucke attempted to do so in the following way: "[M]arginism differed from the earlier economic systems in that it compared units of *want and feeling* instead of *things*" (1921: 226).

> Marginism replaced the objective view of the . . . Utilitarians . . . by a subjective one, the source of value being found in men and not in materials. . . . [W]ants and ideas took the place of wealth and objects in the concrete. Totals and their changes were referred to least doses in successive additions or substractions of wants and values. . . . This reckoning of everything, of prices and incomes, of wealth and of capital, by differentials and margins psychologically measured, is the quintessence of Marginism. It was, in a brief phrase, a theory of least values and productivities, based on premises and definitions for the most part originating in Utilitarianism. (1921: 228 et seq.)

In these considerations two arguments are united: first, the assertion that the schools of Ricardo and Menger are distinguished by the fact that the former builds more on material, the latter more on psychical categories; and second, the idea that the real distinction between them lies in the marginal principle, while the basic psychology is identical. Now, the psychological law that serves as a basis of the marginal principle has been formulated and understood in its full importance only in the nineteenth century. This is shown by Fechner's *Elemente der Psycho-Physik* (1860). But the psychic reality itself, the decrease of the intensity of feeling when equal sensations are repeated, was already known in the eighteenth century. So says Paley (cited in Boucke 1921: 250) in his *Principles of Moral and Political Philosophy* (1785): "[P]leasures by repetition lose their relish. . . . [T]he organs by which we perceive pleasure are blunted and benumbed by being frequently exercised in the same way. . . . [T]here is a limit at which these pleasures soon arrive, and from which they ever afterwards decline." The marginal principle thus appears only as a development and refinement of utilitarian psychology, not as something entirely new.

More interesting and striking is the other argument: Ricardo and his disciples built their theory on an objective basis; they found the source of value in matter. Menger and his followers, however, preferred a subjective foundation; they wished to found their explanation on mind. This is true. But what follows from this argument? It follows clearly and distinctly that the classical doctrine was not yet based on psychology at all, that it indeed presupposed certain observations on the usual behavior of men in economic matters (economic principle), but explained price and wages, interest and rent, independently of all analysis of the soul. This is not true of the theory of marginal utility. It draws psychology into economics, interprets all economic categories in the light of psychology, and is, in fact, a sort of applied psychology. Classicism, the doctrine of labor-value, and neoclassicism, the doctrine of use-value, are not distinguishable as utilitarianism and marginism, but as objective and subjective, as technical and psychological.

This view, opposed to Boucke's opinion, is strongly supported by the fact that—as Boucke must admit—the basis of the marginal utility doctrine is furnished by utilitarian psychology: "Marginism has much in common with both Naturalism and Utilitarianism," he says (Boucke 1921: 226), especially hedonism. "The two ways of looking at economic life and of analyzing price and income overlap . . . they also share in common a few fundamentals that the Utilitarian economists first gave currency between 1820 and 1850" (117). And again, "Jevons made it clear from the beginning that Bentham and Bain had been his mentors. . . . Through Jevons . . . the Utilitarian psychology crept into the marginal interpretation" (236, 254). Most clearly, however, Boucke himself proved that classicism did not build on Bentham's psychology and that the doctrine of marginal utility did so, when he said (240), "Jennings started by showing the discrepancy between Bentham's hedonism and the measuring of values through cost, that is through inert matter," that is, by emphasizing that political economy had not yet used Bentham's psychology, but should use it.

The psychology of James Mill and that of Stanley Jevons are of the same descent. The one is the younger sister of the other. But while James Mill developed his economic theory independently of all psychology, Jevons used it as a key to the world of economic phenomena. It is precisely this which constitutes the difference between classicism and neoclassicism. And what has been said of Jevons is true also of Menger. Boucke's assertion that "the philosophy of Bentham and Mill was British, and not of the continent. . . . The universities at which the Austrians . . . received their training were idealistically toned and under the sway of ideas alien to Benthamism" (1921: 260) is wrong. For it is a fact that about the year 1870 an eminent philosopher following English materialism and opposed to Kantian idealism exerted a profound influence in southern Germany—Franz Brentano, Menger's colleague for many years at the university of Vienna, and the author of the *Psychologie vom empirischen Standpunkt* (1874), a work whose very name discloses its character. His basic thesis was that the method of the natural sciences should likewise be the method of philosophy,—a thesis that must have been very congenial to Carl Menger and brought both men on to common ground.

Boucke's attempt at periodization, the distinction of naturalism, utilitarianism, historicism, and marginism is untenable. Neither can naturalism be opposed to utilitarianism as collectivistic, nor is it possible to draw a strict line of division between utilitarianism and marginism. But Boucke has raised an important problem: the division of the periods in the light of philosophy, and each periodization of development must be justified also from this point of view.

Starting from their philosophical foundations, the three great groups of ideas that are associated with the names Smith-Ricardo-Carey, Sismondi-Marx-Schmoller, and Jevons-Walras-Menger could, perhaps, be distinguished as deism, evolutionism, and sensationalism (to avoid the word psychologism). For Smith, Ricardo, Malthus, and Carey aimed at finding the eternal laws (and that meant the laws instituted by the Eternal) that govern mankind as they govern nature. Thus, in the realm of social science, they fulfilled the program of deism: to show that Providence subjected all in the universe to a great order, in which man is included, an order the unhampered working of which no created being should venture to disturb. Locke, Leibniz, Hume, and Kant were the philosophers of this belief.

Evolutionism, which, as an intellectual movement, is represented not only by Marx, List, Sismondi and Roscher, but also by Ranke, Niebuhr, Cuvier, Agassiz, Lamarck, and Darwin, does not mean to discover constant laws, but to understand the flow of life. In it man first perceived the miracle of growth, the prophets of which were Schelling and Hegel.

Sensationalism, whose characteristic is to regard man even in the bonds of society first and foremost as a natural being, must be viewed in the broader framework afforded by the rise of the exact sciences in the nineteenth century. The development of the psychology of association (Hartley) and of experimental psychology (Fechner) was especially important in this connection. As to their intellectual descent, Jevons and Menger were above all the successors of Condillac, Bentham, Brentano, and Mill.

While Boucke sought to throw light on the history of political economy from the philosophical point of view, G. H. Bousquet (born 1902) takes the natural sciences as his starting point. He views economic theory as an exact discipline; the doctrine of equilibrium is to him the highest achievement of economic analysis. His *Cours d'économie pure* (1928a) aims at establishing a synthesis between Vienna and Lausanne, Menger and Walras, and this endeavor is significant of Bousquet's way of thinking.

Bousquet confesses himself to be a disciple of Vilfredo Pareto, whose work he set out to continue (*Vilfredo Pareto, sa vie et son oeuvre*, 1928b). But he believes that this continuation, although based on the achievement of the master, must still be essentially different from it. For Bousquet sees in Pareto a man who has reached the goal. He says of him—in words which contain at once high praise and faint criticism—"he has almost entirely exhausted the mathematical possibilities which could be found in Walras. . . . With Pareto pure economics reached a degree of abstraction beyond which it is dangerous to go" (1928b: 101, 215). The future of the science, he holds, belongs to the realistic treatment of economic life, however much this must be founded on the achievement of the past, abstract theory. For "pure economics is today completed. It constitutes the past" (Bousquet 1927: x). Progress can only come through delving into the world of facts: "Today it is more than ever impossible to effect progress in theory save by re-establishing contact with reality: before passing on to constructive deduction it is necessary to investigate concrete facts which serve to enlarge the domain of theoretical economics" (5). Bousquet's broad "Institutes de science économique" are meant to aid the mutual permeation of abstract theory and concrete description of the economic system.

In Bousquet, the mathematical and marginalist school overcame the heritage of the nineteenth century, as the historical school had done in Salin. This is above all manifest in the fact that Bousquet—rejecting the old rationalism—fully grasped the importance of the idea of evolution. And it is this new union between the exact thought of the natural sciences and the realistic thought of the social sciences that makes Bousquet's work so interesting. Yet, taken as a whole, his book is more deeply overshadowed by the spirit of mathematics than its author perhaps realizes.

While the historians of political economy who stand under the influence of the cultural sciences, especially history, draw the circle of their studies so wide that it comprises all utterances on economic matters, even if they are not meant to contribute to the advancement of scientific knowledge, the investigators who have been formed by the natural sciences, especially physics, aim at a contraction of the scope of investigation in acknowledging as scientific only those perceptions that have been sought for themselves. This tendency is exemplified by Bousquet's *Essai sur l'Evolution de la Pensée Economique* (1927). He approaches his material with the conviction that only those ideas deserve to be called truly scientific that have sprung from pure will to knowledge, not, however, ideas, that pursue

the "Ought," dream of an ideal, or wish to promote interests. The
economist should regard economic life just as coolly and
dispassionately as the astronomer observes the stars—that is
Bousquet's basic thesis.[10] "The sole and only end of [economic]
theory should be the rational and consistent systematization of concrete
reality without any practical or normative tendency, after the model of
the physical, chemical, or mechanical theories" (1927: 277; similarly
110). Political economy becomes, according to Bousquet, a science
to the degree in which it approaches the natural sciences. "I judge
that it is absurd to study the social sciences otherwise than the natural
sciences. . . . The natural sciences should be the guides and models
of the social sciences" (151 note).

As the scientific spirit as Bousquet understands it, the spirit of
impartial and disinterested investigation, appeared in political economy
very late, it is clear that he regards our science as essentially modern,
even more modern than any other historian. He devoted, however, a
careful study to the "psychological origins of economics" and this
leads him down to those ideas that are in his view (one should say in
the view of the natural sciences) prescientific, that is, to those
economic considerations that did not spring from the motive of pure
will to knowledge, but from practical, political, humanitarian, ethical,
and religious, or juristic and philosophical motives—to those economic
considerations that, according to Bousquet, preceded the science of
political economy, just as astrology preceded astronomy and alchemy
chemistry.

"The first incentive," Bousquet says (1927: 3-4) "which led man to
make contact with economic facts is the desire to do practical work,
to give counsel with the object of being useful, which in its simplest
and barest form aims at the enrichment of the individuals." As an
example he mentions Columella's "De re rustica," a book which he
regards in every respect as prescientific: "Neither objectively nor
subjectively has he anything approaching an economic doctrine. . . .

---

10. That in the end he even dethrones his own ideal as "faux dieu" and preaches
scientific nihilism is of no interest in the present connection. However he judges it
in the final stage of his investigation, he adheres to this ideal; whether God or idol,
he reveres only this spirit.

To discover what ought to be done is . . . the sole purpose of Columella's explanation."

The conviction here expressed, that the practical interest of men in economic matters (as in all other phenomena of nature and society) is older than their theoretical interest, is undoubtedly sound, as mercantilism and physiocracy prove. But is Bousquet equally correct in depicting the will to enrich the individual as the earliest motive of reflection on national economy? Certainly not. Political economy can only originate in the wish to promote national economy or national welfare (by replacing the practical viewpoint with the theoretical, if for a moment we share Bousquet's thesis), not in the wish to promote private economy or private welfare (for this has a different object). Columella was a predecessor of Young and Thaer, but not of Ricardo and Thuenen; the science of private, not of political, economy derives from him.

"In a sphere somewhat higher, but still very near [to that of Columella] we find another tendency which attracted the attention of men towards the economic world—that which aims at the enrichment of the state" (Bousquet 1927: 6). This interest grew out of the one just mentioned, since public property was originally regarded as the property of an individual, the prince. Representative of this stage in the development of economic thought is Justi. Bousquet's views compared with those of Columella indicate great progress:

> What constitutes the superiority of that novel conception of the economic problem is that the study of public finance . . . puts us for the first time into contact with the economy of a whole category of individuals and not of a single individual. . . . The finance of the state . . . brings us nearer to the true question of Political Economy: the study of the relations which arise between different individuals on account of their economic activities. (1927: 8).

Bousquet considers this approximation to reality as the objective achievement of the Cameralists; he emphasizes, however, that subjectively they had not yet come to think of science in the strict sense of the word, as Justi definitely states that disciplines that are not serviceable to our duties, but only broaden our knowledge, must be regarded as mere ornaments.

Is it justifiable to acknowledge Justi as a precursor of political economy? Not more indeed than Columella! Here also a fundamental difference in the object of discussion is to be stated: public finance taken as a matter of scientific investigation is as sharply distinct, and to be distinguished, from national economy as private economy—the approximation that Bousquet thinks discernible is an illusion; such an approximation cannot and does not exist, neither objectively nor subjectively. For the object of the science of public finance, different as it is from national economy, demands also a discipline different from political economy: a discipline that must be in its whole essence normative and cannot therefore follow the model of the natural sciences. Man may contemplate the order of national economy as he does the order of the firmament; both are before and above him. The system of state economy, however, is human work; it is under him. In national economy perception is the end of thought, in state economy it is critique. Bousquet does not take this into account. He says half-bewildered, half-disapproving:

> Even today the discipline which is pompously called "Science of Public Finance" is still subjectively almost on the level of the cameral sciences. Read the work of Leroy Beaulieu which bears that title: it gives you without cessation precepts as to what ought to be done; there is no question of a coolly disinterested study of the subject. (1927: 9)

Herein, however, there is nothing to wonder at or to reject: thus it was, thus it is, and thus it will remain. Even that part of the science of public finance that is nearest to pure theory, the doctrine of the shifting of taxation, cannot avoid judgments of valuation. If it states that a financial burden imposed upon a certain social group by the legislator is being shifted so that in the end it falls on another class, it states implicitly that the finance bill, as it does not achieve its aim, is bad, and no will to objectivity is capable of changing anything in this respect. No thought on public finance can therefore be regarded as antecedent to political economy and least of all to political economy conceived as a natural science.

A further stimulus to the study of economic problems is, according to Bousquet, derived from the ethical and religious tendencies of the mind that precede the purely scientific interest. "Man is an animal . . . which before concerning itself with intellectual and scientific questions is also a religious animal" (1927: 14). An example is Thomas Aquinas. But do his works reveal an embryonic form of

economic science? This question is not easy. It may be answered in
the affirmative in so far as the object of St. Thomas's considerations,
individual town economy, was a precursor of modern national
economy; and in the negative in so far as this system was subject not
to invisible, but to visible laws, laws of tradition and town
government, so that the treatment was necessarily less causal than
normative. While the problem in modern national economy is: how
does the price fix itself? In the medieval town economy it was: how
is the price to be fixed? Hence the fundamentally different character
of economic doctrine then and now! Hence the ethical treatment in St.
Thomas, which Bousquet sharply rejects (because he judges it
according to absolute standards and does not interpret it in relation to
its time). "By definition, religion and morals are absolute and so they
lead us beyond the sphere of logic and experience. . . . That tendency
. . . escapes all scientific discussion" (1927: 14, 18). Where there is
conscious organization as in the domestic economy of Columella, in
the state economy of Justi, or in the town economy of St. Thomas,
Bousquet's "attitude scientifique" simply cannot exist.

As Bousquet concentrates his attention on the attitude of the
theoreticians, and not on the object of the theories, he is not aware
that with the discussion of Monchrétien (the prototype of the older
mercantilists) he enters upon new ground. For the men of this group
already had national economy in view, which, in its full development,
certainly offers a picture similar to that of the universe—the picture of
a seemingly unordered but in reality ordered system—and may
therefore be investigated according to the principles of the natural
sciences. Yet it was not the will to perception, but only the will to
promote national or human welfare that directed thinkers like
Monchrétien toward economic life, and this is the reason why
Bousquet regards them only as forerunners of economic science, not
as its founders. Not the "right" object, but the "wrong" motive
(which alone interests him since he intends to deal exclusively with the
"psychological origins" of political economy) seems to him decisive:

> The belief that there are means by which one can with a single stroke create
> something new and eminently beneficial to the human race has profound
> roots in the psychological constitution of man. . . . In the beginning many
> thinkers were animated by a sentiment of this kind which led them to devote
> their attention to the problems of economic life. (1927: 10)

This point of view—"that tendency to make economic science a doctrine having as its aim the realization of human happiness" (12) —Bousquet most decidedly rejects.   "[I]f mercantilism had an important objective significance in the evolution of economics [by its contribution to our scientific knowledge], the subjective tendency which it imposed on its adherents [as to the end of our scientific endeavor] had a retarding influence on the progress of the science" (13).

This judgment on early mercantilism, although founded on correct observation, is erroneous in its absolutism.   Monchrétien and his contemporaries no longer had before their eyes a town economy ordered by human laws as had Thomas Aquinas, but on the other hand not yet a national economy ordered by superhuman laws as did Léon Walras.   They saw the principle of exchange economy dominant in foreign trade, they comprehended that it strove to extend itself to the whole, they were rightly convinced that it represented a higher stage of development: hence their practical tendency that must be understood from their time and recognized as necessary in their time.   If Cherbuliez said, "economic motion is the product of certain moral forces, as mechanical motion of certain physical forces," and Bousquet (1927: 115) assents, both speak the language of the age of free exchange.   For the mercantilists, economy was something else, above all probably a product of certain regulations and as such an object of science as is law, but not as is nature.   Thus, the economic theory of mercantilism had partly to be normative.   The more the system of governmental tutelage was overcome, the more the system of the free play of forces was realized, the more the economic discussion became a "coolly disinterested study of the matter."   Thus, the view of mercantilism on the tasks of our science was not absolutely wrong, but relatively right—the mercantile system was the political economy of a time in which economic life was being freed, but not yet free, from conscious-molding by public interference and therefore did not yet represent the impressive spectacle of a spontaneous order that had to be achieved before economic life could be treated according to the principles of the natural sciences.

In the last place among the "currents of thought from which economic science has arisen" Bousquet mentions philosophy:

It gave to the economists the idea of society as a problem to be studied. .
. . Before it could study economic life objectively the human mind had to
make an immense effort to understand that there was a problem of society.
. . . It is impossible . . . to grasp the psychological genesis of our science
without giving attention to the fruitful contribution of the politico-juridic
philosophy of the past centuries. (1927: 19-20)

Bousquet names Hobbes, Locke, Grotius, Pufendorf, Montesquieu,
and Rousseau, and with good reason! For in so far as these thinkers
formed the concept of civil society, which coincided with the concept
of national economy, and in so far as they studied the social side of
the dominant unity of life, the economic aspect of which was first
comprehensively described by Adam Smith, they were predecessors
of the fully developed political economy. However, a distinction
between economic and sociophilosophical literature in the age of early
capitalism, as Bousquet suggests, is hardly possible, because men like
Locke and Grotius were not only philosophers but also economists,
and men like Becher and Malynes not only economists, but also
philosophers, and moreover because all thinkers of those centuries
whether they approached the problems from one side or the other,
served the same end: the understanding of the newly arisen modern
society as it was organized by the division and integration of labor.

How then, in the last analysis, did political economy originate?
Bousquet[11] thinks that it developed from the union, realized in Smith,

---

11. Bousquet does not clearly express himself on the origins of political economy; but
he probably regards Adam Smith as the founder. He says (1927: 23 et seq.):

> Until about the middle of the 18th century we have to deal only with
> fragmentary works. . . . Did they form a Political Economy? No:
> subjectively, these treatises do not envisage a scientific problem, objectively
> . . . they were lacking in solid reflections and reasonings which should not
> be too strongly imbued with the prejudices of the time. . . . But this mass
> of works has at least prepared the psychological [sic] setting in which
> Political Economy could arise and develop as it did in the classical school.

However, Bousquet does not include Quesnay's circle in classicism; it is still
"animated by anti-scientific tendencies" (310). "A history of economic science . . .
must keep . . . to the psychological constitution of its authors. . . . Under this aspect
the physiocratic doctrine is not opposed to mercantilism, it is its continuation and
development" (54). Smith, on the other hand, although "not a pure scientific spirit,

of the knowledge gathered by the preclassical literature with the scientific attitude appearing in socioeconomic thought for the first time in David Hume, whose discussions seem to Bousquet "almost always disinterested investigations" (1927: 53). "The *Wealth of Nations* can best be understood by the combination of the Essays of Hume and the preclassical systems" (53).

The same considerations by which Bousquet was led in the solution of the problem of the origin of our science, also govern his periodization of development: here, too, he views theoreticians and theories in the light of his ideal of a disinterested conception of the economic problems and thus reaches four groups: the preclassical system, the classical system, outsiders of the classical system, and the scientific systems. These descriptions, however, conceal Bousquet's true principle of division, which can be found only by a closer analysis of his book.

Bousquet examines the preclassical literature as typified in four characteristic representatives: Genovesi, Steuart, Cantillon, and the physiocratic school. Nowhere does he find the spirit of scientific and disinterested treatment (to which, however, Cantillon was already very near):

> Preclassical economics was the product of a still unclear conception of the social sciences; it had not yet succeeded in freeing itself from the psychological [sic] tendencies from which it had originated. During that period the economists aimed at practical achievements and concerned themselves with the good order of finances, they propounded doctrines intended to secure the happiness of the human race, they judged moral problems, they devoted themselves to philosophical dissertations. (1927: 52)

Even Quesnay[12] belongs to this category: "All physiocracy remains

---

treats his subject with calm and clarity" and that gives him in Bousquet's eyes an epoch-making importance.

12. It could be urged against Bousquet that Smith, too, had practical aims in view, perhaps not less than the physiocrats. He says in the introduction to book 4 (Smith 1904: 395; [Smith 1976b: 428]): "Political Economy . . . proposes two distinct objects; first to provide a plentiful revenue or subsistence for the people . . . and secondly, to supply the state or commonwealth with a revenue sufficient for the

enclosed in a frame-work of moral ideas" (46). Thus, economics before Smith is to Bousquet (who, being concerned only with the attitude of the theoreticians, consciously passes over the doctrinal contents of the theories) an "economics . . . animated by anti-scientific tendencies" (310).

In the age of classicism—Bousquet studies above all Adam Smith, Say, Malthus, Ricardo, Mill, and Ferrara—traces of purely scientific treatment (treatment as conceived by the natural sciences) appear for the first time, especially in Say and Ricardo, later on in Senior, Cairnes, and Cherbuliez. "The men who created this classical theory undoubtedly had the will to study the facts . . . which is at the root of all scientific work, of all scientific theory. But, save for very rare exceptions, the classicists never allowed that tendency to prevail . . . though, on the other hand, it is never absent from their endeavors" (1927: 119). Thus, in the vein of Bousquet one could entitle the chapter on classicism "certain scientific tendencies become visible" (311).

"On the march of the classical system" are men like Marx, List, Sismondi, and Bastiat, and schools like those of historicism, romanticism, socialism, and anarchism, all (with the single exception of Marx) negatively judged by Bousquet, because they cause economics to deviate from his ideal. "On the march of the classical system the will to build a theory, the desire to study the facts objectively, is entirely or almost non-existent." Under this negative criterion Bousquet collects the different authors opposing the Ricardian School, who—as he is convinced—should not appear at all in a competent history of economic science (1927: 120, cf. especially the footnote). Of the doctrines that attacked classicism between 1820 and 1870 he says:

> Under the objective aspect they have but one common link, that is their

publick services. It proposes to enrich both the people and the sovereign." Bousquet tries to meet this objection by the assertion that Smith's theoretical work is contained in the first two books of his *Wealth of Nations* while what follows constitutes only a sort of appendix. In the first two books, however, knowledge is the only aim followed. Against this the critical query has to be raised whether Quesnay's "Tableau" taken in isolation must not equally be acknowledged as pure science in Bousquet's sense? This question is certainly to be answered in the affirmative.

> being almost without exception void of theoretical value. Subjectively they
> present . . . in general a common psychological basis. This basis is formed
> by the sentiment of pity for the disinherited classes, by the sentiment of
> humanity and philanthropy. . . . Economic science can glean hardly
> anything from these doctrines. (1927: 165-66)

Bousquet does not even notice that he has driven from the sanctuary the creators of the idea of evolution, to which he himself adheres (254 et seq.).

The last chapter is devoted to the "Scientific Concept of Economics Adopted by the Austrian School and Pareto"—the word science again used in the strict sense describing mainly the natural sciences. Here the evolution perfects itself: the endeavors of the Austrian School and the school of equilibrium "to introduce objectivity into the social sciences are entirely analogous to the victorious attempts of Galileo . . . to make disinterested science triumph in the domain of physics. . . . In this point they have reached the definitive stage of all science" (1927: 216).

Taken as a whole, Bousquet's principle of periodization rests on the same fundamental idea as the traditional scheme: on the comparison between classicism (which is to be valued positively) and its adversaries (to be valued negatively). Bousquet only modifies the argument; he does not oppose abstract and isolating analysis to concrete and synthetic description, nor deduction to induction, but pure striving after knowledge and investigation for practical and ethical motives. This, however, does not improve the matter, but rather makes it worse. For the two tendencies compared by Bousquet were active side by side not only in classicism but also in historicism.[13] Max Weber must be classed with Cherbuliez for he

---

13. Moreover, it must not be forgotten that the younger historical school (and just this distinguished it from the older one, more perhaps than the fact that it abandoned Smith's doctrine to a still higher degree) conceived political economy similarly to Bousquet, in the manner of the natural sciences; not indeed in the manner of mathematics and physics, but in the manner of zoology and botany, that is, those disciplines, which observe, describe, classify, in short, inductively investigate the phenomena of the external world. If Bousquet says, "Scientific theory . . . consists in an ordered gathering of facts" (1927: 313), he should have treated Schmoller in a different way. This was exactly what he aimed at. (Cf. e.g. *Zur Litteraturgeschichte der Staats- und Sozialwissenschaften*, 1888: 165).

also a strong advocate of a strict distinction between the "Is" and the "Ought." Subjectively, as regards the scientific character of the treatment, there is no clear (and above all no necessary) contrast between classicism and historicism. And objectively? Bousquet says of the followers of historicism, comparing them to the classics: "Their contribution to the science of society, conceived as a picture of reality, was almost nil" (1927: 120). A man who wishes to be only a theoretician but not a sociologist could be forgiven for such an erroneous judgment. For in pure theory Schmoller and his disciples have left no trace. But pure theory cannot be identified with political economy and still less with the social sciences in general; Bousquet himself propounds the postulate that was the kernel of the program of the historical school and at the same time marks its lasting achievement: "Political Economy must be built into sociology, and that the classics neither knew nor could or would do" (122). Thus, in his mouth the assertion that social science has not been advanced by historicism is inexcusable. Classicism and historicism are not to be distinguished as scientific and unscientific, as achievement and nonachievement, but only by the idea of development, which the one possesses and the other does not. He who does not understand this point will never be able to comprehend the evolution of economic thought.

Like all who approach the past with fixed dogmatic convictions, Bousquet is inclined to degrade the history of the science to a previous history of his own doctrine. He thinks it more important to depict the truths than the errors of the past—truth and error distinguished according to the standards of Pareto's doctrine, which Bousquet regards as the last word of the science. Such an attitude implies in principle a contraction of the scope of the investigation; nevertheless in one place Bousquet advocates its extension. He wishes to give to Francesco Ferrara the place that he merits. Even if one does not go so far as to regard Ferrara as superior to Mill, one must agree with Bousquet on this point: Ferrara was certainly much more important than Bastiat; but while the leading histories of doctrine that we possess, Haney, Scott, Gonnard, and Gide-Rist, devote much space to Bastiat, they hardly notice Ferrara.[14] Here a revaluation seems to be

---

14. The reason may be simply that Ferrara wrote in Italian, and Italian is not generally known. But this reason is not a valid one.

necessary, and Bousquet did well to demand it.

The investigations of Boucke and Bousquet were discussions of the fundamental problems of the history of economics rather than representations of its gradual evolution.   Therefore, they left the historiography of political economy more or less where they found it, in spite of the great and fruitful influence which they were destined to exert upon its future development.   The first decisive step beyond Gide and Rist was made by an American, William A. Scott, who wished to write a comprehensive survey of the past of economic thought, which, viewing the whole from the standpoint of modern theory, should make the great outlines of evolution discernible.

William Amasa Scott (born 1862) is one of the leading representatives of the marginal utility school in the United States. The fact that in 1903 he edited a translation of Boehm-Bawerk's "Recent Literature on Interest" proves this intellectual relationship.   Scott's principle work is *Money and Banking* (1st edition 1903).   In the new edition of Ingram's *History of Political Economy*, published by Ely in 1915, the additional chapter "Austrian School and Recent Development" is from Scott's pen. He was especially fitted for this work not only because he so intimately knew the theory of marginal utility, but also because he had as much understanding for adversaries as for those who shared his views—a merit that is particularly manifest in the book *The Development of Economics*, which he published in 1933.

As to the origin and previous history of political economy as a science, Scott entirely followed Joseph Schumpeter. He, too, believed that the union of two streams of thought in the physiocrats and Adam Smith created political economy: a philosophic one, the beginnings of which date back "at least" to the ancient Greeks, and a practical one, which only from the sixteenth century grew in volume and importance. But he only offers lip service to this theory and starts his considerations with a short survey of the mercantilist doctrine without following Aristotle, Plato, Stoa, Epicurus, Roman jurists, and Christian theologians more closely,—obviously because his feelings rightly told him that Schumpeter's thesis is after all only half-true. "Our first task will be the explanation of the sources from which Adam Smith derives his materials and his inspiration. Of these the chief were the Mercantilists and the Physiocrats and the economic life of the periods in which they lived" (Scott 1933: 4). So in the end—in spite of Schumpeter's model—even Quesnay and Turgot become mere "precursors."

The strict sense Scott regarded political economy as modern is exemplified by his representation of the development in four stages. He treats first mercantilism and physiocracy as "The Background of the Classical Political Economy" and then "The Development of the Classical Political Economy". The third chapter discusses "Early Critics of the Classical Economists," and the fourth covers "Attempts to Reconstruct the Science." Here the conviction is clearly manifest that classicism and neoclassicism are alone to be regarded as the science. For Scott, in spite of his great understanding of history, is after all a conscious follower of the Austrian school. The third chapter, which binds together men so utterly antagonistic as Lauderdale, and Müller, Bastiat and Sismondi, simply because they were all critical to the classical school, is characteristic in this respect.

It is for the same reason that Scott, like all theoreticians, chooses the narrower circle of thinkers in the delimitation of his material. Saint-Simon, Owen, Fourier, and Blanc, indeed appear in Scott's book, but only 40 out of the 540 pages are devoted to socialism (including Sismondi). In doing so, however, he exceeds the right measure. The space of hardly four pages, in which Marx's theoretical work is treated, is of course insufficient to convey even a faint idea of the immense system of thought that this man has left, and Scott should not have forgotten that socialism not only formed social ideals and propagated social reform but also cultivated a social theory that has not been the least contribution to our science.

Scott offered to the Anglo-Saxon world the traditional picture of the history of economic doctrines in a new form, as was natural with a man belonging to the older generation. The attempt to reach a new exposition and interpretation of the past of economic science was undertaken by a member of the younger generation: Erich Roll, who, like Boucke and Bousquet, sought to combine abstract theory and concrete realistic sociology and thus to overcome the old narrowness. Before his *History of Economic Thought* (1938) he published different historical and theoretical writings (*An Early Experiment in Industrial Organization*, 1930; *About Money*, 1934; *Elements of Economic Theory*, 1937).

Erich Roll (born 1907)—strange as this may sound—envisages a synthesis between Walrasian economics and Marxian sociology. He conceives "economics as the study of the disposal of limited resources with alternative uses" (Roll 1937: 16) and describes our science in the vein of the Lausanne school:

> The economic problem is . . . essentially a problem arising from the necessity of choice—choice of the manner in which limited resources with alternative uses are disposed of. . . . We study . . . those acts of choice which habitually occur in the market. . . . It is these market transactions which obtain a quantitative appearance and become, thus, capable of measurement—again one of the preconditions of systematic study. . . . Now in so far as we can develop our original definition of economics, the conclusions which we can derive from it will be. . . applicable to all societies, and will thus become very similar to the generalizations of the physical sciences. The laws of choice like the laws of gravitation, will be independent of the legal and political frame-work in which they work.

So far Roll goes with the Lausanne school; but not farther.

> We do possess a body of generalizations of such universal validity. . . . But we shall find that in order to give these generalizations some measure of concreteness . . . we shall . . . have to make certain assumptions about the social frame-work in which they work. We shall accordingly discover that below the highest level of abstraction . . . our analysis and our conclusions are determined by the social system which we are examining. (Roll 1938: 13, 15, 16 et seq.)

Roll holds the teaching of the mathematical school to be unassailable, but not sufficient in itself: "Economics started as a practical subject concerned with the betterment of the conditions of humanity. However austere a scientific discipline it may become, it will always be necessary to put it in its proper setting of social and political ideas." How he himself envisages the formation of the science is indicated in the following words, cautious though they are:

> The formalist school which has greatly developed during the last sixty years, is split in those who . . . wish to preserve the concept of utility and those whose desire for scientific rigour has led them to concentrate on the mathematical treatment of measurable quantities and increments. There can be no doubt that it is this latter method which has produced the more imposing results in recent years. The unity of the two sections persists in

their common desire to avoid reference to social institutions and to establish laws similar to those of the physical sciences. The unifying principle of their analysis is that of choice, or substitution, which can be regarded as a natural datum; while the unifying principle of the Marxist system is the class nature of society, a social datum. (1938: 266 et seq.)

It is a union of the formalist economics of Walras and the realist sociology of Marx that Roll has in view.

To Roll political economy is the doctrine of capitalism and for that reason he regards it as essentially modern.

> Capital, labor, value, price, supply, demand, rent, interest, profit—these are the elements of capitalism and of its theoretical analysis. The earliest systematic development of these concepts is to be found at the end of the seventeenth and the beginning of the eighteenth centuries. The particular set of material conditions to which they refer was not present in developed and comprehensive form at any earlier stage of human history. (1938: 22)

Before that time "we can only expect statements of an economic character to the extent to which certain of the material conditions of a commodity-producing society were already present" (22). So far so good. But in spite of this judgment Roll begins his considerations still earlier than even such historians as Espinas or Gonnard: with the Old Testament. He is of the opinion that already in those times society possessed some characteristic features of modern capitalism, and names private property, division of labor, market exchange, and money. But this is to bring back through a window the error that has been driven out by the main door. For private property, division of labor, market exchange, and money are as old as—or even older than—human history. Whether primeval communism was reality or legend, science does not venture to decide. The first division of labor existed, as Marx so splendidly said, between man and woman and hence before all culture. Exchange was carried on already by the nomads, and Babel, the town of the confusion of languages, was a great market centuries before the Bible. The origin of money is lost in the twilight of early history. Even capital is extremely old; the bow of the hunter, the herd of the herdsman, the plow of the husbandman were capital. But that is not the issue. Political economy is not simply the doctrine of capitalism as Roll thinks,[15] but the science of the laws of national economy founded upon capitalistic private property, general use of money, division of labor, and market intercourse between all members of a nation, and that it what constitutes its exclusively modern character.[16]

Roll divided his book into eight chapters: (1) "The Beginnings" (Antiquity and the Middle Ages); (2) "Commercial Capitalism and its Theory" (the Mercantile System); (3) "The Founders of Political Economy" (Petty, Locke, North, Law, Hume, Cantillon, Steuart, Quesnay and his school); (4) "The Classical System" (Smith, Ricardo, Malthus's doctrine of population); (5) "Reaction and Revolution" (Malthus's theory of crises, German romanticism, early socialism); (6) "Marx" (this chapter occupies the center of Roll's work; while the earlier systems of thought are more or less sharply criticized, the theoretical achievement of this thinker is represented with great appreciation); (7) The Transition" (historicism, Jones, Say, Cournot, Lotz, Thuenen, Torrens, James Mill, Bailey, Lauderdale, Whately, Lloyd, Longfield, Senior, John Stuart Mill); and (8) "Modern Economics" (from Gossen to Pareto). If we survey this principle of division, the leading idea of which is not easily found, we cannot help perceiving in it a certain inconsistency: the preclassical writers are grouped according to economic history, the postclassical according to

---

15. Even if one would adopt Roll's standpoint, consistent thinking should lead to the conclusion that only the sixteenth century developed the phenomena that form the basis of political economy. Up to that time not even interest could find recognition, a sign that capital had not yet unfolded and proved its productive forces—a sign that economy and society were still precapitalistic.

16. Roll says (1938: 44 et seq.): "Industry . . . was not highly developed in Rome. And in the medieval world too . . . industry remains confined to a small local market or to a few products of outstanding importance in long-distance trade." "With its still predominant natural economy, difficulties in transport, restricted trade, and local markets, early medieval society was not a suitable environment for an unrestricted play of the forces behind supply and demand" (49). Property was divided between peasant and noble, the division of labor was confined within the boundaries of a town or a manor; market and money were only a little superstructure on a broad basis of natural economy—such were the Middle Ages during which the preconditions of political economy were entirely nonexistent.

intellectual history. The first chapter contains the economic thought of precapitalistic times; the second depicts the reflection of commercial capitalism, and the third describes the formation of doctrines accompanying the growth of industrial capitalism. The fourth chapter treats the classical system as the doctrine of fully developed industrial capitalism. And then the principle of division changes; for the next three sections describe "the reaction and criticism . . . and the gradual transformation . . . into a new body of orthodoxy" (1938: 196), first late feudal and early socialist opposition, then Marxism, and in the end declining classicism developing toward the system of marginal utility. The reason for this change is that Roll, taking over the Marxian scheme, regards industrial capitalism as a uniform concept, as a fixed category, and in his preoccupation with the (more apparent than real) constancy of its characteristics (profit greed, class antagonism, and the like) he forgets the fact that economic reality went on changing after Ricardo's death, creating in new stages new theories. Had Roll been truly consistent, he would have elaborated, even for the post classical dogmas, a scheme of periodization on the basis of economic history, which could have accepted high and late capitalism as its fundamental notions.

What characterizes Roll's book is the sound delimitation of the field to be investigated. The thinkers and thoughts that best represent the intellectual tendencies of the past are as appropriately chosen as the theories and theoreticians that have formed the modern science. Of the qualities that should distinguish the historian, Roll possesses one in a special degree: the feeling for the correct selection from the fullness of phenomena, which it is the task of historiography to represent in the unity of their development.

In spite of all differences in particulars, the historiography of political economy created by the theoreticians, as we have now followed it from Cossa to Roll, shows three typical tendencies: (1) as to the problem of the origin of the science the inclination prevails to transfer the beginnings into the eighteenth century—whether Cantillon, Quesnay, or Smith is praised as its real founder—because the conception is dominant that economic theory is a systematic science and cannot therefore be conceived before the appearance of a system of ideas, before the breakthrough of the idea of system; (2) as to the problem of development, the division into schools is usually preferred, because the theoreticians direct all their attention to the doctrines and therefore the diversity in particulars impresses their minds more strongly than the unity in general; and (3) in the solution of the problem of character they mostly follow the tendency to draw the circle of their investigation as narrow as possible,—because they adhere as a rule to the ideal of the natural sciences that regard all perceptions as void of value that do not seem to embody eternal truths. In all these decisions, however, the spirit of rationalism is immanent, which believes that behind the multiplicity of phenomena a unity of concatenation is to be found hidden, the discovery of which is the great mission of human reason.

4

The Intellectual Stages of the History of Political Economy

When did political economy arise? What were the phases of its evolution? What thinkers belong within its circuit? Three difficult questions—three unsolved problems!

If we survey the historiography of our science, it may seem impossible to reach a generally accepted solution. This is not surprising, for behind the three questions is the great fundamental problem that looks so simple and is still so difficult to solve: what is political economy? What tasks has it to fulfill? There are as many answers as there are investigators.

And yet, a definition of our science acceptable in all camps is by no means an indispensable condition for establishing the foundations of the historiography of economic doctrine. If it were so, all our endeavors in this direction would be in vain. Happily it is sufficient to find out what must be understood as political economy in the historical sense—and from the nature of the problem this cannot be quite so controversial as the same question put in a dogmatic context.

In his classical book, *The Character and Logical Method of Political Economy* (1875: 35), Cairnes describes the scope of the science in a striking simile that today would probably meet with general approval. He says:

What Astronomy does for the phenomena of the heavenly bodies; what Dynamics does for the phenomena of motion; what Chemistry does for the phenomena of chemical combination; what Physiology does for the phenomena of the functions of organic life, that Political Economy does for the phenomena of wealth: it expounds the laws according to which those phenomena co-exist with or succeed each other; that is to say, it expounds the laws of the phenomena of wealth.

This coexistence of the phenomena under observation, political economy has in common with the exact sciences: astronomy studies the system of the stars, mechanics the system of powers, chemistry the system of elements, economic analysis the system of market relations. And everywhere the same is to be seen: although the parts of these systematic wholes are seemingly independent of one another, they still unite into a perfect order, and we cannot explain this order but by assuming that hidden laws are active in the universe, which, from the chaos of the parts, form the cosmos of the whole. To perceive these hidden laws is the endeavor of the human mind. Its results constitute the science. This is what Cairnes wishes to say.

On the basis of this conception of the essence and tasks of political economy the question now arises: has the human economy always been a system governed by a secret law similar to the order of the firmament? To answer this question in the affirmative, as has often been done in an exaggerated analogy with the exact sciences would mean to disregard the findings of the science that alone is capable of giving the answer: history.

The economic activities of man took place, at least in their essential parts, through hundreds or even thousands of years within units of life that owed their order not to a hidden but to a visible law, not to a superhuman but to a human law, in a domestic or town economy. In order to know how production and consumption were constituted on the ideal manor of the ninth century it is not necessary to describe it and then to analyze it; a study of Charlemagne's "Capitulare de villis" is sufficient. And the same is virtually true of production and consumption in the medieval town, although here a primitive exchange is already inserted: the minute economic legislation of the town, for example, of Strassburg, reveals to our eyes the whole mechanism of the division and integration of labor that operated within its walls.[1]

---

1. As in the consciously organized economic systems of the past, so in a consciously organized economic system of the future, no political economy in our sense could

Not so in modern national economy and in the modern state! What distinguishes the Middle Ages economically from modern times is the fact that the single units of life then produced almost all the goods that they consumed, while today hardly anyone produces all the goods that he needs. Or, in other words, production and consumption were then consciously coordinated; today this coordination takes place independently of the individual wills by the mechanism of the market. Organized and free economy, natural and exchange economy are opposed to each other. And only the free or exchange economy offers the spectacle of an equilibrium system governed by secret laws that can be investigated according to the same principles as the realm of the stars, the powers, or the elements. *Viewed historically, political economy is the doctrine of the order dominant in exchange economy.*[2]

---

exist. As with justice the Bolshevik Bukharin (*The Economic Theory of the Leisure Class*, 1927: 49): "In a socialist society," which he, as it seems, conceives as a thoroughly organized and centrally directed planned economy, "political economy will lose its *raison d'être* . . . for . . . the causal consequences in the life of the unbridled elements will be replaced by the causal consequences of the conscious performances of society."

2. The theoreticians who stand in the Lausanne tradition will probably reject this description. They base their deductions as a rule on two concepts that seem to be timeless: scarcity and choice between alternative uses of scarce means. In this sense Robbins says in his *Essay on the Nature and Significance of Economic Science* (1937: 16): "Economics is the science which studies human behaviour as a relationship between ends and scarce means which have alternative uses." This definition seems to exclude the restriction of the science to a certain economic order. Indeed Roll, who propounds a similar definition, asserts: "The necessity of choice is independent of the social system in which it takes place" (Roll 1937: 16). Now, man is of course always confronted with the scarcity of provision. Without it there would be not only no economy but also no culture. Human behavior in this situation and toward this situation, however, is totally different in different social systems. The *homo oeconomicus* studied by the classicists and neoclassicists is only one form of the *homo rationalis* typical of modern times. (Even the famous Robinson Crusoe is only the man of modern society in isolation, not some isolated man—such a one cannot exist and least of all as a being capable of reasonable choice.) In the organized or natural economy of the past the *homo traditionalis* was the dominant type. To him the same rules cannot be applicable as to his much younger brother. The view of the theoreticians of the Lausanne tradition is itself characteristic of the mentality of modern man: he is so imbued with rationalism that he cannot understand how the homo sapiens can possibly have acted in the struggle for existence otherwise than reasonably. Yet there were thousands of years of Totem and Tabu.

Keeping this truth in view we shall easily understand why the economic dogmas before and after 1750 were so different in their character. The *communis doctorum opinio* delimits the two periods by emphasizing that not until Cantillon and Quesnay does the idea appear that economic life is ordered by natural laws and that these laws must be conceived as a system. Before that there were only normative judgments on economic matters or at best isolated laws. True! But the science has the task of finding the cause behind this empirical statement. It lies in the transition from domestic and town to national economy, in the transition from natural to exchange economy. The idea that natural laws are operative in economic life could be conceived only after an economic order above the individuals and independent of human will had become discernible in modern national economy—an order similar to that of the firmament. However, as long as the order of economic life, as on the manor or in the town of the Middle Ages, was instituted by man and molded by his will, economics had to be a normative discipline, a normative discipline like the art of legislation. Where the science faces superhuman laws, it asks: what is? Where it devotes its endeavors to human laws, it asks: what is to be done? Thus, Cantillon and Quesnay did not discover new truths in an old science but created a new science, the science of national and exchange economy.

But the sentence: *natura non facit saltum*, is true even here. Political economy, like exchange economy, did not suddenly enter upon the world but developed slowly and laboriously. The beginnings of neither can be grasped with exactitude; the stream of life is not measurable with a yardstick. But this we may say: the principles of free exchange as well as their intellectual reflection appear first in the sphere of money and circulation. This is because the sphere of money was, so to speak, the sphere of market and market exchange in a feudal world, and its extension was at the same time the extension of the exchange economy driving back the system of natural economy. It first conquered those domains that had always been the freest: foreign trade and then commerce; in a later stage industry; and only after some centuries the citadel of tradition, agriculture.[3] As soon as

---

3. How in the agricultural system of those centuries feudal and capitalistic elements (i.e., elements of natural and exchange economy) combined into a transitional form I intended to show in a book *Der landwirtschaftliche Grossbetrieb im Zeitalter des*

this had happened, and Quesnay's work proves that it happened about the middle of the eighteenth century, a comprehensive analysis could arise that formed the laws of exchange economy hitherto grasped only in isolated observations into a system corresponding to that already existing in fact. But these individual laws before 1750 were germane to the system of laws after 1750, and their discussion is the first task of any historian of political economy.

These considerations make it possible to judge confidently the problem of the origin of our science. It arose neither in the fifth century[4] B.C. nor in the eighteenth century A.D., but accompanied modern exchange economy in its development, the first beginnings of which—if a certain time can be stated at all—should be sought in the sixteenth century.

The perception that political economy constitutes the science of exchange economy was by no means alien to the age of Quesnay and Smith. We find it clearly expressed by a thinker of that period, Sir James Steuart. "Civil and domestic liberty," he says in his *Inquiry into the Principles of Political Economy* (1805: 200-1), "introduced into Europe by the dissolution of the feudal form of government, set trade and industry on foot; these produced wealth and credit; these again debts and taxes; and all these together have established a perfectly new system of political economy, the principles of which it is my intention to deduce and examine." The words of this statement may be a little primitive, but the idea they express is clear and true.

If political economy constitutes the science of exchange economy,

_____

Feudalkapitalismus, the publication of which was prevented by the outbreak of war in September 1939.

4. Only one more problem presents itself in this connection: did not antiquity also develop an exchange economy? The discussion on this point between Karl Bücher and Eduard Meyer is well known (Bücher, *Beiträge zur Wirtschaftsgeschichte*, 1922; Meyer, *Die wirtschaftliche Entwicklung des Altertums*, 1895). Our view on this question, a compromise, has already been outlined in the text: Meyer is right in asserting that antiquity reached a high stage of evolution, but Bücher is not wrong in maintaining that this evolution did not lead to a full development of a national and exchange economy. In other words, antiquity did not make national and exchange economy the dominant system—the absence of a political economy in our sense at once explains and confirms this fact.

not only its origin but also its scope is strictly limited: all perceptions concerning the character of exchange economy—and only those perceptions—belong within its circle. Historians like Roscher had too broad a conception when they included all utterances on economic matters, even judgments without perceptive value. Scientists like Bousquet have too narrow a conception when they wish to include only exact analyses but not perceptions connected with judgments. Here too the middle way must be chosen. Socialism especially belongs to the history of economics in so far as its exponents (as social critics) have something to say on the character of exchange economy (as had Karl Marx), but not if they moralize (as did Ruskin or Tolstoy) or indulge in fancies (as did Fourier and Bellamy).

Thus, the historical interpretation of political economy as the science of exchange economy gives us the answer to the problems of the origin and essence of our discipline, the solution of which is the condition of a historiography of doctrine really fulfilling its tasks. But does it also offer a key to the problem of development? In fact it does and here also the truth must be found between the extremes.

The historians of the science who followed Wilhelm Roscher as their model took the principle of periodization as a rule more from the general history of intellect and culture than from political economy. The periods that they envisaged were too broad; only an indistinct, hardly perceptible idea unites the thinkers whom they connect. Their adversaries, who adhered to the principles of Eugen Dühring grouped the theoreticians according to their dogmatic quarrels as they appear in actual discussion. The schools that they construct are certainly too narrow:[5] hardly two authors can be reduced to a common creed, even if they are germane in a deeper stratum of their thought, as is often revealed by retrospective consideration. The adherents of historicism are prone to forget that they are concerned with the past of a *science*. Their opponents on the other hand fail to realize that it is the *past* of a science that is to be studied. But it is at the same time the past *and*

---

5. Gide and Rist, in their treatment of Lexis's lifework, show how unsuitable is the periodization of development according to schools. Although they appreciate Lexis they devote to him only a longer footnote because he "belonged neither to the historical school nor to that of state-socialism" (Gide and Rist 1909: 534)—as if one could only acquire civic rights in the science by submitting to a school!

science with which the historiography of political economy has to deal.

A new periodization that starts from the idea that the perception of the character of exchange economy must be regarded as the task of economic science does full justice to this twofold aspect. The thinkers of the past then appear as columns of workers in the same work taking their place in succession, and the visible results of the common endeavor are the milestones of the way traversed. Each new generation indeed does not continue where the old left off, but we may assume that on the whole more is built up than demolished. This results in, so to speak, strata of knowledge, and the intermediate bases between these strata are the new fundamental perceptions that have made epochs. They divide the evolution of political economy—the evolution of the science that in this light appears neither as the overcoming of error by truth, nor as a sequence of products of equal value, but as the modest progress of the knowledge of our economic system. This progress is the thread that we may follow through the past; it leads us by stages to the economic concept of the present, which is perhaps not truer but certainly wider than that of the past.

Now, there are four great fundamental perceptions that strike the eye in a survey of the history of doctrine. The first asserted itself by 1570-80 and consists in the realization that national economy is the modern economic unit. The second broke through about 1750-60 and is embodied in the idea that the exchange economy of modern times must be conceived as a system of interdependence. The third appeared between 1820 and 1830 and showed that national and exchange economy studied by the science can only be valued as a historical category. The fourth and last fundamental perception was reached by the science between 1870 and 1880: the perception that it is the psyche of man in which and through which the laws of the present-day economic system operate. Thus, the history of political economy is divided into four periods: from the origin of socioeconomic thought to the perception of the interdependence of all phenomena; from the perception of the interdependence of all phenomena to the discovery of the principle of evolution; from the discovery of the principle of evolution to the pursuit of economic analysis into the individual psyche; and from the foundation of the science on psychology to the present day.

A preliminary stage of the analysis of national and exchange economy is to be seen in the different money theories that appear as soon as money begins to undermine and transform natural economy. However, as long as the circulation functioned without difficulties, the phenomena of the means of circulation remained uninvestigated. Only when problems arose did men set out to analyze its character and operation, and it was public administration that caused such problems to arise. Jean le Bon, King of France, changed the nominal value of the *livre tournois* between 1351 and 1360 more than seventy times, creating much confusion in the economic life of his country so far as it was already subject to exchange economy,[6] and thus he evoked a monograph, the first that deserves to be included within the scope of economic science: Nicole Oresme's work *De origine et natura, jure et mutationibus monetarum*, which was written about 1360. The description of bimetallism propounded in this treatise by this future bishop of Lisieux—building on the doctrine of his master Johannes Buridanus—starts from the perception that the value of money is based upon the use-value of the money-metal, that the rate of value between gold and silver is therefore formed in commercial intercourse (according to secret market laws), and that legislation should follow the relation thus created. He offers herewith a genuinely scientific analysis of a partial domain of real exchange economy that is thoroughly modern in character.[7]

Interest in the problems of monetary circulation never ceased in the two centuries that followed Oresme's publication. It may suffice to mention Copernicus and the Saxon mint discussion. A new and powerful incentive, however, came when by 1560 the broad stream of gold from Mexico and Peru poured forth by way of Portugal and Spain into Western Europe and revolutionized the traditional price system. The ablest French thinker of the time, Jean Bodin, then turned toward economy and gave in his *Réponse à M. de Malestroit touchant le fait des monnaies et l'enchérissement de toutes choses* (1568) an analysis of the great inflation that clearly grasped the primary reason of the rise in prices. "[T]he principle and almost sole

---

6. It came even to a revolt at Paris under Etienne Marcel.

7. Cf. also the perception that the debasement of the coinage constitutes in fact concealed tax, and "Gresham's Law."

[cause of the rise] (which nobody has so far touched) is the abundance of gold and silver" he says (cited in Baudrillart 1853: 169), "which is today greater in this kingdom than for four centuries." It was not human mint laws, but superhuman market laws that increased the prices. In his interesting *Etude sur Jean Bodin* (1876: 66) Edouard de Barthélemy judges that "in his Réponse Bodin expressed for the first time some of the essential ideas of Political Economy with clearness, with fullness, with a correct feeling of the existence of natural economic laws superior to the arbitrary arrangements and conjectures of authorities." But Bodin—and this is the epoch-making fact—did not stop with monetary theory but expressed for the first time in his *Les Six livres de la République* (1576) the fundamental principle of mercantilism:

> As to raw materials imported from foreign lands it is necessary to lower the duties and to increase them for works of handicraft and not to permit that these should be brought in from foreign lands, nor should raw materials like iron, copper, steel, wool, flax, raw silk, and other similar articles be suffered to be carried away, thus the subject may gain the profit of his work and the prince the impost. (1593: 877)

By prince and subject the theoretician of modern public law means the government and the members of the national economy, which later appeared in the modern state as a visible unit. He thus only raised into a principle the idea that his contemporary René de Biragues applied in practice. We read in an edict of 1572 by the precursor of the great Colbert:

> In order that our subjects may the better devote themselves to the manufacture and processing of wool, flax, hemp, and bast which grow and abound in our kingdom and land, and make and draw the profit made by foreign countries which come here to buy them generally cheap, carry them off and process them and then import the cloth and linen which they sell at an excessive price we have ordered and now order that in future it will not be lawful for any of our subjects or any stranger under what reason or pretext soever to transport wool, flax, hemp, and bast outside our kingdom and land. . . . We also expressly forbid all import into this our kingdom of all cloths, canvas, lace, and purl-lace of gold or silver, likewise of all velours, satins, damasks, taffetas, camlets, canvas, and all sorts of striped material or material containing gold or silver . . . under penalty of the confiscation of the said merchandize. (Baudrillart 1853: 14 et seq.)

Thus, from the time of Bodin and Biragues national economy became the object of all labors in science and reality and Francesco Ferrara not without reason judged that we must regard Johnannes Bodinus as in a sense marking the beginning of the evolution of political economy. Indeed he heads the long line of authors who between the middle of the sixteenth and the middle of the eighteenth centuries devoted themselves to the study of economic life and are traditionally summed up as mercantilists.

In close connection with Johannes Bodinus stands the unidentified Englishman known only as "W.S. Gentleman" thought to have been William Shakespeare, William Stafford, and lastly John Hales. His "Compendious or Briefe Examination of Certayne Ordinary Complaints of divers of our Countrymen in these our Dayes" (also called "A Discourse of the Common Weal of this Realm of England") was first published in print in 1581, although the editor, Elizabeth Lamond, has made it seem probable that the dialogue originated as early as 1549. Not only does the writing propound in monetary theory many opinions similar to those of Bodin (cf. 1593: esp. 71 and 109) but it leads also to the conclusion that only by a national trade and monetary policy can the foundations of a national prosperity be laid. This advocate of mercantilism compares the inhabitants of England to the passengers of a ship and expresses in this simile the common destiny of all members of the national state and the national economy.

In the period of roughly a hundred and fifty years after Johnannes Bodinus the mercantilistic view of economic life developed greatly, increasing both in depth and breadth. All parts of exchange economy were investigated and the more ground capitalism gained from feudalism, the more comprehensive became the scope of economic science. In agricultural production, however, the traditional economic methods survived until far into the eighteenth century and consequently what literature offers on this subject is almost exclusively rules of art, not laws of economy. A comprehensive analysis of national and exchange economy was possible only when the last remnants of domestic and natural economy disappeared, which took place by 1750.

The first to see modern exchange economy as a system of interdependence and to perceive the mutual concatenation of all members of a people in production and distribution seems to have been Ernst Ludwig Carl, the author of a three volume *Traité de la richesses des princes et de leurs états et des moyens simples et naturels pour y parvenir, Par M. C. C.d.P.d.B. allemand*[8] published in 1722-23 at Paris. The basic idea of this very remarkable work[9] which, as the preface says, aims at describing all realities of national economy and all perceptions on national welfare in their essential and systematic connection according to a uniform method, may be summed up as follows:

> The natural order of economic life unites men in a common production founded upon the division of labour and secures the maximum of well-being to all. The social economy constituted by the natural economic order is the collaboration of the individual economies connected with one another and bound together by mutual dependence. The goods produced are directed by interchange to the place of their use and consumption. In this interchange the price brings their income to all producers. (Tautscher 1940: 99)[10]

Here a modern comprehensive theory of production and distribution

---

8. Carl Conseiller des Princes de Brandebourg. Tautscher (1940: 80) lays claim to honors that he did not merit when he says: "The solution of the pseudonym has now been achieved," as if he had accomplished it, for already Roscher (1874: 376) ascribes the *Traité* to the "Bayreuther Carl" without, however, noticing its importance.

9. Tautscher, the rediscoverer of Carl, reproduces in his article the following definitions (1940: 90, 92, 93), which strike us as strangely modern and remind us even of Menger: Goods are only those things which serve for the satisfaction of human needs (Traité I: 34, II: 460); the importance which goods have for the satisfaction of human needs constitutes their value (I: 47); Goods not directly serving the satisfaction of needs acquire value if they serve for the production of goods serving directly the satisfaction of needs (I: 34 et seq. and 60).

10. It is absurd to transform the solution of the problem of the origin of political economy into a matter involving national pride. Had Carl not known Boisguillebert, had he not changed feudal Germany for highly developed France, he would never have become the author of such a treatise. The creation of political economy is the result of a fruitful collaboration of the leading nations. Here as everywhere Turgot's word is true: "He who does not forget that there are political states separated from one another and diversely constituted, will never treat well of any question of Political Economy" (Letter to Mlle. Lespinasse of 26 January 1770, Turgot 1770: 800).

founded on the knowledge of the character of national and exchange economy is presented to us.

In spite of the high level, however, which economic analysis reached in Carl's work, his *Traité* had hardly any influence on the further development of political economy. More successful seems to have been his contemporary Richard Cantillon whose *Essai sur la nature du commerce en général,* which was quoted by François Quesnay and Adam Smith, appeared in 1755 (but was probably written as early as 1725). In the twelfth chapter of the first part of this work he gives his description of distribution, which, however primitive it may appear, marks an epoch because it starts from the social product and shows how it is measured out to the different classes of producers. He suggests that the produce of the soil—which he identifies, anticipating the physiocratic theory, with national income—is divided between farmers and landlords (in a relation of two to one), and that the incomes of all other producers, especially those in trade and commerce, must be regarded as derived earnings. He assumes that half of all the inhabitants of the state live in towns, and half in the country; he then investigates how the economic circulation of money and merchandise takes place in such ideal conditions. While the mercantilists had only analyzed a single section of the whole or at best juxtaposed some partial pictures, here the essence of national economy as an economic system is fully grasped. "The importance of Cantillon" F. A. von Hayek says in the preface to his edition of the *Essai* (1931: xxxiv), "seems to lie in the fact that he was the first to succeed in permeating and describing almost the whole field of what we call Political Economy."

Cantillon furnished the basis on which Quesnay could build. The latter's *Tableau oeconomique* came to be published three years after Cantillon's *Essai.* Schumpeter emphasized the essential point in saying (Schumpeter 1914: 44) that the comprehensive survey of the economic process achieved by the physiocrats is expressed in three concepts: circulation, the social product, and distribution. But behind these three notions is a further image, a new perception: national economy is no longer viewed only as a geographical but as a systematic unit, as an all-embracing process of the national division and integration of labor (realized in the social product and reflected by distribution), which is performed in economic intercourse (by the circulation).

With Cantillon and Quesnay opens the great age of economic theory that reached its climax in David Ricardo. Not unjustly described as classicism, it first gave a comprehensive analysis of exchange economy as a system of interdependence. It showed how the market combines the seemingly independent individual economies into a great order, and how this order appears as the expression of the highest rationality. But this rationality they conceived in the style of their time as something absolute, something timelessly correct, as an emanation of an unchangeable reason of the universe. What unites all thinkers of this period is the common conviction that the laws of national economy found by them were natural laws, similar in essence to the laws of gravitation. Karl Arnd, one of the epigones of Smith and Ricardo, formulated this view perhaps most distinctly. "Political Economy is a science which brings those unchangeable natural laws into prominence on which the economic life of the peoples rests. These natural laws are based on the inner nature of men and things and are as eternal and unchangeable as the physical laws of the universe" (cited in Mombert 1927: 477, 353). The classical economists, like their contemporaries, all viewed the past à la Rousseau. In the beginning there was an age of nature. Unreason made man disturb the harmony of the natural state and mankind sank into the misery of the historical epoch. The reconstitution of the natural order, they believed, would create a new age of harmony founded upon eternally unchangeable laws—secret laws, the revelation of which is the task of political economy. This scheme, however, was only the result of rationalistic speculation, to which the idea of evolution, the great discovery of the nineteenth century, was still unknown. For the classicists, Marx justly observes (*Misère de la philosophie* 1847: 113, 160, 94),

> the institutions of feudalism are artificial institutions, those of the bourgeoisie natural institutions. . . . The economists explain how production goes on within the given framework—it is . . . the error of all economists that they represent the conditions of the bourgeois production as eternal—but what they do not explain is how these conditions themselves are produced, that is to say the historical movement which gave them birth.

To the treatment of this problem, the growth of national and exchange economy, the science, which prior to 1820 had been concerned exclusively with its structure, turned in the romantic age, with increasing interest.

The first writer who refused to regard Smith's doctrine as a collection of universally valid laws was Adam Müller with his *Die Elemente der Staatskunst* published in 1808-09. He endeavored to prove (Müller 1936: 307) "that the Political Economy of Great Britain, however solid may be its basis, and however applicable it may be to the nature of that island, cannot serve as a scheme and model of Political Economy in general," because in different times and places there are different conditions—a fact that, as the inhabitant of a country that was still half-feudal, he easily realized. In his work the dynamic interpretation of economic life is foreshadowed.[11]   Müller writes,

> The political science which I aim at shall conceive the state in its flight, in its movement, and therefore I am not fully satisfied with any of the hitherto propounded theories on this matter. . . . They are, to use a simile from the medical art, exhaustive in the anatomy of the state, but if the whole phenomenon of the life of the state is to be properly grasped, they themselves lack the indispensable life. (1936: 10)

He goes on to say,

> Our usual theories of the state are agglomerations of notions and therefore dead, useless, unpractical: they cannot keep pace with life because they are

---

11. More cannot be maintained. An analysis of Müller's work proves that in many points he had not overcome rationalism—however his present-day admirers may represent him.   Just one example: in methodology he was inclined to prefer deduction. He places at the beginning of his considerations "three simple ideas, understandable even to children, apparently self-evident, such as used to be placed at the head of any science e.g. mathematics from which the whole science starts and to which it incessantly returns" (23). Cf. also "Prolegomena einer Kunst-Philosophie," *Vermischte Schriften* 1817: 263 et seq. esp. 272. Similar traces of rationalism we find in Müller's philosophy of law (cf. *Elemente*: 36), of the state (e.g., 150), of history (e.g., 138), and in many other respects. On economic life Müller says: "All commodities as ... all persons have a tendency to disperse and to bring themselves according to general laws of nature into equilibrium.... This is an institution of nature" (275). Cf. on this point Knies, *Die Politische Oekonomie vom Standpunkte der geschichtlichen Methode*, 1853: 22 et seq.

> based on the illusion that the state can be understood entirely and once for all; they stand still, while the state progresses into the unending. . . . The state is not only the union of many families living side by side but also of many families following one another; this union should not only be infinitely great and intimate in space but also immortal in time. The doctrine of the connection of the generations following one another is an empty page in all our theories of the state and here-in lies their great defect. (17, 40)

The overcoming of which is the task of the future.

If we regard the program laid down in 1843 by Wilhelm Roscher in his *Grundriss zu Vorlesungen über die Staatswissenschaft nach geschichtlicher Methode* as characteristic of historicism, we must place Simonde de Sismondi beside Adam Müller at the helm of this intellectual movement. Roscher, as we have explained, advanced four points into the foreground: the sociological and historical aspects of exchange economy, the comparative method, and the idea of relativity. All these principles were already most clearly proclaimed in 1819 by Sismondi in his *Nouveaux principes d'économie politique*. He says, citing Smith against Ricardo whom he wishes to criticize,

> Adam Smith considered Political Economy as a science of experience. . . . He recognized . . . that it can only be founded on the history of the different peoples, and that it is only from a judicious observation of facts that one can deduce principles. . . . He endeavored to examine each fact in its social position and never to lose sight of the diverse circumstances with which it was connected. . . . One must in general avoid absolute propositions in Political Economy, and likewise abstractions. (1819: 57, 49, 288)

These words are almost spoken in the vein of Schmoller, Smith's "new disciples in England have thrown themselves into abstractions which make us entirely lose sight of the ground. The science is so speculative in their hand that it seems to detach itself from all practice" (58). Even the great Scot is blamed because of his rationalism:[12] "Adam Smith conceived the science as exclusively

---

12. Nevertheless Sismondi proves himself to be partly a child of the eighteenth century. The second book of his investigation ("Formation et progrès de la richesse") constantly makes use of the "solitaire" that is, a Robinson Crusoe, and comes to judgments like this: "The wealth of all is but the sum-total of the wealth of the

submitted to calculation, whilst it belongs in some respects to the domain of feeling and imagination which cannot be calculated" (56). For Sismondi (as for all followers of the historio-sociological movement) political economy is not a *science de calcul* but a *science morale* (288), that is to say not a natural but a cultural science.

In the generation after Sismondi these principles were developed, in France the emphasis being more sociological, in Germany more historical (Saint-Simon and Comte[13] on the one side, List and Roscher-Hildebrand-Knies on the other side of the Rhine). In England, however—after Mill had taken half a step in this direction[14]—Marx created a great synthesis between French sociology, German philosophy of history, and British economics. In teaching that while it is true that the economic system of the present is subject to fixed laws, these laws are not eternal like those of nature but changeable like those of society, he harmonized the old doctrines with the new and overcame their apparent antithesis by a higher

---

individuals" (1819 II: 63), a view the atomism of which was rejected by fully developed romanticism with its organic concept. The third book, however ("De la richesse teritoriale") shows already a strongly developed historicism. The argumentation often reminds the reader of Schmoller's "Grundriss."

13. Schumpeter's rhetorical question: "What has Comte's world of thought"—and that of Hegel who is mentioned in the same connection—"to do with the historical school?" (Schumpeter 1914: 103) appears simply incomprehensible. Common to Hegel, Schmoller, Comte, and Ingram, is "only" the idea of evolution—that is the dominant idea of the post-napoleonic age, which is in intellectual history sharply severed from the eighteenth century, the children of which were Smith and Ricardo.

14. In the *Principles of Political Economy* Mill says: "The laws and conditions of the Production of wealth partake of the character of physical truths.... It is not so with the Distribution of wealth. That is a matter of human institution solely.... The distribution of wealth ... depends on the laws and customs of society. The rules by which it is determined ... are very different in different ages and countries" (Mill 1909: 199-200). Cf. also Mill's very interesting letter to Comte of 3 April, 1844 ("I shall take special pains to separate the general laws of Production, which are necessarily common to all industrial societies, from the principles of the Distribution and Exchange of wealth, which necessarily presuppose a particular state of society."). Cf. further his *System of Logic*, 1843. This division of the theory of production and the theory of distribution, however deeply Mill may have conceived it, cannot be defended, because the process of history comprehends all parts of social life alike.

concept of the world and knowledge.[15]

However, what is common to the historio-sociological school and classicism is the practice of taking the things of the external world, especially of course the phenomena of economic life, as they appear to the senses. This is clearly manifest in the basic notion of theory, the notion of value. "The value of a thing," says John Stuart Mill in his *Principles* (Mill 1909: 478), "means the quantity of some other thing, or of things in general, which it exchanges for." To have overcome this materialist concept and thus opened up a new epoch in the history of doctrine, was the merit of Stanley Jevons and Carl Menger who published their books in 1871, after the earlier attempts of Gossen and Jennings (as well as Ferrara) pointing in the same direction had come to naught. Menger was fully aware that by his psychological considerations he had promoted and deepened the analysis of economic phenomena:

> As a more thorough investigation of the psychic facts makes the perception of the external things appear merely as the influence of the things on ourselves which come to our consciousness i.e. in the last analysis as the perception of a state of our own person so all the importance which we ascribe to the things of the external world is, in the last analysis, only a result of that importance which the conservation of our being in its essence and its development, i.e. our life and our well-being have for us. Value is therefore not anything inherent in the goods, not any attribute of them, but merely the importance which we ascribe to the satisfaction of our needs or to our life and our well-being, and which we consequently transfer to the economic commodities as the exclusive causes thereof. (1934: 81)

In the same sense Jevons means (1931: 37) that "the ordinary necessaries and conveniences of life, such as food, clothing, buildings, utensils, furniture, ornaments, etc.," material things, are "the immediate object of our attention," and therefore, the first object of the science. But—and this is new in his work—"pleasure and pain," that is, psychic magnitudes, "are undoubtedly the ultimate objects of the Calculus of Economics." Thus, both overcome Mill's materialism. Value, says Menger (1934: 86), is no "independent thing existing for

---

15. As in a flashlight we discern the whole contrast between Smith's school and Sismondi's followers in Marx's work: "Proudhon does not know that all history is but a continuous transformation of human nature" (Marx 1847: 144).

itself. It is a judgment which men engaged in economic activities form on the importance of the goods at their disposal for the preservation of their lives and their welfare, and so nonexistant outside the consciousness of those men." And Jevons (1931: 43) says: "[U]tility, though a quality of things, is *no inherent quality*. It is better described as *a circumstance of things* arising out of their relation to man's requirements." A revolution, comparable to the Copernican turn in Kant's work, has here been achieved.

That the pursuit of the market phenomena into the psychic sphere in fact represents a promotion of the science, and neoclassicism stands above classicism and must not be viewed beside it (as if it, as the subjective school, had only sought a different but equally valuable approach to the solution of the problems as the objective) is best shown by Cairnes's work.[16] A follower of Mill's theory of the cost of production at a time when Jevons and Menger had already annunciated the new principles, he preferred the subjective and psychological interpretation of the decisive concepts. Costs of production are to him less wages and profits than labor sacrifice and abstinence—hence in the first place internal categories and not external things.

On the foundations laid by Jevons and Menger economic science has ever since continued to build. If we survey its evolution, we see it divided into four sections: Bodinus and Hales; Carl, Cantillon and Quesnay; Müller and Sismondi; and Jevons and Menger mark the boundaries between the periods. But this division of the history of doctrine can only be well founded if we not only suitably place the milestones but also prove the thinkers and thoughts within these epochs to be germane in character. Now, as we have already emphasized in discussing historicism, it is difficult to find a distinct principle common to Mun and Schröder, Ricardo and Carey, Marx and Schmoller, and Wieser and Edgeworth. The life of the science was too rich to admit of a quick schematization. Over the centuries,

---

16. In a certain sense Ferrara too must be mentioned at this juncture. Cf. Bousquet, "Un Grand Économiste Italien Francesco Ferrara," *Revue d'histoire économique et sociale*, 1926: 351 et seq. He interpreted Carey's theory of the costs of production, or rather reproduction, subjectively and psychologically. "Value is but a judgment of our mind. . . . Value exists in the intellect of man" (355).

however, not only the doctrinal content of political economy has changed, but also its position in the system of sciences, and that may help us in securing our periodization of the past. The scholars who have opened the four periods came from four different worlds: Bodin, the author of the *Six livres de la république* was a lawyer; Quesnay, the author of the "Recherches philosophiques sur l'évidence des vérités géométriques," was at heart a philosopher; Sismondi, the author of the *Histoire des républiques italiennes du Moyen-Age*, was a historian; and Jevons, the author of the *Principles of Science* was by instinct a mathematician. Thus, political economy approaches now one, now another, branch of knowledge, and that clearly reveals its historical course and change of character.

The first period headed by Bodin, economics is closely related to *jurisprudence*, especially administrative law. What Boucke (1921: 28) says of Justi is more or less true of all mercantilists: "Social phenomena are narrowed down to questions of administration in the belief that this is the central theme of economics." What measures were to be taken, that is to say, what legal commands were to be issued, in order to overcome natural economy and to foster the growth of exchange economy was the basic problem of political economy between 1570-80 and 1750-60.

In the second period of evolution, opened up by Carl and Cantillon and decisively influenced by Quesnay and Smith, economic science is in its very roots connected with philosophy and theology or rather what unites both—*deism*. To the followers of Quesnay "Théocratie" and "Physiocratie" were synonymous: the great order of nature that they proposed to investigate was to them the law that Providence, the Highest Being, the Author of Nature, the Founder and Legislator of human society had given to the universe. "All our interests, all our wills tend to unite" says Mercier de la Rivière (cited in Gide and Rist 1909: 9) for his century, "and to form for our common happiness a harmony which we can regard as the work of a beneficient deity who wills that the earth should be covered with happy men." In the same vein Bastiat spoke later the great words: "The social mechanism . . . reveals the wisdom of God and proclaims his glory" (*Harmonies économiques*, 1851: 8). To perceive the "prestabilized harmony," which the Creator has given to his creation, was the end of economic thought between 1750-60 and 1820-30.

In the third period of the history of dogmas, beginning with Müller and Sismondi, economics shows a clear tendency to blend with *history*. Gustav Schmoller, in whose lifework historicism has found its purest embodiment, expressed the conviction that only "laborious special investigations on economic history . . . can afford the right basis to give to economic theory a sufficient empirical substructure." What he once said of himself is characteristic of his whole school: "Whether the future judgment will be that I failed as a historian because I was at the same time an economist, and as economist because I could not cease to be a historian, I must leave undecided. I can only be both at once and imagine that I owe the best of what I am capable of achieving to this combination" (cited in Mombert 1927: 472, 475). The endeavor to grasp life in its historical fullness led to the developments in political economy between 1820-30 and 1870-80.

Finally, since the last quarter of the nineteenth century, since Menger and Jevons, economic theory has come nearer and nearer to *the exact sciences*. "The Theory of Economy," says Jevons (1931: vii), "presents a close analogy to the science of Statical Mechanics, and the Laws of Exchange are found to resemble the Laws of Equilibrium of a lever as determined by the principle of virtual velocities." And Pareto says more directly still (*Cours d'économie politique*, 1896: 2): "The science of which we undertake the study is a natural science like psychology, physiology, and chemistry." The contrast between this view and the historio-sociological as well as the deistic-philosophical and the practical-administrative concepts of the past is manifest.

Thus, the history of political economy has realized itself in four sharply discernible stages. The external view of its development is clear: but what were the internal forces that moved it forward? A deep problem is latent in this question, and it is to the solution of this that we now turn.

II

The Fundamental Problem:
Reality and Ideas

5

The Critical Approach

Scire est per causas scire [One knows through knowing the causes]. This principle of all perception is true for the human world in the same way as for nature. For whatever one may think of the insoluble problem of free will, it is certain that the rational actions of men, viewed in their social interplay, seem not less subject to laws than the phenomena of nature, and it is this fact that makes a social science—as a science in the strict sense of the word—possible.

Scire est per causas scire. This principle is as true of the past as of the present. We see in the past much that we are incapable of understanding at first sight: the idea that a people is the richer the more gold it possesses; the idea that all wealth comes from the soil; the idea that the value of a commodity in exchange is determined by the labor time used in its production, and the like—in short, ideas which today are generally regarded as absolutely wrong but were in their time generally regarded as absolutely right. What circumstances induced our ancestors to believe what we cannot believe? As long as we are ignorant of the roots from which the theories of the past have sprung, we shall not possess a history of political economy that really fulfills its task.

Justus Moeser, the great precursor of modern historiography, once said (*Patriotische Phantasien*, 1774: 38): "If I come upon an old custom or use which does not at all agree with the views of later generations, I ponder over it in the conviction that the ancients were after all no fools, until I find a reasonable explanation." In these words the essential mission of all scientific contemplation of history is expressed—a mission that W. J. Ashley formulated for the history of economic doctrine as follows: "The theories of the past must be judged in relation to the facts of the past, and not in relation to those of the present. . . . [N]o great conception, no great body of doctrines which really influenced society for a long period, was without a certain truth and value, having regard to contemporary circumstances" (Ashley 1888: x-xi). To discover the kernel of relative truth, which the theories of the past centuries drew from their time and possessed for their time, is the mission of the historian of political economy.

A critical examination of literature will show how little labor has hitherto been spent on the solution of this greatest problem of the historiography of economic doctrine. According to the endeavor to understand economic thought from economic reality, the works published since Roscher and Dühring fall into three groups:

> 1. Investigations that implicitly or explicitly reject the concept of causality[1] (critical and valuing approach). These are characterized by judging the theories of the past according to the views of the present, asking how much absolute truth there is in them. The idea of development, the idea of relativism, are foreign to them.
>
> 2. Investigations that do not judge the concept of causality and confine themselves to depicting the views of the past as correctly as possible (purely descriptive treatment). Here two types are to be distinguished: one is the endeavor to show the history of economic ideas in its concatenation with the general history of thought; the other is an attempt to represent it within the framework of social and

---

1. The word *causality* has not, of course, in this connection, the strict meaning that it possesses in the physical sciences. Only he who believes in determinism could maintain that there is a *necessary* connection between what Marx called the material "substructure" and the intellectual "superstructure." Yet the nonexistence of a necessary, that is, mechanical, connection between facts and ideas does not exclude the existence of a free, that is, social, concatenation between them.

economic reality without, however, offering or consistently seeking any causal interpretation. The main end of the investigations of either type, however, is simply to isolate the essentials from the confused mass of ideas that has been handed down to us.

3. Investigations that accept the concept of causality (historical and explanatory approach). It is their aim to reach, by delving into the life of the past, knowledge of how and why the theories that have been propounded and transmitted arose. The conviction that the economic ideas must be understood as the natural products of the real and ideal order of society and economy of their time is the foundation of research here.

The critical approach to the past has found its purest expression in Eugen Dühring's work. He draws a sharp distinction between the history of economic facts and the history of ideas and scientific pronouncements on those facts, and places this discipline of intellectual history above that of economic history. "With the facts"—so much indeed he admits (Dühring 1900: 14)—"develop also ideas on them." But—and here he expresses his conviction—it is to him a "confusing superstition annihilating science, that there are no absolute truths but only conceptions corresponding to individual historical constellations" (10). Thus, Dühring vigorously rejects the assertion that Carey's system presented itself, so to speak, spontaneously as a result of the American development. He regards such a view as an attempt to veil the importance of individuality and it is precisely in individuality's creative power that he believes he has found the source of all ideas.

To Dühring, the apostle of personalism and contemporary of Nietzsche, economic ideas are, like lyrical poems or moral actions, expressions of concrete individualities who bear their law in themselves and do not receive it from outside—and therefore he deems it necessary to study the thinkers in order to understand the thoughts. The "individual characters and morals," he believes, had the greatest influence on the formation of the doctrinal systems (12). In the discussion of the physiocratic doctrine, whose partiality for agriculture Dühring wishes to explain, he deduces the one-sidedness and particularity of this theory from Quesnay's character. "Let us remember," he says, "that Quesnay was educated in the country and always retained a special predilection for rural life" (107). What a poor interpretation! Should we not rather seek the reason in the distress to which Colbertism had reduced French agriculture? A similar personalistic "explanation" is offered by Dühring with regard to the teachings of Smith: "His logic corresponded a little to his character which was marked by a lack of really active energy or rather energy capable of action. It consisted therefore more in passive drifting in the direction of a principle once adopted than in evoking creative forces for the adjustment of contradictions" (147). And similarly Friedrich List's theories, especially their weak points, are attributed to the personal qualities of their author.

Beside these individual causes and in connection with them, Dühring regards the political conditions as the basis for the formation of ideas. They are, in his view, much more important than the economic realities. He freely admits (1900: 236) that he starts from the sentence "that the political constellation is the last and decisive determinant of the economic situation, and that the opposite relation represents only a reaction of secondary importance." This view leads him to the assertion that David Ricardo's theory of rent can only be understood "from the character of party relations" then existing, or to say it more concretely (184), from the political contrast between landed nobility and bourgeoisie, the interests of which Ricardo is alleged to have served. This doctrine, however, bears its refutation in itself. For even if we were to make the (unjustifiable) admission that Ricardo formed his theory of the differential rent not in the interest of knowledge, but in order to serve a party cause, the question would still remain: whether the opposition between landed nobility and bourgeoisie was in its roots a political opposition and not rather an economic conflict, which, in turn, developed and maintained the political feud.

Besides the psychological and political viewpoint, there sometimes appears in Dühring (but not very often) the racial motive.[2] However,

---

2. One illustration may suffice to show how near Dühring was to the ideology and language of National Socialism. He declares: "The modern spirit of the peoples and above all the nordic-germanic, is the source from which we have to draw to render harmless the anti-aryan spiritual robberies of demoralizing Judaism which excavates the soul and distorts reason" (1900: 591).

such a motive does not appear in the form of national delimitation, for Dühring was, as a true child of his time, a convinced cosmopolitan. The place of the nation is occupied in his self-willed thought by another group: the tribe. Smith was not a Briton, but a Scot, Carey not an American, but an Irishman, List not a German, but a Swabian (with all the faults and merits of the "general nature of the Swabians").   For himself Dühring claimed now and then Swedish—today one would perhaps say Nordic—descent (1900: 512). Yet for the interpretation of ideas, the racial element seems to him as secondary as the political element, and it is only the creative individuality, conceived as timeless, in which he wishes to seek and find the ultimate origin of all thought.

Nevertheless, in spite of his fundamental attitude, Dühring cannot avoid using economic history in the explanation of one theory or another.   So he admits "that the first more serious attempts at economic orientation took place, and had to take place, where exchange and science were first . . . stipulated" (1900: 37), and the clearness of his words would almost induce us to believe that he was aware of the necessary internal connection between them. But this was not the case. Yet sometimes he knows quite well how to deduce ideas from reality. To make clear that there were good reasons for the mercantilist theories on the functions of the precious metals and the importance of an active trade balance, he has recourse to the "expedient" of examining the historical conditions under the influence of which they arose, and he uses this method, which he has rejected in principle, not without success. He believes that the acquisition of precious metals must not be regarded as the *aim* of mercantilistic policy, and that their influx, as the result of an active trade balance, was appreciated only as a *sign* of a favorable economic activity. Even if this view is not quite correct—the acquisition of new means of circulation was in fact an aim of economic policy when trade and commerce were hampered by the scarcity of money—it still represents a serious attempt to realistically fathom the meaning of mercantilism.

Such attempts at a causal explanation of the successive economic theories of the last two centuries are, however, very rare with Dühring, and the reason is mainly that he did not conceive the history of socioeconomic dogmas as a historical discipline. He starts from the statement (which, it seems, will not meet with general approval) that in a science, in which there is hardly any unity among the scholars, the history of doctrine belongs to the "actual material of present-day discussion" (1900: 1) and he holds that it is not sound historical knowledge but fixed theoretical convictions that constitute the most important prerequisite for an adequate history of political economy. It is a function, in the last analysis negative, which he assigns to the historical investigation; it should, according to his view, value and sift, select and reject—in short, measure the ideal systems of the past by the standard of the writer's own view. Only from this standpoint does Dühring's work become entirely comprehensible, comprehensible in its great merits and in its still greater defects.

It is the consideration and judgment of the past from the tribune of his own infallible intellect that, at the same time sublime and ridiculous, characterizes all Dühring's labors. He does not ask: what did the thinkers of the past achieve in their time and for their time? Rather, he asks: are their ideas stepping-stones to my theory? If so, they must be praised. If not—woe betide them! Dühring's conviction of the truth of his own system makes him blind to the greatness of other people's ideas and—degenerating in the end into a disease —makes him regard all other thinkers as enemies who deserve only hatred and scorn. His adversaries are to him a "body of squinting reptiles," "unspeakably silly," "idiots," "disgusting figures of social pathology," "logical and economic stutterers," "dogs," and "nonsense-scribblers." Ranke is to him the "shabby, confused, utterly reactionary petty-historian of Berlin" (1900: 348); Pasteur is a "vaccinator of canine madness" and a "helper of all sorts of poisoning of the human race" (618). Even the lofty figure of Kant, the long deceased, is not too high for Dühring. Kant lacked, so he says, "the great heart for humanity and the outstanding character, which is inconceivable without practical sensibility" (240)—a judgment that, of course, cannot reach the author of the Kritik der praktischen Vernunft [Critique of Practical Reason] and the manifest Zum ewigen Frieden [Perpetual Peace].

Yet it is not because of these exaggerations that Dühring's work appears erroneous and even unscientific to the critical reader. It is the fundamental idea of the whole book that justifies an unfavorable judgment. Apart from the fact that studies of individual characters cannot explain ideas that governed whole peoples and periods,—the

study of Dühring's character could not explain to us why he believed
in the existence of natural laws in economic life as did other children
of the nineteenth century who were "personalistically" of a different
stamp. It could at best teach us why he hated all those who adhered
to a different opinion, yet this does not interest the historian and
economist, but only the psychologist and psychiatrist—it is simply
inadmissible to treat and judge the intellectual products of the past
according to the notions of absolute "right" and "wrong."[3] Anyone
who undertakes to write a history of political economy must not
—however much his work may be meant to serve the present—be
completely void of historical sense. He must have understanding for
the essential difference of present and past, and this understanding is
denied to Dühring who always puts the egocentric question, as to
whether an older theory is true or false when compared with his own
view, as if he were discussing theses from the contemporary combat
of ideas.

It would nonetheless be unjust to condemn Eugen Dühring too
harshly because of his critical attitude toward the theories of the past.
Two other great minds of the nineteenth century, equal in the force of
their personalities, opposed in the direction of their thought, treated
the history of doctrine in the same way: Francesco Ferrara and Karl
Marx.

Franscesco Ferrara who, with Henry Carey and Frédéric Bastiat,
formed the great triumvirate of economic liberalism at the height of its
development, expressed his view concerning the ideas propounded in
the past as editor of the classics in the *Biblioteca dell' Economista*.
Also, his eighteen prefaces have been independently published in four
stately volumes as *Esame storico-critico di economisti e dottrine
economiche del secolo XVIII e prima meta del XIX* (1889-91). He,
too, conceived evolution as a progressive approximation to his
standpoint. "From century to century the observations multiply and
with them grow the abstractions . . . and lastly the abstraction at
which we have arrived and to which Political Economy finds itself

---

3. Thus, for example, Dühring says (1900: 26), that the Middle Ages were "totally
unscholarly," "in almost all fields of knowledge only a great desert." As if Dühring's
time had possessed so many men who could in spirit and achievement be compared
to a Thomas Aquinas!

bound is that which has been aptly called satisfaction of human needs." This concept, however, is the center of the science as seen by Ferrara: "Political Economy has the task of explaining . . . all phenomena which are found to be connected with the satisfaction of men's needs" (Ferrara 1938: 18).

In opposition to Dühring, Ferrara clearly felt the essential connection between economic history and the formation of dogmas. "The importance and the value of doctrines has its reason in the facts; we shall never comprehend why our forefathers during more than three centuries have accumulated so many works on money, if we do not know what factors have during those centuries influenced its practical use" (1938: 17). But, and herein he thinks like Dühring, "nothing was more remote from his mind than the idea of a relativity of scientific perception" as says Battistella in his monograph (Rome 1924, cited in Bousquet 1927: 103) on him. "The science has for its aim the truth, which is one and eternal," we read in one place (cited in Bousquet 1926: 353). He was so convinced of the eternity of economic truths that he thought it proper not to develop his own system independently, but to propound it in the critique of older theories (in the above mentioned prefaces). Characteristic is the way in which he brings his theory of value before the public: interwoven into an introduction to Ricardo's *Principles*, so that it appears as a refutation of the labor theory of value.

It follows from this whole procedure that Ferrara, like Dühring, did not aim at understanding the theories of the past, but at their judgment and valuation. To take but one example chosen at random; the theory of the wages-fund is to him simply an error that he rejects as such and to which he opposes as truth a wages-theory in the line of his fundamental concept, based on the principle of the costs of reproduction.

However, Ferrara was a representative of classicism and not a follower of historicism. So his attitude to the history of doctrine is hardly surprising. It is different with Marx whose philosophy of history grew out of the romantic ideas of development and relativism.

To Karl Marx all the cultural phenomena of a time are products of its socioeconomic groundwork. This general truth he regards especially applicable to economic thought. Marx writes in the *Misère de la Philosophie* (1847: 99 et seq.)

The same men who establish their social relations in conformity with their material productivity produce also principles, ideas, and categories, in conformity with their social relations. Thus these ideas, these categories, are as little eternal as the relations they express. They are historical and transitory products. . . . Economic categories are only the theoretical expressions, the abstractions of the social relations of production.

In this sense political economy is to him "produced by the motion of history" (119) and classicism is the reflection of capitalism. "Ricardo," he says (20, cf. also 25, 49, 117), "has expounded scientifically . . . the theory of present-day society, of bourgeois society," and on Quesnay he expresses himself in a similar vein (93).

These prolegomena seem to justify the expectation that Marx's *Theorien ueber den Mehrwert* (written in 1861/63 and published by Kautsky in four volumes in 1904) also rest on the idea of relativism. But it is not so. Even here we have before us a work of critique, not of historiography, of economic doctrine.

Like Dühring and Ferrara, Marx views the achievements of the past as leading up to his own work. Thus, he interprets the evolution of the doctrine of value as a progress: "In the monetary and mercantile system value is represented . . . as money; with the physiocrats as the produce of the earth, as produce of agriculture, lastly with Adam Smith simply as a commodity" (1904, 1: 280). Hence, the mercantilists only understood the form of value and the physiocrats already saw the meaning of value-in-use; with Adam Smith, however, "both conditions of the commodity, value-in-use and value-in-exchange, are united" (281), and that sets the stage for Marx's doctrine.

And as the doctrine of value, so the doctrine of surplus value: its growth, too, Marx believes, can be traced through economic literature until it appears fully developed in his works. "Before the physiocrats surplus value—that is profit in the shape of profit—is explained merely from exchange, from the selling of a commodity above its value. . . . To the mercantile system surplus value is only relative; what the one gains, the other loses" (1904: 29, 47). "The physiocrats transferred the investigation of surplus value from the sphere of circulation to the sphere of production proper and thus laid the foundations for the analysis of capitalist production" (35). Thus, was opened up the right way along which Adam Smith made great progress.

> With Adam Smith . . . it is social labor in general without regard to the
> use-values in which it is represented, the mere quantity of necessary labor,
> which creates the value. Surplus-value . . . is nothing but a part of that
> labor, which the owners of the objective conditions of labor appropriate in
> their exchange with living labor. With the physiocrats surplus-value appears
> . . . only in the form of the land-rent. With Adam Smith, land-rent, profit,
> and interest, are only different forms of surplus-value. (149)

In Marx's view this is indeed a valuable perception, but it does not yet
contain the full truth. We find it only after classicism has reached its
climax.

> The foundation and pivot of the physiology of the bourgeois system . . . is
> the determination of value by labor-time. This is Ricardo's starting point.
> . . . This is . . . the great historical importance of Ricardo for the science.
> . . . The way Ricardo shows up and declares the economic contrast
> between the classes is closely connected with this scientific merit and thus
> the historical struggle and process of evolution is conceived and discovered
> in its roots. Carey therefore denounces him as the father of communism"
> (1904, 2: 3 et seq.)

And Marx, we must add, assigns to him the same role. Petty,
Quesnay, Smith, Ricardo are all, in Marx's interpretation, pioneers of
the theory of surplus-value, his precursors.

But whenever these thinkers differ from the Marxian canon, which
happens constantly, he does not hesitate simply to accuse them of
error without asking what historical circumstances may have called
forth their differing ideas. So he says of the physiocrats: "The
economists err in regarding the industrialists only as a class working
for wages" (1904, 1: 328), and of Ricardo we read that "he commits
a grave error in not further investigating the constant part of capital,
in neglecting it" (177). The idea that industry in the France of 1750
may have been mainly handicraft working for wages and manufacture
of luxury-goods equally subservient to the nobility, that capital in the
England of 1810 may still have generally consisted in tools and
therefore been related to the head of the laborer, thus offering the
aspect of a variable asset, does not enter his mind.

Sometimes, however, the historian in Marx overcomes the
dogmatist; then we find passages that prove that he was capable of

deep understanding of the ideas of the past. As, for example, in the point just mentioned, the relation of constant and variable capital, which is of decisive importance for comprehending the labor theory of value in general, and the wages-fund theory connected with it in particular, is discussed in a chance footnote (1904: 352) that leads straight to the heart of essential facts. We read there: "Smith committed the error of identifying the mass of productive capital and the mass of that part of it which is destined to provide for the means of subsistence of productive labor"—hence total capital and wages-fund, or total capital and variable capital—"But the great industry was in fact known to him only in its beginnings" (cf. also Marx 1847: 137).

In discussing productive and unproductive labor, Marx casts a penetrating side glance at mercantilism (1904: 255).[4] In the countries into which the precious metals flowed, he argues, wages, because of the inflation ensuing there, "did not rise . . . in the same proportion as the prices of commodities . . . and thus . . . the rate of profit increased. . . . This was a reason, if only indistinctly felt, why the mercantilists pronounced the labor applied to those branches of production [which attract gold] to be alone productive." Even if this point is not decisive in the analysis of mercantilism—it shows great understanding, which, however, is very rare in Marx's work.

One of the most striking examples of a rationalistic and unhistorical conception of the history of economic doctrine is afforded by Joseph Schumpeter's essay. The idea that relative truth pertained to the changing theories is entirely foreign to him, and he regards the progress of development as the progress of the knowledge of an essentially unchangeable object of investigation—as if the order of the human world was as eternal as the order of the firmament, as if economics was of the same character as astronomy.[5] Any page of

---

4. In this point Marx may have been influenced by Hume's essay "Of Money."

5. He says indeed of the classicists (1914: 62): "Certainly the facts known to the authors of this period determined their thought just as each science depends at any given moment on the accumulated stock of material." But he still regards political economy as essentially equal to the natural sciences: the material is existent since time immemorial is unchangeably given, and is only little by little prepared and made accessible. He speaks of "known facts" that determine thought, not of "existing

Schumpeter's treatise will serve to prove this: it is a collection of absolute judgments and although the judge is wise and conscientious, he nevertheless infringes upon the laws of higher justice because he measures everyone according to the outward appearance and fails to penetrate to the internal causes and motives. It would be easy to multiply examples, but a few illustrations will suffice to characterize Schumpeter's method.

That England gained the leadership in economic science and Germany was for a long time only the rearguard, Schumpeter does not explain by the fact that the Western nations developed exchange economy a hundred years earlier than Central Europe. He attributes it to a merely external cause, the greater importance of public discussion in the political life of Britain, which favored the origin of an economic literature. By this unrealistic judgment he bars the way to the perception of the reason that caused the essential difference between English mercantilism and German cameralism. He says: "The economics cultivated in England was the science of national economy, the economics cultivated in Germany the science of state economy. . . . While in England . . . the merchant wrote for the merchant, in Germany the official wrote for the official" (1914: 34). Why this should have been so, Schumpeter does not explain. The profound difference, one which at first sight appears to be national, in the literature of the seventeenth and eighteenth centuries is the result of a difference of phases: the modern economic system developed from regulation to liberty, and while England by 1700 was already near the state of freedom so that the merchant and national economy stood in the foreground, Germany had not advanced far beyond the state of regulation, so that the main interest centered on officials and state economy. Indeed, every comparison between English and German social science must in the end go back to this basic fact of historical development.

Although Schumpeter does not appreciate the mercantilists he still endeavors to make their doctrine understood, and, following instinct, he maintains that "they cannot possibly have seen in the acquisition of precious metals the ultimate end of economic activities" (1914: 38). Thus, he stands very high above the many who, like Karl Walker

---

facts"—an essential difference!

(1895: 13), speak of a "Midas delusion." But his interpretation is purely rationalistic and totally unhistorical. He says: "The identification of wealth with the possession of gold and silver loses its doubtful character if in those passages which may be quoted in support of the allegation we substitute index of wealth for wealth" (1914: 38). By such speculations, however, the meaning of mercantilism cannot be fathomed: only a thorough study of the object of perception, which that doctrine had as its basis, can show the way toward the correct interpretation.

Schumpeter's lack of historical understanding also prevents him from fully comprehending physiocracy, and the relation of *ordre positif* and *ordre naturel* is a special cause of difficulty for him. The warm advocacy of the *ordre naturel*, he thinks, for which even divine sanction is appealed to, "gives to the whole system an unscientific and finalist aspect" (1914: 41), while the main achievement of Quesnay was analytical and must therefore be regarded as strictly scientific. Thus, the two parts of the system are contrasted as if they were distinguished by different methods theoretically possible side by side, while in reality the relation of *ordre positif* and *ordre naturel* must be comprehended from the historical point of view (as successive): the *ordre positif* was the existing social order of France in 1750, which was to be analyzed, and the *ordre naturel* was the future social order of France, which was to be presented as a program. Not two theoretical methods are here before us but two historical concepts of society, one actual and one to be realized; economic theory and social reform unite in the physiocratic system. What Schumpeter asserts is not true, "that the theoretical picture of reality was viewed as unchangeable"; he can indeed justly say of the physiocrats that "they lacked the idea of social development" (42) because they believed in a natural and therefore eternal and immutable order of reason, but this order was to be established when the *ordre positif* transformed into the *ordre naturel*—and so reality was not regarded as unchangeable but as destined to be changed.

The classical doctrine is, according to Schumpeter, mainly characterized by its abstracting and isolating method, the use of which was justifiable although it was somewhat overstrained.

The breadth of the abyss between theory and reality, and the full importance of what is today called the difference between real object and object of

> perception, they did not rightly estimate. . . . And only late when, as a
> result of disappointments, methodological doubts had arisen and people
> began to examine things more closely, was it realized to what an extent the
> foundations were hypothetical in character. . . . This is manifest in the
> methodological works of John Stuart Mill, Bagehot, and Cairnes. (1914: 66)

Again the difference between the older and the younger classics is to
Schumpeter only a mere difference of method: as if James Mill, had
he made more use of the principle of induction, would have arrived
at the same concept of reality as his son. But it is not so. If the
second generation of the classical school—Stuart Mill, Bagehot, and
Cairnes—discovered a contrast between the teachings of their fathers
and the experiences of their own time, this was due not to faults in the
traditional method, but to the change of reality. There was no abstract
contrast between a real object and an object of perception, but a
concrete contrast between two real objects of perception: between the
economic system of 1820, in which labor still governed the process of
production, and the economic system of 1850, in which the rising
power of capital was already dominant. The change in the theories of
wages and interest (and also the progressive abandonment of the labor
theory of value) perfectly reflects this development. Schumpeter,
however, fails to perceive it; he believes that fathers and sons had the
same world before their eyes—a fundamental error, the consequence
of which is that in his hands the history of doctrine loses its historical
character.

The theory of the wages-fund is in Schumpeter's view

> a good illustration of the character as well as of the merits and faults of the
> classical way of thinking. . . . The whole deduction is based on the opinion
> that in each period of production the wages are advanced to the laborers out
> of the capital of the employer. The theory of the wages-fund suffers from
> the blemish which we often perceive in the classics: it isolates one link in
> the chain of economic connections . . . and assigns to it a causal role which
> it does not possess to this degree. (1914: 93)

The theory appears to him unacceptable, because it carries isolation
too far. The true reason for its obsoleteness, however, lies in the fact
that it could only be upheld as long as of the two essential forms of
capital, the constant and the variable, the latter (the wages capital)
entirely governed production, while the former (machinery) was not

yet developed. As long as this state of things prevailed, and it did prevail in James Mill's and Nassau Senior's time, the individual wage appeared in the isolated factory as well as in the whole of national economy simply as the quotient of the wages fund (which in fact existed) and the number of workmen—a productivity theory of wages could be deduced from real life only after the mechanization of production had created its factual conditions. By the 1860s this point was reached: Longe (1866) and Thornton (1869) showed that a description of capital mainly as a fund of provisions for the workers was no longer possible and thus caused John Stuart Mill's famous recantation of his views on wages.

In the final paragraph of his historical investigation Schumpeter openly asserted the essential equality of all theories heretofore propounded. "Fundamentally the physiocrats already aimed at what we aim at today, and if we concentrate on the matter and not on the form given to it, it is often difficult to find in a vehemently worded contest a correspondingly sharp expression of the objective differences" (1914: 124). Certainly Quesnay wished to fathom the character of national economy in the same way as did Marshall—just as Ptolemy and Copernicus were united in the endeavor to penetrate the laws of the universe. But nature is immutable, and society is constantly changing; so a scientific history of theoretical economics can only be built on the idea of evolution, on the idea of historical relativism, which is foreign to Schumpeter's rationalist thought.

Joseph Rambaud, firmly convinced as he was that above all things temporal there is an eternal truth embodied in revelation and science, was only acting consistently in searching the ideas of the past for their kernel of absolute truth. However, where was the instrument for dividing the wheat from the chaff, the true perception from the error? Our author did not seriously grapple with this problem, and so his method comes in the end to comparing the different doctrines with the teachings laid down in his *Eléments d'Economie Politique* (1895) and judging them according to this standard.

The conception of history adhered to by Rambaud is characteristic of the rationalistic and liberal ideology of 1890. He conceived history not as a progressive development but only as a change of different combinations of pre-established and unchangeable elements. Against Comte, the leading representative of the evolutionist tendency in

France, Rambaud says (1902: 490):

> It is all very well to speak of periods which follow and oust each other: but does not rather the reality of history show us either the coexistence of several states which according to the theory, should be successive, or an incessant movement of flux and reflux which from generation to generation extends or contracts the domain of each general system of cosmology and philosophy?

Arguing against Pirenne and Buecher who declared economic and moral laws to be subject to change throughout history, Rambaud goes on to say,

> The idea of these changes is more than a hypothesis, it is an error. The physical world around us does not change, the moral world within us, represented by ourselves, does not change either. What can and does change is only our more or less exact and more or less complete knowledge of the forces which the physical world comprises . . . it is the more or less great perspicacity which we possess for the perception of the laws of the moral world. . . . The possibility of these changes and their effective realization suffice for the world to have a history, for mankind to have progress, and for the successive ages to present, even as regards economic life, a variety which is one of the beauties of the divine work. (1902: 509)

Where the treatment of the history of doctrine on the basis of this view, which is so characteristic of rationalism, leads may be seen from a few examples.   After describing Plato's social ideal, Rambaud proceeds (1902: 553-54):

> If we now ask what are the weak points in Plato's premises we should answer: 1) that his theory implies the absolute power of the state. . . . Now such a principle would be contrary to the independent rights of the individual and the family which are logically antecedent to those of the state. 2) That this absolute union . . . among the citizens . . . is not the end of the state. Every man [Rambaud quotes here from Castelein's *Socialisme et droit de propriété*] . . . has an aim independent of that of his neighbor and because of this law, the happiness and perfection of any man are independent of the happiness and perfection of his neighbors. . . . 3) That, even if this union should be pursued as the supreme end of the state, it is beyond doubt that the means imagined by Plato could not have reached that aim. In fact discord is never more lively and continual than in a society of collectivism and community of goods.

We see that Rambaud does not ask: what induced Plato to conceive his ideal state along those lines?—but rather, is such an ideal state feasible and desirable? It is not historical understanding but a definite judgment at which Rambaud aimed—indeed a primitive sort of historiography, which is capable of forgetting that 2300 years have elapsed between the time of Plato and the present.

In precisely the same manner Rambaud criticizes his own contemporary Izoulet, whose *Cité moderne* (1895) marks the highest development of the organic concept of society in its materialistic form. The doctrine that the state must be regarded as a large animal, as hyperzoaire, compared with which man, the metazoaire, is only a cell, just as he himself is composed of innumerable cells, called protozoaires, was necessarily repugnant to the extreme liberal Rambaud (1902: 541 et seq.):

> It remains true that the organic thesis, as pushed by Izoulet to its ultimate consequences . . . contains in germ the worst tyranny of all orders. What becomes of man and liberty in this conception of a social being endowed with a soul analogous to our souls and certainly superior to them? . . . The individual merged and absorbed in the social and humanitarian dough has no more might than we assign to the last of our own cells. . . . No philosophical theory has ever dreamt of a more degrading slavery. . . . The triumph of that sociology would be the ruin of all liberty.

In this primitive way the whole history of doctrine is presented and treated. One more example is the labor theory of value. "Ricardo based the value of all goods on the labor which the current production of goods of that sort involved. . . . This formula was no doubt wrong . . . Value, instead of being created by labor, is like [labor] itself derived from our sentiment of need which inspires at the same time the act of labor and the estimate of value" (1902: 377).

After all that, it may seem surprising that Rambaud's judgment on Karl Knies's *Die Politische Œkonomie vom Standpunkte der geschichtlichen Methode* runs as follows (1902: 495-96):

> It cannot be denied that there is an important element of truth in the chapter where he describes the influence which the events and circumstances always exerted on the classical economists and on the special form in which they have expressed their principles. We have ourselves made similar observations as to the physiocrats; one could repeat them for Malthus and Ricardo, who saw England confined within her own boundaries and did not

expect cheap grain imports from America; for Carey who was spared the
disturbing idea that the world is too small for mankind by the proximity of
the far west; lastly for Bastiat whom the very legitimate fear of socialism
threw into the enthusiasm of a liberty full of harmony and wellbeing.

But Rambaud did not really understand Knies's standpoint. He does
not think it possible to explain the ideas of the past from their time,
but at best to excuse them out of their time,[6] his own words prove
this unmistakably.

Of the century of Colbert, Rambaud says (1902: 97): "Mercantilism"
—and it is significant that by this word he describes less a stage of
economic thought than a theory of economic policy erroneous in his
eyes[7]—"had in those times an excuse which it lost later on. The taxes
then flowed in very badly, credit was not yet organized, and even
those who possessed great resources found ready cash only with
difficulty." In this last argument more is contained than Rambaud
supposed.

The thesis of the physiocrats of the exclusive productivity of
agriculture Rambaud treated in a similar way: as an error which,
however, may be excused. "One may see in this doctrine," we read
(1902: 171, cf. also 135), "a quite natural reaction either to the
exaggerations and mistakes of the system of Law, or to the somewhat
exclusive industrialism of Colbert." But, "Whatever excuse [this

---

6. How inconsistent Rambaud sometimes is, is proved by his treatment of Say's
"Théorie des débouchés." He says (1902: 262-63 [emphasis added]),

> The events have shown that the *théorie des débouchés* cannot have the
> absolute character which J.B. Say attributed to it in the belief that nothing
> but products are exchanged with products between peoples: it does not seem
> that he has taken into account the capitals engaged in this movement of
> coming and going operating between the nations. This was no doubt almost
> *entirely correct* in his time, when the movable values were few and small.

But three pages later (265 [emphasis added]) we read: "[T]he *error* of J. B. Say, is
. . . not to believe in an emigration or immigration of capital which superimposes
itself on the *théorie des débouchés* as well as on the balance of payments to keep the
latter in equilibrium."

7. Thus, he speaks of a "mercantilism among the Romans" (1902: 732, 29).

system] may have found then in the relatively greater importance of agriculture as compared with manufacture, commerce, and transport, it was quickly realized that such a doctrine was inadmissible" (186). This superficial excuse for the past is certainly not the historical interpretation of its spirit that Karl Knies had in view!

The ideology of German romanticism, the ideology of Karl Ludwig von Haller and Adam Müller, Rambaud correctly connected with the fact that Germany entered upon the nineteenth century "with a whole set of feudal institutions, which strangely contrasted with the internal system of England and with the equality of civil rights which the revolution had just given to France" (1902: 320). Thuenen's work, on the other hand, appeared strange to him. The abstract character of the "Isolated State" seemed to him to demand a special explanation. "This bizarre supposition," he says (326), "would never have presented itself to the mind of an Englishman: but it is less absurd in the brain of a Pomeranian who knows only the uniform plain extending from Magdeburg to Koenigsberg and from the Carpathian Mountains to the Baltic." This remark is the more interesting because nowhere else in literature do we find an attempt to make Thuenen's way of thinking comprehensible. Yet it is not entirely correct (though not altogether false). Thuenen was led to his theory when, as a guest of his friend Baron Voght in the neighborhood of Hamburg, he was surprised by the singular contrast between two neighboring villages, Gross-Flottbek and Klein-Flottbek, the disciple of Thaer could not fail to notice that here two different systems of cultivation existed side by side and put to himself the question to what causes this contrast might be traced. He discovered the answer in the different distance of the two places from the market of Hamburg. Thus, the connection between abstract theory and everyday practice is even closer with Thuenen than Rambaud supposed.

One problem of the history of doctrine, however, naturally appeared to Rambaud more difficult than all the others: the canonist prohibition of interest. For in this point his two fundamental convictions, his liberal and his Catholic orthodoxy, come into conflict.[8] Willy nilly

---

8. Little inconsistencies are simply suppressed. Thus, he says: "All the philosophy of the Middle Ages and that of St. Thomas in particular has a marked character of individualism" (1902: 44, cf. also 533). Not only the *catholiques sociaux* whom he

he avails himself of the explanation offered by historicism; this explanation in fact reconciles both views and makes reprehensible the change in the attitude of the church toward interest.

> St. Thomas faithful in all to his thesis of the gratuity of credit, did not even admit of selling at a higher price in the case of a deferred payment. . . . But it would be unwise to judge these rules without reference to the time when they were given. In fact, when the market was very narrow, without efficient organization and without active industry, at a time when great enterprises were restricted to erecting churches and feudal fortresses, opportunities for the productive employment of money were lacking. There was only room . . . for consumptive loans . . . which were so easily usurious and so strictly condemned by the Church. . . . We must descend to the 14th and mainly to the 15th centuries in order to find that the prohibition really constitutes a hindrance to productive enterprise. (Rambaud 1902: 59-60)

The church conformed to this development, first by creating an exception to the rule, and then by dropping the rule itself:

> [T]he actual solutions of the Church are connected with the theory of the *lucrum cessans*, in which already the greater part of the schoolmen saw a legitimate title, not indeed of a formal usury, but of an equivalent interest. In the 19th century it is in fact certain that there are always possibilities to employ with profit all available sums of money so that *lucrum cessans* can be assumed in a general way instead of having to be stated, as [was necessary] in earlier times, for each particular operation that took place. We believe therefore that ecclesiastical legislation, interpreted in this sense, escapes the reproach of self-contradiction which has so often been brought against it. (1902: 317)

Thus, with Rambaud a necessity becomes a virtue: had he investigated the relative truth in the economic theories with the same care as the relative justness of the canonist attitude, he would, no doubt, have reached a different concept of history than his *Histoire des Doctrines Economiques* presents.

Like Eugen Dühring, Othmar Spann conceives the history of doctrine as the science whose task it is to judge of the content of truth

------

tries to combat with these assertions, but also the science will oppose him in this point.

in the theories created in the past.

> The exposition of the theories will always be followed by a critical discussion of their main ideas. . . . This critical and comparative method is . . . the most effective for the study of the history of doctrine, seeing that the writing of history lacks sap and vigor unless the historian acquires a characteristic outlook of his own. The notion that he who is perfectly impartial has also a standpoint reminds us of an attempt to breathe in a vacuum. . . . That towards which the great interconnection of the systems points—therein is inherent the higher system which must supply the standpoint of the historiographer. (1932: xv)

In these words Spann touched the fundamental problem of all historiography: the relation of past and present. And he is right in saying that the historian must consciously adopt a definite viewpoint; the viewpoint of the present. In so far as our system of knowledge is composed of elements that have been brought forth by the labors of the past, the outlook of the present appears as the higher system and affords the right vantage point from which to survey the development. The historiographer approaches his material not without preconceptions but as a living individual of his epoch, and all attempts to reach a science free of valuations (an attempt undertaken by Max Weber) will be frustrated by the fundamental fact of our existence: our indissoluble connection with space, time, and society, which have molded us. If the great historians of the 1870s mainly studied antiquity and the Renaissance and those of the present fervently seek the clue to the problems of the Middle Ages and Counter-Reformation, this is only a reflection of a change of our social system from freedom to organization, which governs all our thought and being—even if perhaps only the future may be capable of proving in retrospect how thoroughly our age was dominated by this great transformation.

Hence, we cannot reach absolute knowledge—in historiography as little as in political economy—as long as we do not succeed in making the impossible possible, or to raise ourselves above ourselves. But does this mean that we are entitled to subject the past to our absolute judgment? By no means! While the historiography avoiding valuations overlooks the fact that the thought of the present is shaped by present-day life, the valuing historiography forgets that the thought of the past was similarly determined by its contemporary conditions. We cannot simply, as Spann thinks, compare the results of the newer sciences with those of the older and thus describe both systems (1932: vii)—for in such a way we should compare the incomparable. We shall never succeed in measuring the past by the standards of the past, but neither may we judge it according to the standards of the present: true historiography aims at *understanding* the past by the past.

Spann, however, does not study the facts of the centuries gone by to comprehend their ideas; indeed, the point of view from which he describes the development of economics is not even the complex system of knowledge of the present, but simply the definite economic and social theory that he himself has propounded.

> When we take a general view of all the trends of economic science, we are led to the conclusion that there is no unified body of economic doctrine, but that the trends must be classified . . . as individualist and universalist [i.e., collectivist, in the sense of German romanticism and Spann's teaching]. . . . It seems unquestionable, after our critical survey of the whole field, that truth lies on the side of universalism, and that the universalist doctrine will ultimately prevail. (1932: 172 et seq., 184 et seq.)

With these words Spann closes his investigation; but the idea expressed by them is at the same time his starting point. According to it, he distinguishes the individualists, whose blunders are to be exposed, and the universalists, whose truths are to be demonstrated.

While mercantilism "in spite of all defects, was a grand conception of national economy as a true unit of life" (1932: 18) and hence universalist (26), Quesnay and, even more so, Smith adhered to an atomist and individualist view, manifest especially in their making the laws of price the center of theory, instead of—as Spann regards as correct—the connections of productive contributions, the functional system. "For Smith . . . the science becomes first of all a theory of individual economic intercourse, a theory of exchange—this was the real disaster in the development of our science" (15). This wrong course was later followed by Malthus, Ricardo, Jevons, Menger, nay, even by Karl Marx. For "where the malady of liberal economics prevails, there also shall we find the suppurative inflammation of Marxism—and both of them are diseases of the soul" (142).

In opposition to the barren schools of Ricardo (1932: 171) stands the other trend of thought leading from mercantilism through Müller, Thuenen (!), List, and the historians to Spann—to the neoromantic doctrine of universalism which offers "for the first time a basis for a concept of national economy free from the spirit of the natural sciences . . . for the first time an insight into the forms and the substance, the anatomy and the physiology, of the economic life of all historical epochs" (173), a doctrine against which, according to Spann, "serious criticisms . . . have not so far been raised" (174).

Thus, Spann regards the history of doctrine as an eternal struggle between individualist error and universalist truth. But he was himself too much a child of historicism not to realize that all theories of the past were somehow an expression of their epoch, and at times this insight bears fruit. So Spann grasped better than all the others the sense of mercantilism in saying

> that the high appreciation of money was indeed the starting-point of mercantilistic thought, but that it was not an end in itself, but a means of fostering trade and industry, appreciated because of its productive effects. . . . Mercantilist statesmen and writers had good grounds for keeping before their eyes the growing need for money characteristic of the days in which they lived; they learnt a lesson from their study of the quickening results of an increase in the circulating medium—an increase that was above all essential to the transition from a more or less natural economy to a nascent capitalist and mercantile economy. (1932: 7, 14)

Of the physiocratic system Spann judged as follows: "The basic idea of Quesnay, the exclusive productivity of the extractive industries . . . is incorrect" (1932: 44). But, like Marx (1904, 1: 36), he somewhat excused their error by emphasizing that the phenomenon of profit is especially obvious in agriculture (1932: 44). His discussion of the physiocratic idea indeed leads him to the very doorstep of the true interpretation. "The whole was palpably conceived as follows," he says: "A number of agriculturists will engage a man to make sabots out of their wood, another to tan and dress the hides, another to make boots out of the leather. Then it seems clear that the labor of the husbandman is the exclusive source of wealth . . ." (936 et seq.). Had Spann put landowners instead of "agriculturists," and gobelins instead of "sabots," he would have aptly described the conditions that induced the physiocrats to pronounce their judgment on the inability of industry to create wealth: its subservience to the nobility, which, alone in the possession of ample means, drew its riches from agriculture alone.

Although Spann dismisses Smith's doctrine as "true economics of a shopkeeper" (1932: 60), he still judges with historical understanding: "England, as the classical country, as the oldest country of large scale industry, was the soil on which the development of individualist economics could best take place. . . . Smith uttered what was in the air, he gave voice to the individualist spirit of the age" (49, 55). And the attempts to develop Smith's doctrine "involved above all an endeavor to explain the misery of the working classes and all the defects and disharmonies that had become apparent in economic life during the rapid development of the capitalist method of production" (62 et seq.)—Malthus and Ricardo. List and Carey, too, are explained in terms of the circumstances of their time (111 et seq., 124).

But although Spann in this way throws many illuminating sidelights on the ideas of the past, he still presents at the decisive junctures absolute judgments instead of relative interpretations. Thus, his treatment of Ricardo's wage theory is entirely unhistorical and therefore false—it shows "the danger of abstract procedure" (1932: 83) not only in the thought of Ricardo, but also in that of Spann. And as in blame so in praise: an extravagant eulogy represents Adam Müller as a timeless genius, while he only described and interpreted the economy and society of Germany, as Adam Smith had described and interpreted the economy and society of England. Müller did not stand against "the victorious march of an individualist spirit" (97), which in reality conquered nothing but the West; he belonged to the country of "Staatsraison," and himself justly emphasized the contrast between Smith's environment and his own, stressing the only relative importance of both systems of ideas. Here admiration disturbed Spann's judgment, admiration being as bad a guide to historical understanding as contempt.

The question about the relation between facts and thoughts, reality and science, is discussed by Gide and Rist in the preface to the first edition of their work. They do not deny that there is a concatenation between mind and world:

Certainly the influence exerted by the economic environment[9] whence even

---

9. It may be emphasized that the doctrine of environment hinted at by Gide and Rist, which had in France a great number of followers and was upheld by very important men such as Emile Zola (cf. *Le Roman Experimental*, 1880), primarily belongs to

the most abstract economist gets material for reflection and the exercise of
his logical acumen, is indisputable. The problems which the theorist has to
solve are suggested by the rise of certain phenomena which at one moment
cut a very prominent figure and at another disappear altogether. Such
problems must vary in different places and at different times. (Gide and Rist
1909: viii)

The concession thus made to the idea of a causal interpretation of
economic theories is however only slight. It is a matter of course that
Ricardo's "High Price of Bullion," List's "Nationales System," and
Marx's "Inauguraladresse der Internationalen Arbeiterassoziation"
were evoked by the developments of their times. But that is not the
issue. The decisive question is whether Ricardo's and Marx's *whole*
work, not only the problems discussed, but also the *solutions* offered,
can and must be understood with reference to their time, and this
question Gide and Rist answer in the negative.

"It is important that we should remember," we read, "that facts
alone are not sufficient to explain the origin of any doctrines, even
those of social politics, and still less those of a purely scientific
character" (1909: viii). And they seek to establish their view by
arguments. "If the ideas were determined only by time and place,
how could we explain that the same environment and the same epoch
have given rise to heterogeneous and even antagonistic theories—J.B.
Say's and Sismondi's for example, Bastiat's and Proudhon's, Schulze
Delitzsch's and Marx's, Francis Walker's and those of Henry
George?"

This question is only meant as a rhetorical question. Gide and Rist
were convinced that there is no answer to it, that it cannot be
explained why one epoch brought forth different or even opposite
views on the same subject. However, this is not at all a difficult
problem. An age is a unit composed not of mechanically equal, but
of organically different parts—fathers live beside sons, capitalists
beside proletarians, towns people beside peasants, Englishmen beside
Russians. One must know the whole reality to understand the
thoughts that it produced—one must try to grasp the whole complexity
of life to comprehend the ideas that are its highest expression.

Jean-Baptiste Say and Simonde de Sismondi for example! Why did

---

psychology and not to history.

they reach different theories?   The answer is clear: Say was a successor, Sismondi a predecessor.   Say still shared the optimistic conviction of the fathers, who—impressed by the development of material production—were convinced that this world is the best of all possible worlds.   Sismondi, however, already adhered to the view of the sons who had been taught by the sufferings of the time that the capitalist distribution brings as much misery to this world as the capitalist production values.   It is only necessary to compare the trade cycle theories of the two men to understand the contrast and its causes.   And yet, in spite of all differences, how much they have in common as contemporaries![10]   Sismondi expected salvation from a return to small-scale production in industry and agriculture based on the combination of labor and the implements of labor as Smith and Say had envisaged it when they formed their optimistic theories.[11]

In fact, just what Gide and Rist regard as inexplicable must be explained; and if the causes of a phenomenon are not always clear, this does not mean that there are no causes!   "With what historical circumstances," Gide and Rist ask, believing that they are formulating an unsolvable problem or even a mock problem, "are we to connect . . . the simultaneous discovery in three or four countries of the theory of final utility?"   Yet the very fact that in the 1870s the same theory arose in three different places, independent of one another, proves that somehow it must have been in the air.   Or should we speak of chance

---

10. Sismondi himself indeed emphasized the far reaching similarity of his standpoint to that of the Smithian school. Cf. *Nouveaux principes d'économie politique*, 1819, 1: 49 et seq., especially 52. It is even more interesting that Saint-Simon too has much in common with classicism. Cf. Lemonnier, *Oeuvres choisies de Saint-Simon*, 1859, 2: 185 (Lettres à un Américain).

11. The agreement in the fundamental concept of political philosophy is also striking. "A nation is nothing but the union of the individuals of which it is composed." This sentence does not come from Smith or Say but from Sismondi! (1819, 1: 231).

As another contemporary and compatriot who—like Sismondi—preached the return to small-scale production and reunion of labor and property, and thus belongs to Say's tradition, Proudhon should be mentioned. Cf. his *Théorie de la propriété*, 1866, in Roll 1938: 240 et seq.   However—and herein the progress of development is manifest—Proudhon already realized that a certain sector must be left to large-scale industry and for this sector he proposed a sort of socialization by free associations of independent workmen.

in this connection? "Chance," Roscher justly observes (1874: 797) "science calls only those facts which it does not know how to explain!" But there must not be anything in a science that remains forever unexplained, or the science must at least endeavor to explain everything!

Thus, Gide and Rist do not seek to perceive relative truths. They regard it as their first task to describe the ideas that have appeared in the years since 1750. "In a history of doctrines," says Rist (apparently for both), "the ideas are the things which should be made conspicuous" (1909: 270). However, their aim is not the simple reproduction of these ideas, but their critical discussion. It is characteristic of the way in which they treat their subject that both Gide and Rist are prone always to represent the thinkers of the past as precursors of the present—as if historiography only had value from the viewpoint of actual interests! Thus, the physiocrats are above all pioneers of the organic sociology, Henry George, the hedonists, the free-traders, as well as the modern advocates of agricultural protectionism—if they were alive today, Gide says, they would be supporters of protective tariffs on agricultural commodities![12] Furthermore, the physiocrats are also the forerunners of the mathematical school and the pacifist movement. Condillac is a forerunner of Jevons and the Austrians, Turgot a forerunner of Boehm-Baverk, the Abbé Galiani a forerunner of historicism, Adam Smith a forerunner of Duerkheim, Say a forerunner of Walras, even Malthus a forerunner of prehistorical sociology, and so on—the list could be easily increased. The search for such connections is in itself of course no offense against the principles of historical investigation (although it always implies, as in the case under discussion, the danger of conceiving the past merely as a preparation for the present and thus of failing justly to estimate its proper value). But Gide and Rist do not stop at that; they add dogmatic *valuations* from the standpoint of modern doctrine, which—even if not regarded as composed of definitely conquered truths—is made the touchstone of right and

---

12. Similarly Rist believes Friedrich List would advocate tariff reductions in Germany and America today, and Gide maintains Carey would propound a different view on rent today. Both authors obviously have only the present in mind.

wrong.[13]   It is the (supposed) absolute truth from which they start and toward which they strive, and they bring all ideas before its tribunal. No wonder that the teachings of the physiocrats are disposed of as mere "errors." "The predominant position which land occupied as an agent of production: this was the most erroneous and at the same time the most characteristic doctrine in the whole Physiocratic system" (1909: 13).

Yet Gide himself felt that there were sound reasons for this error:

> [T]his illusion is not difficult to explain from the historical circumstances in which the Physiocrats lived. What did they see? One section of the community, nobility and clergy, lived upon the rents which their land yielded: their luxurious lives would have been impossible if the earth did not yield something over and above the amount consumed by the peasant. (1909: 18)

But these words spoken in passing (apart from the fact that they show only why Quesnay's school regard agriculture as productive but not why they regard industry as sterile) are not meant to be an explanation of the relative truth, but at best an excuse of the absolute error of the physiocrats whose theory and system according to Gide simply rest on a "prejudice."

More fortunate was Rist in another connection, however, where the concatenation of reality and science is especially obvious: in the interpretation of J. B. Say. He aptly shows how the industrialization of France, just beginning when Say first wrote and then making rapid progress, changed the ideas of this man—how each new edition of his *Traité* was more under the influence of industrialism than the last. It is not by chance that the classical description of the entrepreneur's role in modern economic life was offered by J. B. Say.

Especially valuable is the contribution that Gide made toward the understanding of Ricardo, in deducing his theory of rent from the history of the time:

> Ricardo so often represented as a purely abstract thinker, was in reality a

---

13. Characteristic is the following sentence of Rist: Proudhon's fundamental idea "deserves to be included in a history of doctrine because it contains truth mixed with error." (1909: 341).

very practical man and a close observer who only brought those facts into words which were then occupying the attention of both public and Parliament. For rising rents, following upon rising prices, constituted the most striking phenomenon in the economic history of England towards the end of the 18th and the beginning of the 19th centuries. (1909: 169)

Up to 1794 the price of wheat was roughly 60 s a quarter; it then rose constantly and considerably, and that by no means only because of the war and the blockade. "The available land became insufficient for the upkeep of the population and . . . new land had to be cultivated, wherever it was, even the worst. . . . In 1813, a Commission appointed by the House of Commons to inquire into the price of corn came to the conclusion that new lands could not produce corn at a less cost than 80 s a quarter" (169). Here we have the law of diminishing returns—indeed here we have the whole doctrine of distribution and the whole pessimistic picture of future development sketched by David Ricardo.

Such attempts to explain theories from their environment are, however, rare in Gide and Rist's work, but often thinkers are accused of error, where they—for their time—only spoke the truth. This is, for example, the case in Gide's judgment on Malthus.

> The error with which we may justly reproach Malthus is to have confused entirely different motives. The sexual and the reproductive instincts are by no means one and the same. Only to the first can be attributed the character of irresistibility which he wrongly attributes to the second. The first is a mere animal instinct which rouses the most impetuous of passions and is common to all men. The second is above all social and religious in its origins, assuming different forms according to the exigencies of time and place. (1909: 153-54)

Well! But in Malthus's time the exercise of the sex instinct was for most people in no way separated or even separable from propagation. To satisfy the sexual instinct meant to bring children into the world; and now that the two things have been separated, Malthus's verdict has become obsolete. But that doesn't make it less correct in his time—a fact for which, however clear it may be, Gide shows no understanding.

Of the attitude of both authors who do not set out to seek the relative truth of all theories, but accept or reject them according to whether or not they fit into their own system, the following words of Rist are likewise characteristic. "Sismondi and Smith both fell . . . into the same error as Malthus and Ricardo who imagined that high wages of necessity multiplied population. Today facts seem to show that a higher standard of well-being, on the contrary, tends to limit it." (1909: 222-23). Certainly, but we must not try to judge Sismondi, Smith, Malthus, and Ricardo according to the facts existing by 1909 —we must understand them from the circumstances of their time, and then we shall perceive truth where Rist sees error. Gide and Rist have no historical sense. Examples like this clearly prove their opinion that the theories of the past can be treated like those of the present. They do not aim at understanding but at judging the doctrinal systems. Their book is a discussion of actual ideas rather than a description of views outgrown:[14] this statement comprises all that need be said for the characterization of their work, its merits and its faults. This statement, however, at the same time comprises the ultimate judgment on the character and value of the critical concept of the history of economy doctrines.

---

14. For example the chapter on Malthus or on "The Associative Socialists."

6

The Descriptive Approach

The historians of political economy who have so far been reviewed discussed the theories of the past as if they were theses of the present. This conception overlooks the fundamental fact of all history: that in the course of time sense turns to nonsense and truth to error, so that the children cannot be competent judges of their fathers. Against the men whose work will now be surveyed, the same reproach cannot be made. They clearly understood the independent value of the past. But they did not get beyond an externally correct description of development. They showed, indeed, how, but not why, things happened. This is their achievement and this was their limitation.

Alfred Espinas, for example, knew no connection between economic reality and economic science. "The development of wealth must not be confounded with the history of the science which studies wealth"—so runs the first sentence of his work (1891: 19). And in its motivation he thinks proper to emphasize that Egyptians, Assyrians, Babylonians, and Persians too had an active economic life, but that only among the Greeks, who were intellectually on a higher level, did a thinker arise in Socrates to investigate the phenomena of wealth. But this argument, plausible as it may sound, is not decisive. A flourishing economic life does not by itself produce an economic science[1]—only the rudest materialism could maintain this. So long as it presents no urgent problems (as in the ancient empires of the East) it remains unanalyzed. But in the age of Socrates and Xenophon, Plato and Aristotle, the economic life of Attica presented an urgent problem: the old system of natural economy began to give way to exchange and money economy, and this development evoked the earliest economic thought; thus, it did not arise without external cause. The problems of the time indeed determined even the content of that thought: the great philosophers, as Espinas himself points out, thus giving the clue to the correct interpretation (1891: 50), belonged to the aristocracy or at least took its part. Their conservativism is thus explained; their predilection for agriculture and their disinclination toward handicraft and money-trade, as it is most fully developed in Plato and Aristotle, were social prejudices similar to the disinclination of the petty nobleman of Eastern Prussia of yesterday and today toward the *parvenu* from trade and industry.

How incapable Espinas was of perceiving the facts that conditioned the theories is manifest in the following sentence: "In fact, says Aristotle, it is in the family and for the family that all wealth, that all goods are acquired; it is in the family that they are consumed. Here we have an essential feature by which the economics of Aristotle differ from modern Political Economy" (1891: 39). He conceives the difference as a difference of opinions. The idea does not enter his mind that in one case it is modern national economy, in the other ancient domestic economy that is under consideration. Certainly, Aristotle too pursued economics—but to him it was the doctrine of the *oikos*, not, as to Adam Smith, the doctrine of exchange economy: the two systems of ideas have indeed no more in common than their name.

The dogmas and laws of the Middle Ages, which arose from the undynamic natural and subsistence economy of the time and which

---

1. It is surprising to come across such a view in Roscher's writings: "As astronomy on the basis of a mere calculation asserted the existence of a planet at a certain spot which observation afterwards really discovered, so I was long of the opinion that so highly developed a national economy as the Dutch in the 17th century . . . could not possibly have been without a correspondingly great economic science" (1874: 222 et seq.), a conjecture which has been confirmed by Laspeyres's research.

were destined to regulate and preserve it, are to Espinas only "errors of opinion," a "collection of wrong ideas" (1891: 78). He reproduces the arguments that are to be found in Lactantius against the loan at interest: it is inhuman because it exploits the distress of the debtor, and unjust because by the exaction of interest, it robs him of his property. But he does not realize that these arguments can only mean the specifically medieval borrowing in times of need, the merely consumptive usurious loan; for the productive loan, which did not exist in Lactantius's times, does not exploit any distress of the debtor, but helps him to gain riches, and does not take from him a single penny but adds to his fortune by its productivity.[2] Yet in Espinas's uncritical and unhistoric view, a loan is simply a loan, and he does not perceive the change of reality behind the change of thought. The discussion between Jourdain and Espinas, whether the doctrine of usury of the schoolmen was borrowed from Aristotle or originated in the Roman philosophers, is only of secondary importance. Whether the one authority is quoted or the other, it is reality from which the prohibition of interest in the Middle Ages can and must be understood.

However, it is precisely in this connection that Espinas spoke the words that are so surprising in his mouth: "Generally the economic doctrines are the reflection of a social state and reveal the more or less conscious needs of each epoch" (1891: 89). But what he goes on to say only proves his lack of understanding of the inner concatenation of science and reality. He is of the opinion that the real reasons for the prohibition of usury were simply the disorders and wars of the transitional period between antiquity and the Middle Ages, and the hostility against interest "diminished . . . from the moment when feudal society forming itself united step by step the conditions of a civilized society." The strangely unhistoric character of this view is obvious. He believes that in *any* ordered economy interest is at home—even in the feudal, precapitalistic system, before the rise of exchange economy. Thus, he totally misunderstands the essence of the medieval economy from which the canonist doctrine sprang. Its attitude toward interest is and remains to him a "préjugé" (90) and

---

2. That the church objected only to loans at interest to the poor, not to all loans at interest without distinction, was proved by Marco Mastrofini, *Le Usure*, as early as 1831.

even a "préjugé antiéconomique" (110).

Espinas is as incapable of comprehending the newer developments in the history of economic thought as he is of the older ones. Thus, he expresses himself on physiocracy without understanding: it is to him "a chimerical philosophy" (1891: 214). Indeed, he says (220) that "the pretended new science was on the whole nothing but a collection of postulates aroused by the needs of the country" but he views its origin exclusively from the political angle. The physiocratic doctrine is a protest "against the abuses of the monarchical regime" (227) and as such Espinas seeks to interpret it. But he explains only its call for freedom, not its economic theory. On the essential point of the position of agriculture in Quesnay's system, of the connection between science and reality, he says nothing, yet it is exactly this that is to be explained, that is to be made understandable! Physiocracy remains to him simply an accumulation of wrong ideas, and only Adam Smith was the first to perceive truths. Only of him Espinas says: he "leaves the domain of chimeras to enter that of experience" (289). He is to Espinas the "founder of Political Economy" (269), or rather, the founder of the doctrine governing modern times.

Espinas, in surveying the whole evolution of economic doctrine, thinks it possible to perceive a double progress: first, the conquest of mysticism by naturalism (we should say reason), that is, the separation of economics from morals and the establishment of its independence as a science; and second the progressive growth of its object. "Domestic in ancient times . . . it became political towards the end of the Middle Ages; then it had for its object the interest of a single nation only; soon afterwards it rose to the conception of a universal and human interest." (1891: 347), a development in breadth which was accompanied by a corresponding development in depth: "The phenomena which it embraces are more and more complex; it is far from the timid observations of Socrates to the immense variety of facts comprised by the economic literature of the globe."

Thus, Espinas sees in the sequence of the doctrines a teleological evolution to greater and greater perfection. "The economic art follows in its variations a pre-determined course." And yet his investigation is not really historical. It lacks the perception that the products of different periods are *different in their essence*: Socrates and Smith are not simply distinguished by the fact that the one had domestic, the other international economy, that is to say, a broader field in view. The difference is less quantitative than qualitative. But Espinas has no sense of this distinction. Like Dühring he treats the uncomprehended views of the past exactly as the supposed errors of his contemporaries; as timeless blunders and no more. The opposition of Aristotle to chrematistics is in his opinion germane and ever essentially equal to Marx's opposition to capitalism: "It is the naive offence of Aristotle, in view of the great commerce of his time and its rapid profits which renews itself with the modern revolutionary in view of the great industry and its triumphant enrichment!" (1891: 333). Antiquity and modern times, nobility and working class, reaction and revolution, moral considerations and economic analysis—all are the same to Espinas.[3] It was not the viewpoint of history from which he surveyed the evolution of economic doctrines. He describes them, without consistently judging and without fundamentally understanding them, and herein ends the contribution that he made to the literature on the history of economic doctrine.

René Gonnard, like Ingram and Haney before him, expressed the conviction that there is a constant interrelation between reality and science, facts and doctrine. "If it is according to its fruits that we should judge a tree, it is also true that the knowledge of the tree allows us to foresee what the fruit will be, and a complete science embraces both points of view." But while Ingram was prone to think the influence of facts on doctrines stronger than the influence of doctrines on facts, and while Haney seems to have regarded the action of the two elements on each other as equally strong, Gonnard is rather of the opinion that science molds life. To deduce the theories from reality was therefore not his intention. "The doctrine," he says (1930: v), "engenders the facts[4] and vice versa. . . . The doctrine is itself

---

3. Cf. also 320, 322. The basic problem of modern socialism already existed in antiquity. "Fundamentally it was the problem that had moved the ancient, Socrates, Plato, Aristotle, and even the Christians, which arose anew in other forms."

4. In this sense Gonnard expresses the conviction that it was the medieval doctrine that created the medieval society—not the other way round. "This doctrine was accepted and obeyed. It permeated legislation, customs and souls; it inspired the corporative spirit . . . it molded the artisan . . . it gave to all the Occident . . . a common ideal of civilization where a latent individualism was reconciled . . . with the

a fact. . . . And the other facts, those of legislation and economic practice, do not assume all their significance, but in the light of the doctrines from which they have issued" (as, however, on the other hand "the doctrines do not display all their sense but illustrated by the facts in the environment of which they were born"). And almost a decade after the first publication of his book Gonnard repeated this creed: "I remain more than ever convinced of the influence exercised by the doctrines on the facts—an influence which is indeed not one-sided but real and strong" (1930: 1). As a motto he put at the head of his work a sentence of Balzac: "*Thought* is constantly the starting-point and the end of all society."

What character Gonnard's investigation of development assumes on the basis of this concept is manifest in the treatment of the medieval theory of usury. He acquaints us with the arguments with which the schoolmen supported the banning of interest that has to be regarded as part of a broader view according to which all gains in the sphere of circulation appear unnatural and therefore immoral and illegitimate: that money is only a means of circulation and all profits come lastly from labor; that one must not accept payment for the use of money because it is a consumable, and not a durable, good; and that one may not demand a recompense for waiting because time belongs to God. He describes to us the exceptions that then opened the door to interest: the *damnum emergens* [when lender incurs a loss], the *lucrum cessans* [when lender forgoes profits], and the *periculum sortis* [when there is a high risk to the lenders capital]. But he does not say what was at the bottom of the whole view that so greatly surprised modern times: the fact that the Middle Ages practically knew only consumptive loans, which indeed do not justify interest, but hardly productive loans, which create surplus-values and thus make the payment of interest a matter of course.

It is not astonishing that Gonnard's basic attitude prevents him from reaching a full appreciation of mercantilism. He justly connects the rise of this doctrine with the rise of modern capitalism and modern monarchy, explaining how new social and political facts created the conditions of a new economic dogma. And he puts—if only in a footnote—the question that leads straight into the understanding of the

---

eminently social genius of catholicism" (1930: 42).

ideal world of mercantilism, whether the mercantilists sought money because it was made from precious metals, or precious metals because they were wont to be made into money. Rightly he is inclined to prefer the latter view. He says: "Mercantilism was born in the epoch in which the growing preponderance of the merchant and of commercial capitalism asserted itself, and its characteristic was consequently to place in the foreground of all wealth the wealth of the merchant, money" (1930: 48, footnote). In the transfer of the business point of view of the merchant to the whole of society, he sees the soul of mercantilism (and at the same time its explanation): "It regards the nation as a merchant" (142). But he thus totally misunderstands the economic sense and the historical achievement of this theory: its realization that without the extension and acceleration of monetary circulation, the unfolding of exchange economy was impossible—exchange economy which, in the given circumstances, necessarily appeared as the end of all progressive zeal.

Although Gonnard endeavors rightly to assess the merits of the physiocrats he takes no pains to explain the relative truth of their theory in their time and for their time. On the contrary he is inclined to believe that Quesnay confused value and matter (1930: 214) in the sense that only newly created matter appeared to him as newly created value. But he touches the interesting question that could lead to a better interpretation: why did the physiocrats succeed only in France and Italy, but not in England or Germany? And it is characteristic of Gonnard's attitude that he indicates a totally abstract reason: the circumstance that Quesnay's doctrine with its predilection for agriculture and its belief in a good providence is reminiscent of the Catholic doctrine of the Middle Ages and could therefore find no understanding in the Protestant countries. But this way leads one astray.[5] The reason simply is that the agrarian and social constitutions of England and Germany could not confirm such a

---

5. The church historian David Ogg argues in the other sense: France remained Catholic because it lacked the class which in other countries formed the basis for the spread of the doctrine of predestination (be it of the Jansenistic or of the Calvinistic stamp)—the class whose predominance excluded an agrarianism of Quesnay's type in a country like England. Cf. *The History of Christianity in the Light of Modern Knowledge*, 1929: 660.

doctrine. In England by 1750 the country was as capitalistic as the town, in Germany the town was still as precapitalistic as the country. A doctrine, the basis of which is the contrast between a precapitalistic agriculture and a capitalistic industry, could arise neither here nor there.

It is obviously not part of Gonnard's plan to study the mutual concatenation between dogmas and facts. *Ad narrandum scribitur historia*, he says (1930: 685), and this is characteristic of his purely descriptive approach, *non ad probandum* [history is written to describe, not to prove]. And still there is one element to which he ascribes strong influence on the formation of ideas: the "ethnical factor" (344, 369) plays a special role in his treatise.[6] "It has been said that science has no fatherland: if this is true it is at least also certain that the doctrines . . . have one" (447). Gonnard writes:

> It is not unimportant to reveal the Hebrew origin of David Ricardo, especially if we compare him with Karl Marx. The most rigorous theoretician of the liberal school and that of collectivism strangely resemble each other in the turn of their thought. In spite of the opposition of their conclusions, the same ethnical influence marks their doctrines: both are pitiless logicians, dialecticians who construct by reasoning an abstract and syllogistic economic dramaturgy with only that difference that Marx spreads over it a cover of facts, while Ricardo disdained to do so. (344)

But Gonnard leads his own argument ad absurdum. He heads the chapter devoted to Marx with a word of Bernard Lazare (499): "The instinct of revolution is the very genius of Israel"—an instinct which the "forty-fold millionaire" Ricardo did not share with the starveling Marx, in spite of all racial propinquity! And it is interesting that in his valuation of Ricardo, Gonnard explicitly accepts the verdict of a man who incidentally was also a severe critic of Marx, Franz Oppenheimer, who by race and descent belonged to David Ricardo and Karl Marx, but not to René Gonnard!

Gonnard devotes special attention to the differences between English and French economic theory. "Could we not go as far as to say," he

---

6. Cf. also (1930: 472). The breakdown of the Chartist movement Gonnard partly explains by the fact that its leaders were "Celts from Ireland" whose national character "shocked the Anglo-Saxon temperament." Further see 492, 533 et seq.

asks (1930: 143), "that there is more similarity between an English mercantilist of the 17th or 18th and an English liberal of the 19th century—than between an English mercantilist and one of his French contemporaries—while there remains a certain doctrinal relationship even between Colbert and Quesnay?" And he opposes the English system of economics "from beginning to end, from the 17th century down to our time" as "mercantile" to the French as "producteur"—an antithesis that bears its criticism in itself. He believes especially that classicism falls into two groups, a French and an English one. French liberalism, as he thinks, is "more dogmatic, more absolute, more disinterested" (1930: 306)—and on this last point he lays particular stress. "One could say," we read in another place (369), "that the chrematistic and a-moral tendency . . . is much less universal amongst the French economists than with the British."

Is it indeed necessary to relate the difference sketched by Gonnard (which by the way is much smaller in reality than his prejudiced judgment would make us believe, for were such men as Charles Dunoyer and de Molinari really so unlike their English contemporaries?) to contrasting national characters in order to understand it? Certainly not! Gonnard himself shows the direction in which we have to seek the true explanation. He emphasizes that on the continent the idea of freedom was understood in a more negative sense (as contrast to state intervention), in Great Britain in a more positive sense (as means to the strengthening of the individual). "The English fraction of the classical school had a more individualist than liberal color; the French group, on the contrary, a color more liberal than individualist" (1930: 370). This difference is explained by reality.

> The state of Napoleon appeared to Say as a menace to economic liberty[7] . . . while in England the government soon assumed an attitude of abstention which reassured the economists. Much later, towards the end of the 19th century, this attitude of the English state changed: but then Spencer expounded an economic anti-statism equal to that of the Frenchmen most absolute in this respect.

Hence, is it not after all historical reasons rather than ethnic that

---

7. This view had already been expressed by Michel Chevalier (Gonnard 1930: 594).

explain the difference? It is just to assert this—with or against Gonnard.[8] If liberalism in England really assumed a somewhat more extreme form than in France, it is not due to a characteristic of the English being more open to mammonism, but to the fact that capitalism, along with its ideology and ethics, developed more quickly, more thoroughly, and more strikingly in England than in France. Hence its rationalism, its pessimism, and all the other isms that characterize it! We need not dig very deep to find their roots.

Gonnard, however—he cannot be spared this reproach—tries less to understand the national coloring that the different theories assumed in the different countries than to use them to represent French science in an especially favorable light—as if a history of economics was a suitable stage for the display of national pride and prejudice![9] Gonnard endeavors to extol Quesnay's achievement in comparison with that of Smith and Ricardo, Bastiat in comparison with Mill, Saint-Simon and Proudhon in comparison with Marx—his French nationalism is manifest everywhere.[10] French economics, he holds, can be characterized "as science, as moral science, and as science of observation" (1930: 410); thus he ascribes to it the attributes which,

---

8. Gonnard did not clearly formulate his thesis and thus it is impossible to find out whether he regarded the national influences as determined lastly by historical or by racial factors. The latter interpretation is suggested by his comparison of Ricardo and Marx as Jews, the former by the connection of the Russian inclination toward communism, which, as he believes, has its roots in the Russian national character, with historical, geographical, and social elements (he refers to an "egalitarian and communistic race" [1930: 570]). Most unfortunate is the following statement: "A genuinely German and also genuinely Hebrew dialectics . . . these two ethnical features characterize . . . the work of Karl Marx" (499).

9. On the other hand, how broadminded was Francesco Ferrara! He scorned to extol the Italian economists of the sixteenth, seventeenth, and eighteenth centuries for purely nationalistic reasons. "Frankly," he said (cited by Bousquet in Ferrara 1938: 20), "I do not share and I cannot share the enthusiasm which reflects the conventional admiration for the name of every Italian economist."

10. Gonnard has hardly any right to accuse Schmoller of national prejudice, and it must remain undecided who was more affected by this evil. Cf. Gonnard 627, note 4; Schmoller, *Grundriss der allgemeinen Volkswirtschaftslehre*, 1900, 1: especially 151 et seq.

in his view, the ideal science of economic life should possess. But political economy, the formation of which all the leading nations have taken part in, does not agree with the narrowness of a nationalist outlook; and although Gonnard keeps his tendency within certain limits, it still infringes upon objectivity, the cultivation of which is one of the foremost virtues of any historian.

Edgar Salin shares the strong emphasis on the independence of the mind with René Gonnard. To him the successive economic theories are free products of a freely changing spirit, and not faithful reflections of a lawfully changing reality. This is Salin's fundamental conviction; it is well weighed, conscious, willed—but not therefore less onesided and (*sit venia verbo*) erroneous.

Salin not only denies that economic conditions have the power to form scientific ideas and systems and that the intellectual phenomena are only a superstructure above the material substructure (that indeed could hardly be maintained in so crude a form), but he is also reluctant to admit that they necessarily correspond to a certain stage of economic and social evolution (1923: 12)—as if it were possible to imagine that an economic theory could arise that is severed from economic reality and not stimulated and determined by it. Here his idealism is led to its extreme limits, nay, indeed, far beyond them!

"It is . . . not because of economic facts and certainly not because of economic facts alone, that the early Christian time is distinguished by an almost entire lack of economic doctrines," says Salin (1923: 16). However, "what place was there for an economic doctrine among men and in centuries to whom the earth had only meaning as a preparation for the here-after, to whom therefore the political, legal, and especially economic, order of the world appeared as indifferent and transitory?" This rhetorical question leads us entirely astray. In other times too men to whom earthly life was only a preparation for the next world cultivated economic theory—who would deny that Archbishop Whately, Senior's follower in the economic chair of the University of Oxford, was a genuinely religious man, a real Christian?[11] And how closely this was sometimes associated with religion is clearly shown by classical economics, which, from the

---

11. Cf. for example Cardinal Newman, *Apologia pro vita sua*, Everyman ed. 1930: 36 et seq.

analysis of economic life, gained above all the conviction that as in nature so also in society there is a cosmos and not a chaos, that here as there a divine order can be recognized. If in the period that English historiography so aptly describes as the Dark Ages economic life was only seldom the object of thought, this was not due to the devotion and unworldliness of those men but certainly above all to the fact that economic reality, agricultural and traditionalist as it was, offered no urgent problems. This does not run counter to the fact that Salin emphasizes that "the chrematistic style of economic life survived in spite of the predominance of agrarian forms of economy and dominion in those centuries." It is the rule and not the exception, the dominant and not the secondary factor that decides. Salin himself rightly says (1923: 19) that the constant retrogression of Europe to a more rural structure spared the church (and that means science) the necessity of discussing national economy, and only its new unfolding toward the end of the Middle Ages compelled the inclusion of economics in divinity as a frontier province—a very realistic view surprising beside Salin's otherwise too onesidedly intellectual standpoint.

Salin's hyperidealistic concept and its limitations also become manifest where he speaks of the schoolmen and contrasts them with the classicists (1923: 20). The classicists, he says, asked for the inner order of the economic system, whereas the schoolmen asked for the compatibility of actual facts with the dogma. But if we so wish we may without difficulty interpret and describe the problem of the classicists also as a question "of compatibility of actual facts with the dogma," as question of the compatibility of the economic facts of 1750 and 1800 with the dogma of the divine harmony in the creation, and of Adam Smith, Say, and Bastiat too one may say in a certain sense "they put a theological question and give a theological answer." The whole difference is that the canonists had a regulated town economy, the classicists a free national economy, in view. Therefore, the ones asked for the "Ought," the others for the "Is;" and therefore, the ones pursued a human, the others a superhuman, order of things.

Salin's fundamental concept expounded with so much vigor does not prevent him from sometimes adopting a causal explanation reminiscent even of crude materialism in so far as it ascribes the change of economic doctrines to the rise of new interests and groups of interests.

Let us consider only the following (1923: 24):

> While Thomas a hundred and fifty years earlier . . . regarded the
> maintenance of living according to one's station as the sign of just pricing,
> so now after handicraft and merchant families had attained to new riches
> and to the dominating power in the state, no economic doctrine is possible
> which denies all change of economic life. . . . If the economic doctrine of
> Thomas was like the economic life of his time preeminently static, it was
> the task of Bernardin and Antonin to make room for the dynamics of
> capitalism.

Does not this statement imply a coordination—which Salin rejects in
theory—between certain intellectual phenomena and a certain economic
development?!

Not less penetrating, but also not less at variance with his
fundamental attitude, is Salin's attempt at a causal explanation of the
decline of mercantilism. Mercantilism, he says, had been based on
the conviction that the enrichment of one's own country in foreign
trade was conditioned by the impoverishment of the other—and this
conviction, we may add, was then correct as the colonies had to hand
over their money and property to the exploiting countries in which
economic activity was awakened and strengthened by the influx of
wealth. However, as soon as the overseas territories were parceled
out and exhausted a situation arose in which it had to be realized that
a constant profit from trade was possible in the future only if the
commercial intercourse was in the interest of both partners—a
perception that led over to Adam Smith.

This explanation affords a splendid example of a causal interpretation
in the sphere of the history of economic thought, and we must thank
Salin for this hint—even though he himself held theoretically a
different view from the one here actually employed!

Most strikingly perhaps Salin condemns his assertion that there is no
coordination between the intellectual phenomena and a certain
economic and social situation (1923: 12) by his remarks on Ricardo's
relation to the period previous to 1878 (57).

> It is still more important that Ricardo's scheme of an economy of perfectly
> free competition and of a rigid wage held out an attractive ideal to the
> interests of . . . progressing industry and to the profit greed of capital; that
> gave to it the character of the only competent . . . theory: the rational

scheme became the genuine theory of the first phase of high capitalism.

That here a strict coordination between facts and thought is clearly suggested cannot well be denied; it only remains to ask whether it would not be more correct from a logical as well as a historical standpoint to replace the coordinating statement by a causal connection. The contact between the Ricardian theory and reality may indeed, as Salin says, have appeared accidental to the Ricardians themselves, as they conceived their doctrine as timelessly valid and correct.   But the historian must reject the notion of accidental happenings, if he is to be a man of science, and in the explanation of the external fact of coordination lies, no doubt, his mission par excellence.

In discussing Ricardo's work Salin points out that, according to this view, two types of economic investigation are possible: on the one hand the type of mercantilism, German economics, that is, the type of doctrine that regards the historical and political elements as indissolubly connected with economic life and indeed views economy always only as part of the supereconomic whole (representatives Adam Müller and Friedrich List); on the other hand the type of physiocrat-classicists, that is, of "pure theory," who work free of social or sociological considerations on a mechanistic and exclusively economic object of perception (Quesnay, Ricardo, and Pareto).   Salin, who decidedly rejects any science that avoids valuations and frankly admits that he belongs to the historio-sociological tradition, knows how to use this division and its kernel of truth without clumsily dividing the mass of dogmas into black and white, right and wrong; and this humanly and scholarly sovereign attitude is not the least merit of his work. For although he is convinced that only List (by the "de-poisoning of cosmopolitanism") and Rodbertus (by "the political restriction of individualism through social conservativism") founded the "true economics" (82 et seq.), he still avoided absolute judgments and well understood how to bring to life the import and meaning of the divergent schools and teachings.

Fred O. Boucke who, both in time and in thought, stands near to Gonnard and Salin, opens his book with a confession of his belief in the idea of evolution.

The whole history of thought testifies to the relativity of our understanding.

> Nothing is quite certain. Nothing holds good for more than a time. . . .
> Everywhere the same law. A becoming, waxing, and waning. . . . The
> genetic principle proves equally fruitful whether we study creed or deed,
> things or thoughts, politics or economics. (Boucke 1921: 2-3)

And he then touches on the basic problem of all historical research,
the question whether objective historiography is possible at all since
even the thought of the present and thus its relation to the past is
determined by its time and only of relative validity. Boucke answers
this question in the negative:

> It is practically impossible to speak of the past without putting into
> it something of the present. . . . Historians consequently dare not
> hope to be mere assemblers of facts, even if they wished to. The
> fact itself is little or nothing, the interpretation much or
> everything. The *value* put upon events of the past is the core of
> historiography. (1921: 2-3)

Starting from these considerations Boucke rejects the teachings of the
materialist conception of history, which implies—though it does not
assert, as Boucke thinks—that objective knowledge of history is
possible if we only abandon the valuing retrospect from the viewpoint
of the present, which applies the ideas of today to the life of
yesterday, and try to understand the individual stages of development
from their socioeconomic structure, thus comprehending the past
through the past. Boucke does not deny that there are connections
between the objective and the subjective, but he does not admit any
sort of economic determinism. "[T]he main point is not whether
cross-references may be advisable or even necessary—for most
historians would grant so much—but whether economic conditions
possess a *causal* force, an exclusive power of explanation. . . . And
here . . . the direct evidence of facts has, on the whole, favored the
opponents more than the friend of the Marxian doctrine" (1921: 7).
Thus, he does not consider the knowledge of economic conditions
indispensable for the explanation of the phenomena of thought.
"Intellectual history stands on its own ground" (8). In these words
Boucke sets forth the principle of his own treatise.

It is impossible at this juncture to discuss the question, which is as
interesting as it is intricate, whether Marx's interpretation of history

may be characterized as determinism and materialism.[12]   Upon the answer to it will largely depend whether this theory should be accepted or rejected.   But even if we leave this problem undecided, we must investigate whether the method suggested by Marx, that is, the deduction of thought from social existence (Marx does not speak of existence in general, and this is important) or of the cultural superstructure from the socioeconomic substructure, must not appear as a heuristic principle of the highest value.   The past is to us at first sight a book with seven seals.   From which side shall we try to open it?   It cannot be doubted that the approach from the socioeconomic side is easier and at the same time more promising.   That the philosophy of the Middle Ages thought a great deal upon the order of seating among the angels in heaven appears to us incomprehensible but it is not difficult to comprehend the feudal system.   Once its essence has been comprehended it is possible also to interpret the legal order of the time; this leads us on to the state; the state to the church; and the church to philosophy.   And all will teach why the Middle Ages cherished the belief in a great order in which all things existing have their predetermined place—God, angels, men, animals, and plants alike.

So much for the importance of the method arising from the Marxian interpretation of history for the historical science.   Its value is independent of the judgment on the correctness of the socioeconomic interpretation of the past.   Yet with regard to the history of political economy we can and must go farther.   For it may seem doubtful that the religion and philosophy of a time can be understood from its economic and social order, but not that economic theory always results from economic reality.   Boucke's counterargument is not sufficient:

> The economic interpretation of history gives us to understand that a more or less fixed ratio exists between systematic thought and the concrete facts of economic life.   Psychology, however, is definite in declaring the flexibility of such a relation. . . .   One stimulus may end in several responses, and one response may have to wait upon a congeries of stimuli, either all issuing outside of us, or partly aroused from within. (1921: 7)

---

12. The best study on this problem is Max Adler's book: *Marx als Denker*, 2d ed. 1921.

By these words only a narrow determinism is rejected, which tends to teach that economic theory is strictly (so to speak mechanically) determined by economic practice and that man reads reality as a child reads a primer, endeavoring to formulate the words that are prescribed. Such determinism would indeed be absurd. It would contradict our inner experience. For in dealing with any problem, are we not capable of deciding on several solutions? Certainly! But this cannot mean that the solution may be conceived or understood without the problem. A stimulus may perhaps cause several reactions—this point may be contested—but reaction and stimulus are still a unity; they must correspond to one another, and be understood through one another. And it must especially appear so in retrospect. The alternative possibilities given in the passing moment when the stimulus made itself felt have, with the exception of one, perished without even becoming perceptible. The one reaction, however, which has turned into reality creates the impression of having been the only result of the incitation, and in a certain sense this is true.

The attempt to separate perception and object of perception is an absurdity. Boucke indeed does not in practice go as far as that. But his interest is not attracted by the problem as to how the dogmas arise from the facts, but by the question of what connections there were between the economic teachings and the philosophical premises on which they rest. It is the task of the critic to investigate how far he has succeeded and whether he has offered an interpretation of the fundamental systematic ideas of the different schools that may claim to be called satisfactory.

Boucke first tries to explain the fundamental thesis of the physiocrats from their basic philosophical concept. He endeavors to prove that the belief in the exclusive productivity of agriculture resulted from their deism.

> The cult of nature was the reaction of modern times against medieval theocracy. The study of substance and space was an attempt at reconstructing an older personalism. . . . So the Physiocrats were consistent in defining wealth as concrete things derived, in one way or another, from the earth. They meant *stuff* when they said value. (1921: 68)

Hence the materialism of the physiocrats, their identification of matter and value, originated in their notion of God "because they saw Him through nature." Smith's labor theory of value too is explained by Boucke from the "naturalistic outlook" (if we may call it an explanation, for he provides only a few hints): "Smith saw the problem from a social standpoint. He emphasized the material origin of all kinds of wealth. He has in mind stuff and energy in discussing value or labor" (88). Hence the progress beyond Quesnay. "[T]he imputation of wealth to labor instead of to nature" Boucke views in this connection: "In line with the ideas of Locke, Tucker, Hume, and Turgot the active agent in production is set apart from all natural resources" (88).

Now in the first place it is erroneous to stamp Quesnay simply as a materialist, for following Descartes's prima philosophia he recognizes two world substances, matter and mind. But quite generally deism is as open to a purely idealistic interpretation as to an essentially materialistic one. Its perhaps highest expression—Kant's "Religion innerhalb der Grenzen der blossen Vernunft" (1793)—sprang from the idealist tradition, and even on French soil Malebranche is opposed to Diderot. The identification of matter and value, or rather the deduction of value from matter, cannot be comprehended from this side. And although we must regard Adam Smith as the successor of Locke and Hume, his materialism was not so predominant and above all not so crude that he should have viewed everything from the material aspect. His philosophy was essentially an exploration of the soul, which had its roots in experience but not in matter. In so far as deism upheld the belief that all is subject to a great law, Quesnay and Smith must be comprehended as its adherents. But what was the character of this law and its parts, on what did it rest and how did it operate?—on these problems nothing followed from the deistic creed. And therefore it cannot have determined, and it cannot possibly explain, the political economy of its time.

Similarly Boucke strives to interpret the essence of the Ricardian doctrine from the underlying philosophy.

> [I]n Utilitarian economics the objective and static version was the only legitimate one. The world was taken to be real, and the usefulness of things as inherent in them. . . . Cost was outgo of materials. . . . Income referred to goods and not to legal rights. . . . Measurement was by a standard accessible to all, namely, by stuff or time, labor being back of both. . . . [T]hough individualism had triumphed, there were echoes of the Physiocratic chant in praise of a beneficent nature. (1921: 162)

Labor appears in this interpretation again as "energy previously spent" (163).

Here it is not difficult to prove that an explanation of the "Utilitarian economics" from Utilitarian philosophy and psychology is impossible. Boucke himself must more or less openly admit that there is a breach between the two doctrines:

> If the Physiocrats had dwelled long on goods in the concrete the Ricardian followers now pointed again and again to values. And values related to facts of consciousness. It was in a way *curious* that with all this revolving about sensations the Benthamites did not abandon at once their objective norms of value-measurement. However, they did not. (1921: 320 [emphasis added])

Indeed they did not! However closely one tries to connect Bentham's psychology and Ricardo's economics, one cannot be understood from the other.

As Boucke regards historicism as a manifestation of the collectivist spirit—"they united in a condemnation of the individualistic regimé and meant honestly to create a new science of society" (1921: 207) —he approaches it from the philosophy of collectivism which, in 1830, however, was still in its beginnings.

> [Historicism] . . . took a sociological view of human nature. It declined to rest content with speculations privately conducted. It looked for a unit larger than the individual and found it in the society of all ages. . . . [Centuries of history were to show what introspective psychology could not. . . .] Society as an organism whose unity every scientist should respect is contrasted . . . with the atomistic view of human and civic bodies which utilitarian economics made the basis of its speculations. In reality society is both more and less than the sum of individuals composing it. To narrow down economics therefore to a science of exchange relations . . . seemed . . . a vain attempt at dodging responsibilities. (214, 216)

Now, historicism as a dynamic and collectivism as a social interpretation of life are, as has already been emphasized, by no means identical. Thus, Adam Müller was near to the one and still far from the other doctrine, and that they often appear together between 1820 and 1870 does not prove any necessary relationship. But let us restrict ourselves to the universalists among the historians and the historians among the universalists! Is the thesis then correct that the philosophy of collectivism was the soil from which their ideas sprang? By no means! Collectivism as a philosophy, especially as a political philosophy and ethics, measures in the end by absolute standards, while all historicism is relativism. Collectivism was either an ideology of estates idealizing the Middle Ages or an ideology of the class struggle bent upon the future. The one believed that actual society nearing the state of perfect free trade was only a deterioration of the ideal social order of the past, the other that the world of today torn by class struggles would give birth to the classless community of tomorrow, in which the motor of history will cease to work. Historicism, however, genuine evolutionism, does not know any form of life that stands out in the great stream of growing and waning, it knows only change as the one eternal thing.

If we wish to connect the philosophy and economics of 1840 we can only do it in the same way as we have connected the philosophy and economics of 1760: by the fundamental idea common to both doctrines, in the one case evolution, in the other the universal law. The economic theories are not conclusions from philosophical premises as Boucke's treatise suggests. Both economics and philosophy are, like all chains in the system of sciences, an expression of the time that has created them, and only by this relation to the same life are they united.

In modern theory, as it has developed since 1870, the concatenation between psychology and economics seems indeed far more intimate. Is not the whole theory of marginal utility only to be understood as a child of Benthamism? Boucke endeavors to prove that this is so, reducing the basic concepts as well as the basic laws of the theory created by Menger, Jevons, and Walras to their supposed basis in psychology.

> The definition and laws of Marginism, which together may be said to constitute its principles, were of course based on its premises. The same circumstances that gave Marginism and Utilitarianism premises in common also gave them a similar superstructure. . . . Marginism consequently had no quarrel with the general drift of Utilitarianism. What it proposed to change, and did change was the standard of measurement for exchange ratios, and the explanations given for the *naturalness* of the pricing and distributing process under investigation. . . . Feelings and marginal valuations took the place of outgo in things or in labor, but otherwise little was changed. . . . Value was an act or a state of consciousness, an

imputation of qualities to things or deeds . . . as exhibited in exchange. .
. . . Concrete objects ceased to be the sole subject of measurement. . . .
Wealth was a fund of values rather than a conglomeration of things
physical. . . . Production consisted of a creation of *values*. . . . Capital
was a fund of values like wealth . . . employed productively. . . . Costs
were . . . outlays of value [labor, pain, abstinence, impatience]. (1921: 287-
93, 305)

[W]ants lay at the bottom of every price and income. The premises [of that
persuasion] were the hallowed competitive ones which fitted in so admirably
with Benthamism. . . . The static individualistic view alone satisfied the
requirements of an exact economics.   Valuations could thus only be
translated into prices; and costs would represent but the obverse side of the
coin. (299-300)

"In the long run or else in an perfectly stationary society, costs and
marginal bids will make a equation" (303). "The *cost* of a commodity
is any *pain* that must be submitted to in order to obtain it," says
Pantaleoni (cited in Boucke 1921: 304 [emphasis added]), and he thus
harmonizes the notion of costs with the hedonistic doctrine of marginal
utility.   For "economic science consists of the laws of wealth
systematically deduced from the hypothesis that men are actuated
exclusively by the desire to realize the fullest possible satisfaction of
their wants with the least possible individual sacrifice."   In these
words Pantaleoni on whom Boucke mainly depends (259) tried to
show that the teachings of modern theory, the teachings of Jennings,
Gossen, Jevons, Wieser, Walras, and Pareto, logically follow from
Bentham's psychology.

Thus, it cannot be doubted that economics and psychology have
contracted an especially intimate union in the theory of marginal
utility. And yet we must not assume that modern psychology offered
the fundamental idea of modern economics.   This arose in truth
directly from the modern development of society, as the basic thesis
of deism had arisen from late eighteenth-century conditions and the
leading concept of evolutionism from early nineteenth-century
conditions.

The application of psychological conceptions to economic analysis
obviously has one prerequisite: man, as he appears to us entangled in,
and determined by, the innumerable interrelations of economy and
society, had first to be conceived as an individual, as a natural being

capable of isolation, before the idea of deducing the social phenomenon of value from his individual psyche could be reached. Only after the conviction had asserted itself that the individual and not the class (or the estate) is the decisive unit in the common life of men[13] could individual psychology be used for the explanation of social economy. A satisfactory analysis of the origin of the utility theory of value must show how this came about, and in this task no philosophy can help. The science of psychology always investigated man as an individual, but political economy learned to see him in this light only by 1870.

However, once this conception has come into being, it is only expedient for economics to use for its purposes the results of psychological research. This has indeed been done, but it has been done less than one should have been led to expect for only a few primitive facts and rules of experience have passed from the one doctrine to the other. "Every layman knows the whole material of the theory of value from his own experience," said Friedrich Wieser (1889: 4) and thus he implied that the idea of marginal utility is owed to empirical introspection rather than to scientific psychology.

Bousquet bases his considerations on a distinction (introduced already by Vilfredo Pareto) that he consistently upholds through his whole investigation: the distinction between the objective and subjective aspects of the history of doctrine. Either (1927: vii-viii) "we study solely the relation in which the theory stands to reality without regard to the reasons which have given birth to it, or to the form which it has assumed; we study whether or not it *agrees with the concrete facts*" —this is the objective viewpoint. Or we take the subjective viewpoint:

> we direct our attention to the form and the origin of the doctrine; we do not then set out to see whether it is objectively correct but seek to give an account of *what the author thought* when he wrote a given passage. We

---

13. Ricardo conformed to the latter conception and it is this that distinguishes classicism from neoclassicism. Cf. the first sentence of the preface to *The Principles*: "The produce of the earth . . . is divided among three classes of the community." The "premises" in psychology were common to Ricardo and Jevons (Bentham), but the economic system had changed between 1810 and 1860 to a merely individualist constitution, and this is the fundamental fact in the formation of economic ideas.

wish to know what motives induced him to formulate it, we are interested in the manner in which he conceived the object of his doctrine, abstracting from its content proper.

Bousquet thus divides the history of doctrine into two disciplines: a history of the scientific spirit and a history of the doctrinal systems. "[T]he facts," he thinks (102-3), "prove the usefulness of our distinction between the objective and subjective aspects of the doctrines. The evolution of the one has absolutely nothing in common with that of the other, and their history is not the same." This is most clearly manifest in the discussion of Walras and Pareto: "[F]rom the material point of view there is no breach between the economics of Pareto and of Walras: objectively we must speak of a Walras-Pareto theory; subjectively these two authors are diametrically opposed" (241), for Walras's ideas sprang from practical motives, those of Pareto from pure will to perception. The picture differs fundamentally according to the side from which we approach it:

> If we wish to know the way in which positive knowledge has been accumulated, the study of the objective contributions of the different doctrines alone is interesting. . . . It is a history of the progress of the economic . . . science which we would thus have to study. . . . The investigation of the subjective concepts of the authors on the other hand is of a psychological nature, it has for its object man with his motives. (1927: x)

Bousquet intends to deal mainly with this latter aspect. "We endeavor in the present Essay" he says (90), "to give an outline of the subjective tendencies which have governed economics."

Bousquet devotes himself to this study starting from the conviction that the development of economic thought reached its climax in the modern marginal utility and equilibrium theory which treats its subject in the manner of the natural sciences.

> The long psychological evolution which economic thought has gone through since Columella and St. Thomas Aquinas is accomplished in Menger and Pareto. Both . . . teach . . . that Political Economy, having become the economic science, should search only for the truth; no practical, ethical, or philosophical, tendency should disturb the disinterested objectivity of the economist. As in the physical sciences the student investigates . . . the concrete reality of the social world exclusively in order to discover its laws;

this is the only aim which he will set . . . to his thought" (1927: 213; cf. also 242 et seq.)

Bousquet now turns to the question whether, and to what degree, the thinkers of the past adopted this attitude of disinterested search for truth, from pure will to perception, which he regards as alone scientific, and judges the different views according to his preconceived ideal. He thus follows the same procedure as Gide and Rist and, like them, he sees in the development an approximation (not indeed a steady, but on the whole a progressive approximation) to his ideal: "The evolution towards a more and more scientific mind is a general phenomenon; it is to be found in all the . . . sciences" (1927: 313).[14] To him also the present is the perfection of the past: "[S]ubjectively and objectively the mathematical system of equilibrium is the crowning of modern economic theory" (242-43). But unlike Gide and Rist he has no doubt that this development of the science toward the present view is only the reflection of the development of life toward the present reality: "In this Essay," he says (40, footnote 2), "we consider mainly the psychological evolution towards the objective point of view in the investigation of scientific problems. It need not be emphasized that this evolution stands in relation to social evolution," an aspect that he does not wish to follow further. In these words lies implicitly an acknowledgment of the historical relativity of the changing motivation of scientific work, which Bousquet in the end acknowledges even explicitly in ranging the "sentiment de la science" as a newer but not higher motive of study beside the "sentiment de l'intérêt personnel, sentiment religieux, sentiment philanthropique ou de la haine des classes" and so on (297 et seq.).

The result of Bousquet's investigations consists in the realization that the scientific spirit, as he understands it, is hardly perceivable in political economy before Menger and Pareto. Of the classicists only Cairnes and Cherbuliez satisfy him, both of whom are in time already close to the schools of Vienna and Lausanne. Among the older

---

14. In a comparison, reminiscent of an almost literally identical simile used by Bousquet, Roscher had said as early as 1851: "As alchemy preceded chemistry and astrology astronomy, so socialism preceded economics proper" (*Zur Geschichte der englischen Volkswirtschaftslehre*, 120). How widespread is the conceited belief of men that they are more clever than their ancestors!

theoreticians he finds only in Senior and Cantillon, to a less degree in Ricardo, Say, and Smith, the conception that he regards as true. Two questions the critic has to raise with regard to this opinion: is it correct? The answer is a simple yes! And: is it fruitful? The answer is a decided no!

The very fact that the postulate: economic science should treat its matter in the same disinterested spirit as crystallography, which first appears after 1860, proves that it is senseless to seek such an attitude prior to this time. It is only possible after the economic system of exchange economy is fully developed and thus presents an aspect analogous to that of other equilibrium systems as they appear in nature. To state this is the task of the historian. And it is only possible as long as the economic equilibrium remains on the whole undisturbed, as long as the illusion is not destroyed that the economic system is a cosmos like the universe. To state this is the task of the theoretician. A theory of crises in the vein of the natural sciences is impossible—here we cannot avoid comparing the "Is" of the disturbance with the "Ought" of the order—unless we blame the sunspots!

But in seeking Pareto's ideas in the eighteenth century, Bousquet does not only err historically—he errs even in principle! For what is it that he does? He looks for the spirit of the natural sciences in the social sciences! No wonder that he cannot find it. The attitude of man, of real man of flesh and blood, to the phenomena of society is necessarily different from that to the phenomena of nature. If Bousquet raises the puritan postulate (1927: 126): "The expulsion of sentiment should be pursued in sociology as in physics or in biology," he demands the impossible. His *homo scientificus* would be a paler ghost than the much condemned *homo oeconomicus*: for the *homo oeconomicus* rests partly on the "Is," the *homo scientificus* entirely on the "Ought." The former is a (never wholly achieved) reality, the latter would at best be a (never wholly achievable) ideal. The laws that determine the rotation of the heavenly bodies may interest us, but in the laws that regulate the distribution of incomes, we are necessarily interested. Nobody will think of calling the order of the stars good or bad, but everybody has his opinion on whether the order of the human world is right or wrong. No will to objectivity can change this fact; even the most objective person somehow and at some time judges on socioeconomic problems. While even the most interested will never and in no way judge natural phenomena. Obviously, what in the one case is sense, is in the other nonsense.

Well, Bousquet will say, but these subjective judgments are no science—science is only concerned with the "Is," but not with the "Ought." Granted! But we must seek the intellectual reflection of the "Is" everywhere it can be found.[15] If the mercantilists said that the state *should* endeavor to allure gold into the country, they said at the same time: there is—in comparison to the needs of circulation—too little gold in the land. If the physiocrats said that the export of grain *should* be free in order to raise the price of wheat, they said at the same time: if and as long as the export of grain is not free the price of wheat *is* lower than the free play of the market would make it. Is this not a scientific statement? Indeed! Every fruitful idea of economic policy has a definite perception of economic theory at its roots.[16] "Before thinking of procuring an abundant revenue to the people . . . the economist pursues and seizes purely scientific truths," says Walras (1938: 13 et seq.). "Pursues"—and not "should pursue"—the connection is plainly necessary.

Bousquet is certainly not wrong in demanding *pro futuro* [for the future] that pure and applied economics should be kept apart: *pro praeterito* [before proceeding] the historian of economic thought must make this separation himself. He must not simply dismiss Sismondi

---

15. Bousquet says (p. 182): "Le Play . . . opines . . . that it is necessary to know the facts before wishing to reform them. . . . Thanks to this idea he has left to us very remarkable studies"—but this is true of hundreds of others who all have a claim to a place in our science!

16. If Adam Müller in one passage (cited in Bousquet 1927: 147) says that rational agriculture is a source of sin and injustice (and must therefore be rejected) because it puts labor, money, and man in the place of God, even these words contain a scientifically correct, though hidden, perception: the perception that rational agriculture (with intense application of capital and labor) is, under the given conditions, impracticable in Germany—and this opinion was quite correct in view of the scanty population of the territory under consideration and its lack of industry.

or Marx as unscientific[17] because they combine pure perception and practical postulates. He must isolate and describe the one and push the other aside; only so does he secure a comprehensive view of development. In the end a historian who absolutely followed Bousquet's principles could not act otherwise: Cherbuliez, so highly praised by Bousquet, wrote not only his strictly disinterested study "Précis de la Science Economique" but also—what his admirer does not know or does not mention—a passionate polemic that bears the characteristic title "*Le socialisme, c'est la barbarie!*" Here Bousquet would have to advocate the inclusion of one work in the history of the science and the exclusion of the other. But whether we separate different books of one author, or different chapters in one book (as in Smith; see Bousquet 1927: 60 et seq.), or different sentences in one chapter, or different parts in one sentence, is fundamentally the same: in the thinking brain of the living man all thoughts dwell together—thoughts which, if concerned with nature are always disinterested, if concerned with society will always comprise perceptions as well as judgments.

Bousquet himself indeed admitted that the historian has to seek the perceptions where they can be found: "Le *Promessi Sposi*" he says in his charming way, yet strongly exaggerating, "contain more economic science than all the works of Fourier, Proudhon, Bastiat and the romantic school together" (1927: 140, note 2). And he also felt that the problem mainly investigated by him, the problem of the subjective attitude of the scholars toward science is not so important as the question of the objective contributions to it.   "It is in the aim envisaged that the divergence between scientific and unscientific theory will become visible" (293)—but not what the thinkers of the past have

---

17. On the other hand Bousquet is undoubtedly right in demanding the exclusion of poets like Tolstoy, Ruskin, and the like. Here the science, *our* science, has indeed nothing to glean—here is no perception, but only fancy. It would perhaps be proper to divide the whole of the development into three parts: a history of economic theory (description of the perceptions); a history of economic and social politics (description of the ideas that aim at an improvement of economic life but rest on perceptions); and lastly a history of social ideals (which would deal with the literature aptly labeled "political novels").

willed, what they have *achieved* must interest us.[18] Thus, Bousquet himself says of the arch-fantasist Fourier: "It is of little consequence that, speaking subjectively, we have before us a lunatic; economic science should concentrate on the objective construction of the theory" (189).

Now as regards this second, objective aspect of the history of economic doctrine, Bousquet, rising high above men like Gide and Schumpeter, arrived at the true insight that science and reality develop side by side. He almost advances to the notion of relative truth: "The theories of [a] preclassical scientific economics would not have been analogous to ours and would still have been true" (1927: 262). In three instructive examples, the theory of equilibrium, the principle of population, and the doctrine of money and exchanges, he proves how the change of the facts to be interpreted necessarily caused a change of the interpreting thought. "It is not impossible," he says, thus implicitly outlining the mission of future historians (267), "to recognize in the scientific doctrines the evolution of facts;"[19] and in a simile; "an economic theory is something closely akin to the anatomic description of an embryo, it is only true for a given time." What he says of the present is to a still higher degree applicable to the past: "In order to understand political economy, it is necessary solidly to found it on the realities of practical life" (6).

With this postulate Bousquet stands halfway between historians like Gonnard and Salin who represent the ideas merely in their connections with intellectual history, and the historians who must now be

---

18. In the Marshall Library at Cambridge hangs an old picture representing the poverty-molded face of a workman of early English capitalism. This picture, it is said, induced Alfred Marshall to change from mathematics to economics. Marshall saw it in a curiosity shop and was attracted by its power; it seemed to him to express all the misery of the proletarians' life and made him devote his future to the study of the means for the reformation of social conditions. Thus, from the "unscientific" "sentiment philanthropique" arise great scientific achievements. Bousquet's postulate would close the purest source that leads ever-new students to political economy.

19. Bousquet himself, however, did not advance in this direction. With regard to the mercantilists he follows Sombart's correct interpretation (11, footnote), but the physiocrats he simply reproaches with error (50). Cf. also his similar remarks on Ricardo (85 et seq.) and Marx (121), neither of whom is understood from his time.

discussed, historians like Roscher who indeed view the theories against the background of the material conditions of their time but do not advance to any consistent causal interpretation.

To this group belongs Luigi Cossa. He expressed himself in a positive sense, but with great restraint, on the influence of contemporary history on economic theories. This is manifest in his very definition of the history of socioeconomic doctrines. "The history of political economy is a critical account of the origin and progress of economic theories considered in relation to social conditions, ideas, and institutions" (Cossa 1893: 113). This connection between theories and facts he regards as twofold: (1) the facts to a large degree determine thinking and thought; (2) the theories react on reality and mold it, mainly by suggesting legal and administrative measures. So far so good.

Yet a closer examination of Cossa's treatise proves *in extenso* that he had no exact idea of the concatenation between economic theory and economic life. He sees reality only as one determining element beside, or even after, the intellectual factor. Thus, he says that before the thirteenth century there was no developed economics because: (1) religious ideas were predominant; (2) there was a strong reaction against the materialism of heathen antiquity; (3) natural economy prevailed; (4) international trade had but little importance; and (5) the mundane sciences were in decay. In this manner his argument usually proceeds (cf., e.g., 1893: 168 et seq., 290, 304, etc.). And although he always takes economic reality into account, he never makes clear the decisive influence that it exercised on the formation of ideas.

This is also the reason why Cossa's appreciation of mercantilism, although well weighed (1893: 194 et seq.) still misses the point (208 et seq.). In the end he accuses the mercantilists of having built their doctrine on errors:[20]

> Undoubtedly the mercantilists grossly exaggerated the importance of money, not understanding that its function was purely instrumental. . . . They considered that the balance of trade, and the balance of debits and credits, were convertible, and it therefore never dawned upon them that a nation might go on for a long time importing goods of greater value than those it

---

20. Cf. especially 1893: 239. "[T]heir works, following as they do the false lines drawn by the . . . legislation of the day."

exported without the least danger of exhausting its stores of the precious metals in the process. . . . [T]heir doctrine that exports must exceed imports . . . involved the absurd identification of the interest of the nation at large with those of one class only, the trading class.

Had Cossa's study of contemporary conditions been more profound, he would have come to a different view of the overestimation of money as well as of the confusion of the balances of trade and payments or of the interests of the trading class and those of the nation. To say in brief what will be more fully explained in its proper place: money was at that time of outstanding importance not only in theory, but also in practice, as all tended to the extension of market economy, which seemed impossible without increasing circulation. The balance of payments was then hardly different from the balance of trade,[21] especially as international migration of capital was still not extensive; and lastly trade and manufacture necessarily appeared as more important for national welfare than agriculture, which—still under feudal restrictions—seemed to exclude all progress of production.

Similarly we have to value Cossa's concluding judgment of the physiocratic system. He conscientiously separates the achievements of Quesnay's school from their mistakes. The achievements include: a clear idea of capital, a sense of the importance of agriculture, and the overcoming of the faith in the unlimited power of the state. The mistakes include: a false belief in timeless laws of nature and in the exclusive productivity of the soil, the neglect of the consumer's interest, and the conception of the laissez-faire principle as an axiom. But he shows neither the achievements nor the mistakes of the physiocrats in their dependence upon the time and its problems. "[T]hey stand convicted of many errors" (1893: 271)—this is the verdict at which he finally arrives.

As for the post-physiocratic ideas, Cossa did not search at all for their historical causes. Only in his treatment of Malthus he puts

---

21. Thomas Mun clearly perceived the difference between the balance of trade and the balance of payments. He goes so far as to demand the inclusion of the money spent abroad for briberies by secret diplomacy and of the expenditure of espionage agents; but even his analysis of the international system of payments which aims at completeness shows that it was entirely determined by the commercial exchanges.

forward some sort of explanation. If Cossa said of the history of economic doctrine: "It does not limit itself to a simple chronological exposition of theories, but undertakes to appreciate their absolute and *relative* worth" (1893: 113 [emphasis added]), he has laid down a program but has inadequately carried it out.

Wilhelm Roscher clearly realized that a purely intellectual description of the development of political economy must always remain unsatisfactory. "A mere history of doctrine as is possible for such sciences as mathematics," he says in the preface to his work, "would bear little fruit for economics. Its theories, whether they aim merely at the explanation or also at the improvement of reality, will only be understood by those who know this reality itself" (1874: v). And in another place (659) he expresses the conviction that "the judgment of men on reality" is determined "by this very reality." Yet even Roscher does not aim at a causal connection between reality and science; he at best juxtaposes the two,[22] brings the science into the framework of contemporary facts, but does not trace any interconnections. Sometimes indeed he indicates that the historical concept requires us "to put . . . the intellectual causes above the material results" (120)—a concept that Roscher, however, employs as little in his investigation as the deduction of the theories from reality postulated in other contexts.[23]

But although Roscher did not consistently show how the different dogmas originated in the conditions of their time, he still propounded occasional explanations that are of high value. The principle that should have governed the whole is usefully applied in some parts of

---

22. To this treatise are applicable to a still higher degree Ingram's words on the "System der Volkswirtschaft": "the dogmatic and historical matter are rather juxtaposed than vitally combined" (1915: 201).

23. Sometimes again he expresses the postulate that idealistic and realistic conception should go together. Thus, he says of Canon law (1874: 11): "This whole system of economic doctrine and economic policy is to be explained as much from the . . . characteristics of medieval economic life as from the doctrines of the Christian religion. The one gave as it were the drawing, the other the colors of the picture." But again, these words do not express a fundamental principle of Roscher, but only an idea put forward in passing, which is not followed farther—very much to the detriment of the whole book!

his treatise, and where this is the case, it proves its strength. His discussion of the "relative truth of Colbertism" is of this kind (1874: 232 et seq.). "The postulates of the mercantile system," he says, and here his historicism shows its best side, "need not be excused by the unavoidable imperfection of any commencing science. Still less will he who is historically educated believe that a doctrine which for centuries governed . . . in theory and practice rested on a mere error. No, they were mainly demands which . . . corresponded to a real need," to a necessity of the time from which they must be comprehended. Five points, he says, the mercantilists seem to us to have overestimated, and he gives the reasons for this overestimation: (1) the number of people (a growing population could then only be an incentive and help to economic life); (2) the mass of money (the contemporary progress from natural to money economy necessarily increased the demand for money); (3) foreign trade (Italy, Holland, France, and England possessed no gold and silver mines of their own so that they could obtain the precious metals only by an active foreign trade); (4) the manufacturing trades (toward the end of the economic Middle Ages when the rural elements so heavily outweighed towns and trades a mature and flourishing state of national economy, which is inconceivable without sound industry, could be fostered by making the export of raw materials and the import of manufactured goods more difficult, thus causing the productive forces to turn toward manufacture); and (5) the activities of the state (the state is called upon to intervene as an educator where the spontaneous development of industry is hampered by superior competition outside, and the egotism of aristocratic classes within, the state). Thus, where others, grossly misunderstanding mercantilism, speak of its errors, Roscher grasped its historical meaning: to be the guide of national economy toward modern capitalism, and herein lies the highest achievement of his *Geschichte der Nationalökonomik*.

Similarly Roscher rightly understood the historical place of Adam Smith. He is of the opinion that every period of economic greatness has two strictly distinguishable phases: a "David's period," characterized by youthful joy in all things new, and a "Solomon's period," which usually brings satiety and opens the eyes to the blemishes of the system. Now it is "the first half of economic prime which is expressed in his writings; just as it was to be found in the contemporary practice of his people" (1874: 596). And all the qualities of Adam Smith's economics, which Roscher calls the "theory of a highly developed national economy," he interprets from his position in, and with regard to, his time.

In opposition to Eugen Dühring and in agreement with Wilhelm Roscher, Hugo Eisenhart in his book expressed the conviction that "history cannot . . . possibly make itself serviceable to a purely theoretical curiosity" (1881: 216) and thus rejected the critical and unhistorical treatment of the intellectual work of the past from the viewpoint of present ideas taken as absolute and infallible. He thinks that "the science in all its great and epochmaking figures, even where it . . . believed itself to be pronouncing general truths, only formulated the needs of its age in a more or less correct way" (218) and that "even great and epochmaking errors never came into being without a kernel of relative truth well worth attention" (205). He goes indeed so far as to regard the history of economic theories as a part of general economic history. A comprehensive history of "real economy," that is, of economic reality, should, according to his view, "absorb into its broader scope the history of economic science . . . in its mutual action and reaction on life struggling for self-understanding" (219), and he assigns to the historical school the task of creating a work of this kind.

The question that directly interests us here, is, of course, how far Eisenhart himself in his study disclosed the concatenation between science and reality, in other words: how far he discovered the relative truth of the individual dogmas. If we go through his work we find with every theoretical system that he regards as essential a description of the factual conditions that governed the respective period: thus he gives us pictures of the real background of mercantilism (1881: 19), physiocracy (30), Adam Smith (42), Malthus (78), Ricardo (82), Sismondi (104), List (138), Carey (178), and Rodbertus (201). But these descriptions—apart from the fact that they are in parts much too narrow to be capable of explaining the essential points, especially in the case of the physiocratic system[24]—convey more an idea of the atmosphere in which the theories have formed themselves than of the roots from which they have sprung. The connection of life and

---

24. On the other hand, the passages on Sismondi and List are very good.

thought is not sufficiently exact to be satisfactory.   Thus, even Eisenhart did not advance beyond a purely descriptive achievement.

7

The Explanatory Approach

The principle suggested by Roscher and pronounced by Eisenhart was made the basis of the investigations by Ingram, Haney, Scott, and Roll. They try to explain all ideas with reference to the period of their origin, and this consistency in their endeavor distinguishes them from the group just considered. Not even they, it is true, arrived in all points at a satisfactory solution of the outstanding problems. Yet nowhere has the science so far been capable of establishing more advanced positions.

The pioneer of the concept that it is the task of the historiography of doctrine to reach, beyond mere description, a causal interpretation of the economic theories of the past, was John Kells Ingram. The editor of Ingram's work, Richard T. Ely, rightly says: "Perhaps the main guiding thread in Ingram's social and economic philosophy was the idea of evolution. . . . Now this idea of evolution means also the idea of *relativity*. . . . [M]en cannot be understood unless they are brought into connection with the life of their own country and their own age" (Ingram 1915: vii). Ingram himself says the same thing. In one place he calls (231) "the relativity both of economic institutions and of economic thought, arising from their dependence on varying social conditions" the basic idea of the historical school, his adherence to which he is never tired of emphasizing. And the following words indicate his conviction:

> The history of Political Economy must of course be distinguished from the economic history of mankind. . . . But these two branches of research, though distinct, yet stand in the closest relation to each other. The rise and the form of economic doctrines have been largely conditioned by the practical situation, needs and tendencies of the corresponding epochs. . . . [E]very thinker, however in some respects he may stand above or before his contemporaries, is yet a child of his time, and cannot be isolated from the social medium in which he lives and moves. (2)

In accordance with this fundamental attitude Ingram seeks to fulfil his mission "by tracing historically, and from a general point of view, the course of speculation regarding economic phenomena, and contemplating the successive forms of opinion concerning them in relation to the periods at which they were respectively evolved" (1). It is his program "to point out the manner in which the respective features of the several successive modern phases [of economic history] find their counterpart and reflection in the historical development of economic speculation" (32).

This program Ingram not only outlined but also executed. To illustrate and prove this, the greater part of his work would have to be reproduced. It may suffice to mention that he makes the disinclination of antiquity towards chrematistics and its predilection for the institution of slavery, especially Plato's ideal world, comprehensible from their time; he causally explains the canonist prohibition of interest; he unveils the historical sense of mercantilism, especially (to use a term of Mises) its interventionism;[1] he depicts the main features of the physiocratic doctrine as products of prerevolutionary France; and he regards, and teaches the reader to regard, even Adam Smith as a child of his time. His deductions are not always exact and not always cogent, but we must not forget that he was the first who

---

1. Yet Ingram's description of mercantilism is not wholly satisfactory; not only does he say too little on its principle of population, but he explains the entire ideology too much from the political side and too little from economy proper. In the text, however, only the principle and method are under consideration, and these Ingram certainly understood rightly, even though some of his positive assertions may be doubtful.

ventured to advance so far.

The ideas of the nineteenth century, however, Ingram did not try to interpret causally. Ricardo's theory, for example, which is indeed a clear mirror of its time, is (like historicism) discussed more than explained. This is the more surprising since Walter Bagehot had, in his *Economic Studies* published in 1880, already revealed the historical conditions on which the Ricardian system had rested. The reason for Ingram's unhistorical procedure in this respect obviously lies in the fact that he, who was born in 1823, regarded the classical school as the dominant doctrine of the present; and the ideas of the present we do not explain—we accept or reject them, and we cannot justly expect Ingram to deviate from this natural attitude that is simply general and human.

Ingram also discussed the relation of the history of economic doctrine to the general history of intellectual evolution and did not fail to realize how closely the two disciplines belong together.

> The movement of economic thought is constantly and powerfully affected by the prevalent mode of thinking, and even the habitual tone of sentiment. . . . All the intellectual manifestations of a period in relation to human questions have a kindred character, and bear a certain stamp of homogeneity, which is vaguely present to our minds when we speak of the spirit of the age. (1915: 3)

But this relation of the spirit of the age to economic thought is to Ingram not a connection of cause and effect, as if the economic dogmas issued from it. This is proved by his whole work. He represents the economic theories of the past in the framework of the intellectual life of the individual periods, but he seeks their reason always in economic reality and nowhere else.

Similarly psychology and characterology are not, or only in a very, very restricted sense, regarded as auxiliary disciplines of the historiography of economic doctrine:

> The particular situation and tendencies of the several thinkers whose names are associated with economic doctrines have, of course, modified in a greater or less degree the spirit or form of those doctrines. Their relation to special predecessors, their native temperament, their early training, their religious prepossessions and political partialities, have all had their effects . . . but, in the main, they are . . . secondary and subordinate. . . . [T]he

> constructors of theories must be regarded as organs of a common
> intellectual and social movement. (1915: 4-5)

The close connection between economic history on the one hand and
the history of economic thought on the other was particularly
emphasized by Haney who in this question as in many others followed
Ingram's example. "That men's thoughts depend largely upon their
surroundings, no one doubts. And so it is that economic ideas, to say
nothing of systems of economics, are colored and limited—determined
sometimes—by industrial environment" (Haney 1936: 4).[2] However,
"this interaction is reciprocal; for opinions and theories once formed
are often tenaciously adhered to, and may become a determining
element in their turn" (4). In another place we read: "Before we can
call medieval thinkers, blockheads, on the ground that they condemned
interest-taking, we must examine their premises and the circumstances
of those premises. Men being in part creatures of their environment,
their thought is often guided and limited by the changing phenomena
with which they are confronted" (6). And Haney rightly explains that
reality not only confronts the theoretician with the problems with
which he has to grapple, but also (at least partly) shows the ways that
he must follow toward his aim.

Yet Haney ascribes only limited importance to the idea of the
relativity of scientific perceptions and thoughts.

> It would be a mistake to maintain that there are no absolute general
> principles, or that all economic thought is the product of the economic
> environment. In fact, in emphasizing the relativity of economic doctrine,
> men have often been too prone to overlook the element of direct continuity,
> which has handed down the theories of individual thinkers or groups of
> thinkers to successors, so connecting one time or place with another in a
> more absolute way. (1936: 769)

It is not the controversy between adherents and adversaries of
historicism, as to whether there are fixed laws in economic life, which
is here considered: for in this controversy the issue was only whether
or not such laws exist *within modern national economy*. In so far as

---

2. Excellent is Haney's remark on the utopias. "'Utopias' are to be considered in part
as protests arising in periods of social crisis and depression" (Haney 1936: 114).

Haney answers this question in the affirmative, he may expect today general assent. For national economy—however much it may have altered in the two centuries of its existence—is historically a whole. The foundations of its character have changed but little, and so far as these foundations are concerned we may believe in certain laws that time and space may perhaps modify, but not overthrow. Thuenen's doctrine of the localization of agricultural production proves correct everywhere where agriculture is governed by the calculating and rational principles of an exchange economy—it was as true in the eighteenth as it is in the twentieth century, it is as true in Germany as in China or Brazil.

But Haney maintains more. He believes in the continuity of ideas in a wider sense, in a continuity beyond the borders of historical epochs. He cites as examples the transmission of the concept of natural philosophy from the Greeks through the Romans and schoolmen to the physiocrats and classicists; the continuation of the discussions on the barrenness of money from Aristotle to the mercantilists of 1690; and the influence of the Greek ideas concerning labor on Cicero, through Cicero on Hutcheson, and through Hutcheson on Smith. But these examples cannot support Haney's thesis; indeed, they prove, if we regard them more closely, the opposite.

The belief in the existence of an ideal natural law in fact outlasted the centuries; and it will outlast centuries even in times to come. So long as individual men and social groups are dissatisfied with the existing social order, the positive law, which is condemned, will be contrasted with a higher law exalted above all judgment. This is manifest in the revolutionary movements of the present. Thus, we may indeed call the idea of natural law eternal. But only the form, or rather the name, is unchangeable. The content changes with the centuries. "This entirely formal idea," Gonnard rightly says (1930: 14 et seq.), "has constituted a sort of mould through which afterwards the most contrary ideas were destined to flow." The natural philosophy of antiquity was essentially different from that of the Middle Ages, the natural philosophy of the Middle Ages from that of modern times: as different as ancient, medieval, and modern society.

Aristotle's idea of the barrenness of money and Cicero's idea of the importance of labor were certainly operative until the very beginning of the present age. But even these ideas were not independent of time and space; they arose and existed only in a society in which capital did not yet play the leading part, and they had to disappear, as soon as this had changed.

That Haney did not follow the idea of relativity and development to the end is manifest also in the fact that he regards the theories of the past always in the light of three pairs of notions that he conceives as absolute: idealism and materialism, individualism and societism, optimism and pessimism. Idealism he views as generally connected with societism and optimism, materialism with individualism and pessimism. Obviously such a conception must contain the danger of offering violence to the manifoldness of history. Haney is certainly right in endeavoring to find the connections between economics and philosophy. But he should conceive this concatenation, in accordance with his subject matter, not systematically but historically. It is of high value to investigate the relations between Hobbes and Petty, Kant and Smith, Hegel and Marx, and Fechner and Menger, but what sense would there be in discussing the question whether Marshall was an idealist or a materialist? The notions by which Haney here seeks to judge are brought to the science from outside, not developed from within, and are therefore ill-suited to their purpose.

A thorough investigation of the relations between the socioeconomic dogmas and the philosophical teachings above them as well as the economic circumstances below them is, for the rest, entirely within Haney's plan since he regards the theories on economy and society as influenced by, and conditioned from, both sides. He endeavored to render the ideas—all ideas—comprehensible from the real and, at the same time, from the ideal point of view, and especially the time before Mill is made accessible to the understanding of the present. But he does not trouble to go into details. He is more interested in the doctrinal contents of the theories and their achievements than in their causation, and although the thoughts propounded up to about 1870 are (sometimes admirably) placed in their historical setting, he does not attempt any interpretation covering all aspects, the fundamental necessity of which he has realized and the suitable method of which he has described.

William A. Scott's *The Development of Economics* also belongs to the tradition that started with Ingram, as the following words from the author's preface will serve to show: "In its development economics has passed through several stages, in each one of which the thinking of the past has been influenced and modified by the economic and social conditions of the period and by thinking in allied and sometimes quite remote fields" (Scott 1933: v). More as to his fundamental attitude Scott does not explicitly say. Neither does the text of the book offer many indications. On Boisguillebert, Vauban, and Cantillon we read (32): "These men were genuine products of the intellectual, social, and political conditions of the period." Do these words imply the view that different writers stood to a different degree under the influence of their time, that the connection between economic life and economic theory is sometimes closer, sometimes looser? A remark on Rodbertus and Marx seems to support this assumption. "The development of a new type of socialism in Germany," Scott says (277 et seq.), "is due more to the genius of two men than to the condition of the country, though the latter furnished the environment in which these men grew up and doubtless determined the direction of their thought." But on the other hand Scott precedes the description of any group of theories with an account of its conditions in contemporary history, thus implicitly admitting that this is everywhere necessary for a true understanding, and he emphasizes with special consistency that even the theory of marginal utility must be interpreted historically (without, however, being able to show how). Before entering upon the discussion of Karl Menger's opinions he says (326):

> To point out the most significant trends in economics during the last half-century (i.e. since the seventies) is difficult, perhaps impossible. . . . Doubtless equally competent observers and students would differ regarding this matter. All would agree, however, that this science has been influenced and to a degree modified by the changes in economic conditions.

Thus, Scott regards his principle as capable of general application, without, however, always making use of it.

Scott regards mercantilism from two points of view: on the one hand as a national policy, on the other as a theoretical system. As to the first side of mercantilism Scott in his interpretation follows Gustav Schmoller, but with the difference that he rightly brings the economic element into the foreground and does not, like Schmoller, represent the political factor as primary. European civilization, according to this thesis, traversed a progressive course from smaller to larger economic units and thereby passed the stages of (family, tribal) town and territorial economy. Scott, in agreement with Schmoller, sees the essence of mercantilism "in the total transformation of society and its organization, as well as of the state and its institutions, in the replacing of a local and territorial economic policy by that of the national state" (1933: 7). In so far as Scott regards the formation of national economy as decisive and not the formation of the national state he certainly brought to light the true kernel in Schmoller's thesis. He admirably describes the transition from the medieval order under which self-sufficing towns and manors governed economic life, to the partly national, but partly already international, economic system of the seventeenth century, in other words: the background of the mercantilistic idea! Nevertheless Scott is in the end incapable of fully overcoming the heritage of Schmoller; he interprets the sense of the monetary and foreign trade theory of mercantilism after all only from the political side:

> [T]he desire to build up a strong navy as an instrument of national defense and exploitation furnishes the key to a large part of the economic history of the time. . . . For the acquisition and maintenance of the ships . . . there was needed a continuous increase of the national revenues and of the volume of precious metals in circulation. By this time England had definitely passed into the stage of money economy. Every increase in the revenue needs of the state, therefore, correspondingly increased the need for coin, and the state's needs . . . could not be met unless the volume of the circulation was constantly enlarged. (15)

In this way the whole theory of the mercantile system is interpreted; an illustration is afforded by the treatment of the—generally neglected—wages principle of the doctrine: "When the ideals of the nation were military aggrandizement and the exploitation of new countries, a necessary consequence of this doctrine was the conviction that wages should be low and food cheap" (18). Scott here wrongly connects politics and economic theory as cause and effect. Certainly they belong intimately together as expressions of the same epoch, but it is not possible to discover a causal bond as Scott does. It was not to increase the ability of the people to pay taxes that the mercantilists advocated an active trade-balance, this aim (especially in the west) was always only secondary, but to foster the welfare of the nation—the welfare depending upon the development of market economy, which, in its turn, presupposed unhampered monetary circulation. It was not to make military success possible that the mercantilists favored low wages, but to support industrial production. It was not "because military power was directly proportional to population," but because "a rapid increase in the number of the people meant a rapidly increasing supply of labor, which was . . . essential to low wages" (18) that they formed the principle of a policy of population, the end of which was the substantial increase of the number of the people. We must not try to explain economic theory from political practice as does Schmoller to whom Scott too closely adheres, however much he shifts the stress to the economic factor: economic theory is the reflection of economic reality, and here alone exists a relation of cause and effect. This criticism of details, however, is not meant to deny or lessen the general merit of Scott in having expounded the relative correctness of the mercantilist teaching for its period: "Criticism of the mercantile system . . . would be easy but useless. . . . When considered with reference to the problems of the time in which it flourished . . . it is difficult if not impossible to find fault with the system" (25)—a fundamentally incontestable opinion!

Physiocracy Scott regards as a "reaction against Mercantilism in France," for, however applicable to its time, "at a later period the mercantile policy became a hindrance" (1933: 27). Here, too, he endeavors to bring the contemporary conditions to life and gives a description of the *Ancien Régime* on the basis of Taine's classical model.[3] He shows the intimate relations between the physiocrats and the *classe des proprietaires* [landowners] whose property in the soil was conceived as a sort of divine institution. And starting from here he explains the doctrine of the barrenness of all nonagricultural production. "In explanation of this attitude may be mentioned the fact that labor did not have in their eyes the dignity it possesses in ours. It is not productive, not even that of the cultivator. In agriculture nature does the producing, not labor" (50). Hence, Scott believes that the doctrine of the physiocrats can be deduced from aristocratic

---

3. Today, however, Taine no longer exercises his former authority. Aulard's life-work has caused many problems to appear in a new light.

contempt for manual work. Interesting though this attempt at an explanation may be, it is impossible to accept it; for Quesnay's life fell within a period in which England's king posed as Farmer George and Austria's emperor laid his hand, symbolically as it were, to a plow, in the time of a sentiment, the gist of which Quesnay himself expressed in his famous motto: *Pauvres paysans, pauvre royaume; pauvre royaume, pauvre roi*! No, the physiocrats had no contempt for the husbandman, they did not think of robbing labor of its value. They came to their opinion because they saw that in their world the riches of the rich were derived from agriculture and all industrial activities confined to making the life of the ruling cast more agreeable—to help in spending the revenues that the peasant in the sweat of his brow acquired for his superiors.

Similarly Scott is not very happy in his interpretation of the great Adam Smith. "In the eighteenth century," he says (1933: 56-57), "evidence . . . of the growth of individual initiative and enterprise appear on every hand. . . . The interpreter of the economic life of this new epoch as well as a product of it was Adam Smith, the founder of the classical political economy." Certainly we must understand Smith's liberalism and optimism in this light; but his teachings only become quite comprehensible when we keep in mind that he thought and wrote at a time when the industrial revolution, just beginning in 1776, had not yet changed the character of English economic life and especially had not yet brought about the separation of capitalists and proletarians nor the separation of the capitalists into rising large-scale industrialists and sinking small-scale craftsmen. Smith's doctrine is the counterpart of an undifferentiated and egalitarian society, and this constitutes its whole character.

With regard to the period from 1776 to 1815, Scott appreciates the conditions that characterized it (and its economic theory): on the one hand the uprooting of a rapidly growing mass of people and their transplantation to new industrial centers, on the other hand the constant inability of English agriculture in spite of all intensification to produce adequate supplies. And he follows a fundamental thesis of classicism to its roots in practice: "[T]he doctrine of diminishing returns in agriculture . . . appeared in connection with the debates in Parliament on the corn-laws that took place during the Napoleonic wars" (1933: 97)—a fact noted earlier by Edwin Cannan.[4] But the central doctrine of this period, Ricardo's labor theory of value, and its central problem, the position of (constant) capital, Scott did not interpret from its time. Here appears even an apodictic judgment: "Ricardo's method of treating the relation of profit to value was unsatisfactory. It was a recognition of the problem without any attempt to solve it" (300). Scott indeed describes "a spread of factories and a corresponding decay of the domestic system of industry" (90) between 1776 and 1815, and "the extension of the factory system to the point of dominance in the industrial life of the nation" only for the time between 1815 and 1848, but he fails to show to what stage in the development of machinery Ricardo's teachings correspond, and how they correspond to it. Ricardo's time was already characterized by the contrast of capitalist and workman but not yet by the dominance of the constant capital. Scott's description of industrial development lacks differentiation without which the progress of doctrine cannot be comprehended.

The same is manifest in the treatment of Senior's theory of abstinence. Scott emphasizes that it leads beyond Ricardo's price theory and replaces it by a theory of the costs of production, thus removing the necessity of making exceptions from the general principle. But he does not tell us the real reason for this new doctrine of the process of distribution: the fact that capital (as a means of production) no longer consisted mainly in tools that appear as an accessory of the worker but progressively took the form of stable machines beside which the worker rather must give the impression of being an accessory so that its role in production and distribution clearly demanded a new explanation.

The period between 1815 and 1848 Scott describes as the period of the full development of capitalism with all its light and dark aspects and of the complete victory of liberalism with all its merits and faults. "The influence of the period on political economy . . . can best be seen in the life and writing of John Stuart Mill. . . . His work marked the end of one period and the beginning of another. . . . [It]

---

4. Cf. *A History of the Theories of Production and Distribution in English Political Economy from 1776 to 1848*, 1893: Chap. 5, par. 4. Charles Gide in this point followed Edwin Cannan.

was preeminently a transitional work summing up and expounding what had been done before and opening the way for new developments of the future" (1933: 130, 151-52). Thus, John Stuart Mill's position in intellectual history is certainly aptly described; it is only regrettable that Scott does not show in detail how Mill's work in fact reflected the transitional character of the age.

Since Scott's description of classicism manifests a constant endeavor to harmonize the background of factual history and the foreground of intellectual history and to combine them into a uniform picture, it is disappointing that with Adam Müller and Daniel Raymond he confines himself to a mere account of their views. Indeed, even Friedrich List who undoubtedly can be comprehended only as a child of his time and his country is not treated otherwise. Scott, it is true, says: "[H]is views evolved gradually under the influence of his observations and studies in Germany and the United States" (1933: 200), but he does not explain the nature of List's experiences, although it must be obvious from whence arose the ideas of the advocate of the young industrial countries in their struggle against the superior power of their older competitors.

Scott also views the origin of older historicism only from the point of view of intellectual history. Hegel's philosophy, the cultural historiography of the Goettingen school, and Savigny's doctrine of law seem to him the sources. He says indeed: "[I]n the second quarter of the nineteenth century the increasing importance and complexity of . . . [social and economic] problems invited a reaction" against the abstract and isolating analysis of economic life (1933: 230), but this idea, which suggests the reason for the origin of the historical school, he does not follow any further.

The striking fact that Carey's *The Past, the Present and the Future* (1848) and *The Harmony of Interests* (1852) on the one hand, and Bastiat's *Harmonies Economiques* (1850) on the other propound parallel, if not identical, teachings, although they arose under different conditions, naturally attracts Scott's attention:

> An explanation is suggested by the conditions with which each man was confronted in his own country. . . . The United States was a new country with vast, undeveloped natural resources. . . . Increasing capital and increasing population . . . had always resulted, and to Carey's generation seemed certain in the future to result, in increasing prosperity for all

classes. There was no visible evidence that they ever had produced or were likely ever to produce the consequences predicted by Ricardo and Malthus. (1933: 231)

It was far otherwise in France where existing conditions rather seemed to offer confirmation of Ricardo's and Malthus's teachings. "There was another factor in the situation there, however. Socialistic agitation was rampant and threatening. . . . For a person like Bastiat, who . . . regarded socialism as a dangerous menace, the problem was to convince the public of the advantages of the present order" (232). Thus, he came to the same theories as Carey (we should rather say that he was induced to take over Carey's theories; we may be more severe than Scott as Carey clearly had the priority in time). Anyone who knows both authors, Carey's natural optimism and Bastiat's purposeful apologetics, will certainly feel the truth of Scott's explanation.

If, however, we carry through the comparison between Carey and Bastiat we find—and this must be emphasized in completing Scott's discussion—that the difference is not simply confined to the fact that one was "a domineering, autocratic type of man who believed ardently in protection," while the other appeared to be "a modest, almost peasant type who believed just as ardently in free trade" (1933: 231). The contrast in the conditions from which they started is above all manifest in the relation of soil and people, which was really only a problem to Bastiat (and to the densely populated France), a problem which he believed capable of being solved in a genuinely French way by a distribution of the given space as wide and as uniform as possible.

Scott's attempt to explain Schmoller's descriptive realism is very interesting. "He was the heir of a tradition which dates back to the Cameralists," he says (1933: 509), "who were primarily interested in training young men for the civil service of their respective states and principalities and who were therefore obliged to deal with the facts and conditions with which civil servants were concerned." For this reason, Scott suggests, he moved descriptive economics into the foreground and economic analysis into the background. This interpretation is hardly acceptable, be it only because Schmoller must in the end be conceived as the representative of a worldwide movement that made its appearance also where the science was not serving administrative practice. How does Scott's argument apply to Auguste Comte before Schmoller, and Thorstein Veblen after him? But even if viewed from a narrowly German standpoint the assertion that Schmoller made a theoretical principle of a practical necessity is not tenable. We shall have to delve deeper. Germany comprised the feudal East Prussia and the highly capitalistic Ruhr. It as yet had no idea of political equality but separated its citizens in the system of class franchise into socially severed groups. Thus, in Germany, with its numerous petty states, which in every respect presented a motley picture, a descriptive investigation was an indispensable preliminary to a scientific economics, while in England, which was in every respect much more uniform, economists could at once proceed to abstraction: Schmoller rightly felt that with regard to Germany he had first to create the necessary basis for a well-founded abstraction, and in these preparations he was in the end submerged.

Of all the historians of political economy Scott most persistently strove to conceal his own opinions: it is rarely that we hear him utter a critical remark: "The method of treatment has been," he says of his treatise (1933: vi), "so far as possible, objective, the aim being accurately to present the thought of the writer under discussion rather than the author's reaction to it." This raises the questions as to whether such objectivity is possible, how far this is the case, and how far it may be regarded as desirable.

Perfect objectivity, freedom from valuation in the strict sense in which Max Weber understood the word, is entirely beyond the reach of any historian of political economy. Let us hear Scott's own words: "[O]nly typical and outstanding authors have been selected for treatment, others being either entirely omitted or discussed in their relations to the former" (1933: vi). Does not this will to selection imply a will to criticism? If Scott touches Walras only in a footnote and Jevons in passing, but devotes much space to Menger, he necessarily conveys the impression that he regarded Menger as in some way more important than Jevons and Walras, and the principle of objectivity is violated.

But if in this way a certain implicit critique is unavoidable, nothing has yet been said for or against an explicit and open critique. Should the historian of political economy on this point follow Scott and abstain, in describing the older theories, from all criticism? Yes, in so far as this criticism tends to subject the past to the same standards as the present. No, in so far as the past has been fully understood in its independent life so that the basis for a just judgment is secured. If —to choose an extreme example—a certain writer once suggested (Bousquet 1927: 220) that the invention of the airplane would solve the social problem because the proletariat, now no longer dependent on free soil, will in the future be capable of living on the results of bird hunting, we may state without hesitation that such a view is nonsense. Within the historical interpretation we are allowed to judge, for in the past also there were consistent and inconsistent thinkers, clear and unclear theoreticians, broad- and narrow-minded men. Yet even here scientific historiography will aim at understanding rather than at judgment.

Erich Roll is firmly convinced—and thus he occupies the foremost position that the science has reached—that a really scientific treatment of the history of political economy must build consciously and consistently on the idea of causality. "The approach of this book," he says of his work, "is based on the principle that the appearance of certain ideas is not fortuitous, but dependent upon causes which can be discovered." And he rightly adds: "This conviction underlies all scientific investigation; without it nothing but mysticism can result." It is economic reality in which Roll seeks the roots of economic ideas: "Economic theories are always, though often tortuously, related to economic practice. Only a study of the interplay between objective conditions and the theorizing of man can provide a guide through the conflict of ideas. . . . [T]he economic structure of any given epoch and the changes which it undergoes are the *ultimate* determinants of economic thinking" (Roll 1938: 14, 16), even if other factors as ideological tradition and practical politics exert some influence beside them.

Roll's book, precisely because it applies the idea of causality to the history of political economy and even tends to make it the foundation of the investigation of development, is the last word of science in our special discipline. In theory Roll has reached perfect clarity, but did he perfectly understand practice? This must now be investigated.

Roll tries to comprehend mercantilism as the doctrine of commercial capitalism and he rightly rejects the view propounded by Schmoller to the effect that it can be interpreted from a narrowly political standpoint (as the doctrine of the means to the formation and strengthening of the national state).[5] He proves that the state and economy of that time reacted upon each other: trade strengthened the state (by the creation of a public treasure) and the state strengthened trade (by the protection and expansion of its markets). And he endeavors to deduce the main thesis of mercantilism from reality. "[A] high regard for money," he states (1938: 67), "was common to all mercantilists. They looked upon the economic process from the point of view of the primitive stage which capitalism had reached—its commercial phase—and were thus led to identify money and capital." This identification Roll regards as decisive; it is not incomprehensible from its time. "[T]his popular notion is explained by the fact that treasure—that is, money—is the earliest form of wealth, once private exchange and a medium of exchange have become established social institutions" (66). The mercantilist era "knew capital only in its primitive monetary form, and the confusion which was later so much derided was perfectly compatible with its own economic experience" (69).

Yet, in spite of his will to comprehend the theory of mercantilism, and in spite of his knowledge of the time, Roll in the end descends to the old practice of accusing the mercantilists of blunders—he speaks of primitive monetary errors (1938: 112) and mercantilist superstition (118)—and thus his interpretation does not reach its aim.

> Nevertheless, the mercantilists were led into many notions which are now seen to be erroneous. They ascribed . . . a definitely active force to money. . . . Where money was scarce, trade was sluggish; where it was abundant, trade boomed. Ironically, however, their high regard for money led them to reject the defenses of usury. . . . They returned to the views of the Canonists. (69)

This attitude, Roll thinks, can be deduced from their interests:

---

5. A similar definition, but one that puts the decisive factor into the foreground is to be found in Schumpeter who speaks of "means to the creation of national economic territories" (1914: 37). In justice, however, we must point out that even Schmoller by no means judged onesidedly when he said that mercantilism was "in its innermost essence nothing else than the formation of the [modern] state—not however only the formation of the state, but formation of the [national] state and of national economy at the same time" (Schmoller 1884: 43).

> The mercantilists believed that money was productive, but, because they were anxious to obtain money-capital, their interests clashed with those of the providers of it. In their fight against what they considered excessive interest mercantilists were not above using the arguments of those who would have condemned no less strongly the merchant's profit. (69)

Behind Roll's considerations is the old and erroneous conception, which is most clearly manifest in Gonnard (1930: 48 et seq.), that the mercantilists only transferred notions of private economy to the whole of society, but did not take up any standpoint of national economy proper.[6] If we free ourselves from this idea the way to the right understanding is open. The mercantilists started from the conviction that exchange economy can only unfold if market transactions increase and market transactions can only increase if there are sufficient means of circulation; hence their teaching—little money, little exchange, little trade; much money, much exchange, much trade—a teaching that perfectly suited a society changing from a state of natural to a state of money and exchange economy. "If Money be wanting," says Malynes (cited in Heckscher 1935, 2: 217), "Traffic doth decrease, although commodities be abundant and goods cheap." Because the mercantilists conceived money from the viewpoint of national economy—as helper in the market, not of private economy—as capital, they could advocate a strict limitation of interest. In their attitude there is no inconsistency, no irony, no breach. Yet it must be properly understood.

With regard to physiocracy, Roll likewise upholds the traditional view. He explains it on the one hand as a reaction against Law and on the other he tends, like Gonnard (1930: 213 et seq.), to represent its thesis as built on an erroneous identification of matter and value. "It was Law's merit," he says in one place (Roll 1938: 119), "that he contributed to the creation of those conditions which inspired physiocratic thought. For the only sort of property which appeared to have remained intact during the postinflationary slump was land." But more important is the other argument:

> The physiocrats tried to discover the concrete form of productive labour.

---

6. On page 101 he describes the fundamental concept of mercantilism as follows: "Wealth is the same as commercial capital (represented by money)."

> They had no clear idea of the distinction between use-value and exchange-value, and they thought of the surplus entirely in terms of differences between use-values which had been consumed and those which had been produced. The *produit net* was not a surplus of social wealth in the abstract (exchange-value), but of concrete material wealth of useful goods. It was this approach which led the physiocrats to single out one particular branch of production as the only really productive one. . . . [In agriculture] the amount of food consumed by the labourer and what is used as seed is . . . less than the amount of produce raised from the ground. It is the simplest and most obvious form of surplus. (134)

Therefore, the physiocrats understood this simple form of surplus while they failed to understand the more complicated formation of profit in industry. Roll here (as in many connections) follows the analysis given by Marx in his *Theorien ueber den Mehrwert* (1904, 1: 33 et seq.).

These considerations of Roll, however, like those of Marx, offer no causal explanation of the origin of the physiocratic doctrine,[7] but an absolute judgment on its content.[8]   This explanation is not

---

7. Marx says, however, in passing (1904, 1: 41) that the physiocratic doctrine corresponds to "the bourgeois society in the epoch in which it breaks from feudalism. Its starting-point is therefore in France, in a preeminently agricultural country, not in England, a preeminently industrial, commercial, seafaring country," and thus he comes near to the historically correct interpretation without, however, following it further.

8. In other respects, too, Roll's description of the historical position of the physiocrats is unfortunate. "The natural order," he says (1938: 137), "was an anticipation of utilitarianism at a time when the economic and political conditions were not really ripe for it." This judgment is at variance with Roll's correct fundamental thesis of the causal connection of reality and science: a period only creates those doctrines for which the economic and political conditions are existent—or else where would be the causality? Roll also goes astray in saying: "It is this fact [of anticipation] which explains the contradictions of the physiocratic system itself"—the contradictions between the defense of the landed interest and the demand of a single tax, between the "rearguard action on behalf of feudalism" and the "looking through capitalist glasses" (138). Contradictions within Quesnay's system will only be discovered by those who approach it with preconceived and schematic, fixed notions like landed interest or feudalism. The physiocrats were agrarian and social reformers. They did not defend the interests of the existing feudal nobility, but advocated a new order in the sphere of agriculture in which the interests of the farmer who created the rent

satisfactory. Whether an idea of the past appears today right or wrong, primitive or perfect, it demands in any case an interpretation in the light of its contemporary conditions. So does the thesis of Quesnay of the productivity of agriculture and of the barrenness of industry—a thesis that had its roots partly in the contrast between the wealth of the nobility and the poverty of the peasants or workmen, and partly in the opposition between the rural production of food supplies and the town production of luxury goods in the France of the *Ancien Régime*.

The doctrinal system of Adam Smith Roll treats more from a critical than from a historical standpoint. He sees in the great Scotsman "a true representative of industrial capitalism" (1938: 173). Is this true? Yes and no. Smith indeed regarded national economy from the angle of industrial production, but this production was not yet transformed by the technical revolution. Only he who bears in mind that by 1775 industrial capitalism was undergoing a profound change leading from small- to large-scale production and realizes that Adam Smith's ideas were conceived in the significant moment of the great change, will fully understand the immortal work on the *Wealth of Nations*.

The idea of the German romanticists Roll aptly deduces from the economic state of Germany, which was very backward at the time in comparison with England. The theories of Adam Smith necessarily met with resistance in Central Europe because there life still spoke a different language. Roll shows the genesis of the teachings of Adam Müller and Friedrich List from the half-feudal, half-capitalistic environment of the Reich; he neglects, however, to explain from contemporary conditions the contrast between the reactionary Müller (a child of Brandenburg which was still entirely agricultural) and the progressive List (a son of Wuerttemberg which was already well industrialized).

It would of course be petty to base the criticism of Roll's work on

---

should be safeguarded, the income of the proprietor who received the rent should be taxed—a new order destined to lead from feudalism to capitalism. Roll's assertion "that the economic and political conditions which produced the founders of French political economy were not fundamentally different from those which were responsible for moulding the thought of Adam Smith" (146) overlooks the essential point: the agricultural problem of society, and the social problem of agriculture, of prerevolutionary France.

such secondary issues. We must, above all, investigate whether and in what manner he does actually execute the program that he has developed in abstract. In doing this we find that he gives to his interpretation of history a certain turn that makes it problematic: he views the ideas less as reflections of economic conditions than as expressions of social struggles, less as products of economic reality than as embodiments of class ideologies. Thus, he makes a subjective factor the basis of interpretation: the will to assail or defend a given order—as if all economic and social science had sprung from this root!

Roll's method, and at the same time the danger inherent in it, are most clearly manifest in the discussion of Nassau Senior. "The striking feature of Senior's theory," Roll rightly says (1938: 341), "was the admission of the productivity of capital and the introduction of the term of abstinence." Why did he abandon Ricardo's heritage?

> It is difficult not to see in this change a reflection of the altered position of industrial capitalism. The main factor was now, not hostility from the landowners . . . but the challenge of the working class. The theoretical necessity was to remove the antithesis between the two classes of income, profits and wages; that is, to remove the labour theory of value. Capital had to be made as legitimate a source of income as labour; and whatever attenuations Senior's 'abstinence' suffered at the hands of later economists, he clearly meant the term to carry a special moral significance. (348)

Senior—and this is the causal explanation of his position presented by Roll—endeavored to show that the profit of capital is justifiable, and therefore he propounded his theory of abstinence.

The question now arises whether there is not an objective reason that makes Senior's thought comprehensible and enables us to dispense with the subjective element on which Roll founded his thesis. A study of the industrial development of England between 1817 and 1836 allows us clearly to perceive why Ricardo's doctrine was reshaped by Senior: fixed capital had in the meantime substantially extended and strengthened its position in the process of production. Ricardo—at a time when machinery was only in its beginnings—had (like Smith) still regarded capital mainly as variable capital (as wages-fund) or upheld the conception that the capital equipment per individual worker was in all branches of industry (at least in the long run) the same. The question of the productivity of capital could therefore still remain unanswered: once the income of the worker was theoretically determined, the size of profits was likewise automatically fixed. But in Senior's days it was no longer possible to conceive capital merely as the annex of labor force and represent profit simply as a residual income. Such a doctrine would have ill explained reality. Capital was now in an increasing degree fixed capital, and this fixed capital was very unequally distributed through the branches of production. If one compared Ricardo's doctrine with these facts, it necessarily appeared obsolete and a new theory of distribution was bound to arise: a theory of distribution that—like Senior's doctrine—had to accept capital as an independent agent of production and to bring interest and profit as an independent problem to a definite solution.

It is not economic reality from which Roll explains Senior's ideas, but the political discussion or even—let us plainly state it—the contest of narrow interests. Can such an interpretation be scientifically satisfactory? The raising of this question means its negation. In two respects Roll's procedure must be criticized: historically and in principle. His attempted explanation is historically insufficient because he conceives "industrial capitalism" as in itself unchangeable. Not only in the two hundred years between Adam Smith's birth and Vilfredo Pareto's death has national economy, the theoretical object of investigation, changed (although it may now as then be described as industrial capitalism); even in the twenty years between Ricardo's *Principles* and Senior's *Outline* it underwent an essential transformation that necessarily caused a revision of the theories. Only he who keeps in mind the fullness of the changes of life can comprehend the fullness of the changes of science.

But more important still are the objections that must be raised against Roll's method from the standpoint of principle. Is the modern economic science really nothing but a collection of attempts at defending or attacking capitalism? Must all theoreticians of the past be conceived and understood as hack writers of narrow class interests? Roll seems to assume this. Let us follow him through the centuries in his judgement on the leading spirits: "Misselden's immediate motive for theorizing," we read (1938: 76), "was to provide a background for policies designed to foster the interests of the class he represented." The physiocrats are partly characterized "by their passionate defence of landed property" (137). "It has often been said that Adam Smith represented the interests of a single class. This is undoubtedly true not only in a historical sense but even subjectively"[9] (152). Ricardo "was forced by the same social purpose which was inherent in the *Wealth of Nations* to imply the productivity of capital, he was also determined far more than Smith to represent the claims of landed property as economically unjustified" (185). Malthus was "an apologist for feudalism on a capitalist . . . basis. . . . He seems to have aspired to a sort of balance between Whig-aristocratic and primitive industrial-bourgeois elements" (209, 203). "Müller's writings were weapons supplied to a particular social class for use in the political struggle" (217). List "was a champion of industrial capitalism" (229). The late classicists "were anxious to preserve the pro-capitalist element of classicism" (296). Walras (like Jevons) "was led to his economic analysis by a desire to build up a strong case in favour of laisser faire, in answer to an attack by a follower of Saint-Simon" (390).

But even from collective judgments Roll does not refrain. Classicism—"the citadel of industrial capitalism"—"did not ignore the existence and historical development of their own society which they knew . . . to be a society divided into social classes. . . . Apologia for industrial capitalism . . . is implicit in nearly all classical theory" (1938: 355, 369). Modern economics is hardly better, for "it cannot be doubted that there is . . . an apologetic strain in modern theory" (370).

What Roll entirely misunderstands is the motive from which our science—like any other—has sprung and must be comprehended. Science does not arise from the desire to defend ruling interests[10] but

---

9. Cf. on this point Schumpeter (1914: 61 et seq.) who rightly vindicates the "neutrality of the scientific basis." He defends the classicists against the charge "that political tendencies were the premises which determined scientific reasoning," but he fails to understand that it was the economic conditions by which it was determined.

10. Bukharin develops this concept even more fully than Roll (*The Economic Theory of the Leisure Class*, 1927). He simply identifies the classical doctrine with the doctrine of free trade and deduces it from the powerful position of the English bourgeoisie that governed the international markets. "English industry was not obliged to make reference to specifically English conditions as an argument for the erection of customs barriers of any kind. The theorists of the English bourgeoisie, therefore, had no need to turn their attention to the specific peculiarities of English

from the will to understand existing circumstances.[11] The theories that the past has brought forth are reflections of past conditions (not products of past struggles for power) and must be explained from those conditions. The great interpretations of life that Thomas Aquinas and Adam Smith have left, we cannot, like Roll, dismiss as "ruling class ideologies" (1938: 55, 155); they were efforts of the spirit to understand life, endeavors of men to unravel the world, rising from the pure source from which all thought flows: the great desire to fathom the meaning of the universe.

---

capitalism. . . . [T]hey spoke of the *general* laws of economic evolution" (1927: 18). Similarly the historical school is identified with the protectionist movement. "[T]he German . . . tariff movement was the cradle of the Historical School" (19). This is also supposed to explain the predilection of this group or special inductive investigations of the particular problems of individual economic territories: "The rising German industries suffered perceptibly from English competition. . . . [T]he German bourgeoisie was obliged to give exceptional attention to precisely the peculiarities and the independence of the *German* evolution, in order to use them as a theoretical foundation for proving the necessity of 'nursery tariffs'" (18). In these words not even the history of tariff policy and its theory is sufficiently explained (much less anything else), for the English classicist Stuart Mill regarded educative tariffs as justifiable, while the German historian Lujo Brentano rejected all protection on grounds of principle!

11. Roll himself says in his *Elements of Economic Theory* (1937: 30): "Absence of partiality is the most important qualification of the scientific mind."

8

The Material Contents of the History
of Political Economy

If we examine the wide literature devoted to the history of political economy from the viewpoint of a causal interpretation of the doctrines governing the past, the critical eye perceives a very varied picture. It is known what circumstances have evoked and molded the canonist and mercantilist doctrines; some wise things have been said on the sources from which the classical and historicist ideas have flowed, but the genesis of these theories cannot be regarded as clear; physiocracy and the utility theory of value, moreover, are still unsolved problems of historical investigation. Does this imply that there is, as Salin believes, no necessary connection between economic life and economic science? Or must we not at least admit that, as Mombert thinks, such a connection cannot be proved everywhere and that especially the newer dogmas escaped more and more all causal concatenation?

Let us test these decisive questions by the most intricate example: the origin of the doctrine of Menger and Jevons! At first sight it might seem—and the literature has not yet advanced beyond this stage—that the marginal utility theory emerged from the head of its creators as Minerva from the head of Zeus: no source seems to be visible from which they could have drawn their fundamental ideas.

But this appearance dissolves if we widen the view. A closer consideration of the history of economic doctrine during the nineteenth century already serves to show that not even in this case can we speak of a free formation of ideas. Since 1830 there was an endeavor visible in Nassau Senior and still more in Lloyd and Longfield to interpret subjectively the objective categories of the classicists. This tendency became dominant in late classicism; it was brought to logical perfection by the Italian, Francesco Ferrara, and the Englishman, John Elliot Cairnes, working independently of each other. In the meantime two other thinkers likewise investigating separately had made subjectivism the exclusive basis of a systematic theory of economics: the Prussian, Hermann Gossen, and the Briton, Richard Jennings. Without relation to them and without relation to each other Carl Menger and Stanley Jevons then formed their parallel theories. Obviously there are only two alternatives: either we assume that all this is due to chance—or we believe that there must have been a cause that in all these minds, separated from each other in time and space, produced the same effect, inducing the thinkers to choose the individual psyche as the starting point of economic analysis. To the disciple of history as a science there can be no doubt that only the second view is really admissible.

This conviction is strengthened when we compare the history of political economy with the general history of culture. In so doing we readily perceive that by 1870 there was a universal turn from the intellectual type of Schmoller to the intellectual type of Menger and Jevons, a tendency away from the social and realistic aspects of life, and toward the individualist and idealistic aspects. This movement may be briefly illustrated from three spheres of culture entirely severed from economics: the philosophy, religion, and art of this age of transition.

First, as to philosophy: in the same year as Carl Menger's *Grundsätze* there appeared a book by Hermann Cohen entitled *Kants Theorie der Erfahrung* which inaugurated the great Kant renaissance of the Marburg school. As the economists of historicism had exclaimed "no more theory!" so the philosophers of positivism had demanded "no more metaphysics!" As economists like Schmoller had maintained that only the descriptive collection of material could advance the science, so philosophers like Dühring had taught that the expansion of our knowledge of the external world alone was the end of our endeavor: the parallelism of the views is obvious. And Cohen like Menger preached: Back to the intellectual permeation of the phenomena! Back to the use of reason! Back to theory!

A similar development may be perceived in the sphere of religious thought. While up to the middle of the century, in harmony with the universal positivism, the social and institutional, that is, the external, elements of Christianity had above all been stressed (for example, by Montalembert), so now a new tendency springing from the same source as Cohen's idealism and Menger's individualism permeated Europe. It emphasized the personal and spiritual nature of religious experience, thus stressing the individual side of religion rather than its institutional embodiment, the church. The great success attained by Tolstoy in his *Confession*, which was written in 1879, is the best proof.

This change in the spirit of the age is, however, most clearly reflected in the history of art. The part of economic historicism was here played by naturalism: description, or portraying of the external world as it presents itself to us, was even here taken as the ideal (Zola's *Roman expérimental*, Manet's impressionistic painting). In contrast symbolism and expressionism arose after 1870, emphasizing the values of the individual (Rimbaud's lyric poetry, Van Gogh's pictures): experience of the supertemporal and spiritualization of art—these were the watchwords that the young generation of those years readily followed.

Thus, a wider consideration proves that Jevons's and Menger's great discovery was no isolated phenomenon but must be conceived as part of a universal trend of thought. But if this is so, it cannot be denied that there is a latent force behind the seemingly free movement of the spirit, which leads it on—and even with reference to the utility theory of value this raises the great problem, to the solution of which we must now turn.

Among the historians of political economy who accept in principle the idea of causality, the view prevails that the connection between reality and thought, or economic life and economic theory, must be comprehended as a concatenation of *action and reaction*. Ingram and Haney especially upheld this view, which on account of its breadth proved very attractive.

It is, however, necessary to make this conception if possible more concrete and exact. Perhaps it would not be unfair to describe its underlying idea as follows: the economic reality of a time forms the views of the science on this reality, but these views in their turn transform the economic reality so that in the end things and thoughts appear in the same way as determining and determined elements. But the process, as it is generally envisaged, demands time. To borrow Haney's example: "The individualism of the *laisser-faire* economists and statesmen was to a great extent the result of industrial evolution; but in its turn it became a condition reacting upon industry" (Haney 1936: 4). In other words, the economic situation of England, the requirements of commerce and industry as he continually observed them since the end of his Oxford studies in 1746, induced Adam Smith in his book, published in 1776, to advocate free trade; this teaching in turn prompted Pitt in 1800 to introduce free intercourse between England and Ireland, and Peel in 1846 to repeal the corn laws (236 et seq.). Action and reaction are spread over a whole century.

This conception is entirely correct; but it explains the history of economic policy rather than that of economic theory. For the transformation of the economic order is a real and political *process*, its interpretation, however, is an ideal and individual *act*. Therefore its causal analysis must start from a different basis.

This basic idea we possess in the mutual concatenation of all social phenomena in any given moment. The life of a time is a great and comprehensive unity, the parts of which correspond to and are, therefore, only comprehensible with each other. This is especially true of economic reality and economic ideology: economic reality is conditioned by the mind, for it is the thinking man who creates and molds it; economic ideology is conditioned by facts, for it is the objective phenomena that it interprets.   But this necessary concatenation, for the characterization of which one is tempted to borrow from mathematics the idea of the functional connection, can only be asserted if we concentrate on a fixed point in time. For everything is in a state of flux, and however short a period may be, the form and essence of life are at its end different from what they were at its beginnings. A historical analysis that rests on the idea of causality must therefore always try to make a crosscut through historical development, and then things and thoughts do not appear connected with and related to each other in action and reaction but as *mutually conditioned*.

This essential dependence can, however, only be acknowledged as mutual in the full sense of the word, if we take economic reality and economic ideology as comprehensive categories, economic reality for the whole real aspect, economic ideology for the whole ideal aspect, of social economy. If we are only concerned with the history of political economy, reality appears as the determining factor and science as the determined factor—simply because the science aims only at knowledge and not as such at influencing reality. With this limitation (but only with this limitation) Cournot's comparison is true, which represents the relation of the economist to economy as similar to the relation of the grammarian to the language; the work of the grammarian is conditioned by the language, the laws of which he strives to perceive, and any dependence in the opposite direction does not pertain: the science is here only an *ancilla vitae* [slave to life]. But this attitude implies no materialism; as the poet transforms the language, so the economic politician transforms the economic system: we must only discern poet and grammarian, economic politician and economic theoretician, if we mean to write a history of the grammatical or a history of the economic science. In doing so we are soon led to realize that the development of language and economy continually forces the science to change its doctrinal contents, that the mind is here conditioned in its utterances by real life.

We say conditioned, but may we go one step further and assert determined? Here we touch the problem of free will, and it is proper to say: *Ignoramus, Ignorabimus*. But one thing is certain: so long as philosophy and psychology have not established the principle of determinism, we as historians must not postulate it. Our inner experience teaches us that, confronted with a difficult problem of the present, we decide only after a long and painful inner struggle on one solution or the other, and even after having decided we are not freed from all doubts. There is no reason to assume that the thinkers of the past were in a different position. The problems, however, which offer themselves to the perceiving science, to our science, originate in economic life and its solutions must be confirmed by economic life. Therefore, freedom cannot be understood as arbitrariness: only between the possibilities of explanation that reality suggests are we capable of choosing. And although we may assume that we are free to decide in the moment of the choice, as experience seems to teach and the determinists are unable to disprove, this freedom of our choice has perished once we have exercised it. Posterity knows nothing of the inner struggle of the thinker; it sees only the thought that has become history. The individual and free element has disappeared, but the real and predetermined element is still visible. Thus, Petty's or Cantillon's doctrines were in their time conditioned by the circumstances and appear in our time as determined by them. It is the historical perspective that allows us to advance from the assertion that the ideas are conditioned by reality, to the assertion that they are determined by it—provided we do not forget that the formation of ideas has never been mechanically fixed in its time.

So much for the causal interpretation of the economic theories according to their content. To understand the form in which they have been propounded is the task of the biographer rather than of the historian. For here the element of individuality has its place: the enthusiasm with which Ferrara pronounces the word freedom becomes comprehensible if we learn that he has languished in Bourbon dungeons; the fervor with which Bastiat preaches the gospel of optimism is explained by the fact that in his chest raged tuberculosis, which fills its victims with confidence. But that both adhered to the ideology of liberalism, and the ideology of liberalism itself, has its ultimate reason in the history of that time, when the economic order seemed to be, and was, a great and ingenious system of collaboration according to superindividual laws, the free action of which necessarily invited under the given circumstances an optimistic view of the world.

To describe fully the fertility of the conception that has just been outlined, a lifetime of study devoted to the history of political economy would be necessary. The subject under discussion is, however, one of those that can be treated in twenty or in two thousand pages, and so the attempt may be made to interpret in a short sketch the leading theories, paying therein special attention to the physiocratic and marginalistic doctrines because they have not yet been treated from the viewpoint of causality.

The quintessence of *mercantilism*, that is, of the first doctrine that had the system of exchange economy (then still in the course of development) for its object, could be summed up on the model of

Roscher in the following five principles:

> 1. The welfare of a national economy depends upon the increase of the population

> 2. The national economy also depends upon the increase of the mass of precious metals in the country. "Imperli potentia ex civium numero aestimanda est," says Spinoza (*Tractatus politicus*, 1803, 2: 354), and Schröder observes: "A country becomes the richer the more money or gold from the earth or elsewhere is brought in, and the poorer the more gold flows out" (cited in Mombert 1927: 170)

> 3. Foreign trade is to be made as active as possible, for thus it becomes the most important "of the means which make a kingdom without mines abound in gold and silver" (title of Serra's "Breve trattato," 1614)

> 4. Commerce and industry are more important branches of national economy than agriculture. "A Seaman is in effect equivalent to three Husbandmen." (Petty 1899: 259)

> 5. The state—this follows from the four foregoing maxims—is called upon to foster the national welfare by an appropriate policy. Hobbes's *Leviathan* (1651) is the best illustration of this doctrine.

These five programmatical ideas may be explained in the following way:

1. The population of the territorial states, which had been constituted up to about 1600, was remarkably sparse and decreased still further during the murderous wars of the first half of the seventeenth century. But this was not all: the vast majority of the people lived in the country and was either legally or at least factually tied to the soil. If commerce and industry were to develop, this was only possible on the basis of an additional population. Thus, an increase in the number of the people became a condition of the transition to a higher stage of economic life, and opinions like the following appear in their setting far less grotesque than when severed from their time: "If all the . . . People of Ireland, and of the Highlands of Scotland, were transported into the rest of Great-Brittain;

. . . the King and his Subjects, would thereby become more Rich and Strong" (Petty 1899: 285). In that fortunate time every new citizen helped to build up commerce and industry above the agricultural basis.

2. And this is the most important point. The *communis doctorum opinio* maintains that this doctrine originated in the confounding of concepts of private and national economy. What Adam Smith said on this point more than a hundred and fifty years ago is repeated over and over again:

> That wealth consists in money, or in gold and silver, is a popular notion which naturally arises from the double function of money, as the instrument of commerce, and as the measure of value. . . . In consequence of these popular notions, all the different nations of Europe have studied, though to little purpose, every possible means of accumulating gold and silver in their respective countries. (Smith 1904: 396 et seq. [Smith 1976b: 429, 431])

Hence, the whole thesis must be rejected! "Mercantilism is among the economic aberrations what avarice is among the moral" (Emminghaus in Rentsch's *Handwörterbuch der Volkswirtschaftslehre*, 1866).

It is, however, impossible to dismiss the matter so simply. The allegation that the mercantilists were governed by avarice and the Midas illusion, or, as it is sometimes expressed more mildly; that they in their primitive way transferred the notions of the individual, especially the merchant to the whole of society, would be justified only if they had appreciated the gold merely in its function in private economy, as a measure and store of value, not because of its specific function in national economy, as helper in the market and circulating medium. But it is just this second aspect that they emphasize; they never tire of stressing[1] that the gold must not be accumulated as a

---

1. Anyone who doubts the assertion of the text may convince himself by the study of the sources. The following small selection from the international literature will perhaps suffice:

> Bacon, Francis, *Sermones fideles*, 1597, XV, XXXIX, Opera omnia ed. Lipsiae 1694: 1163 and 1206 et seq.
> Petty, Sir William, *A Treatise of Taxes*, 1662, in *Economic Writings* ed. Hull, 1899: 35 et seq.
> Temple, Sir William, *An Essay Upon the Advancement of Trade in Ireland*, 1673: 8.

treasure as the individual and the miser wish, but must circulate unceasingly—as a *pendulum commercii*—because otherwise it is, from the standpoint of society, useless. To quote only one of them: "If . . . [gold] is locked up in chests, it is not gold but a dead and useless rubbish; and the more of it lies sterile . . . the more all commerce and traffic is thereby weakened and impeded" (Lau, *Entwurff einer wohleingerichteten Polizey*, 1717, cited in Mombert 1927: 174). And even Schroeder, whom we mentioned above, states with the greatest emphasis that gold must not be hoarded, but must incessantly change hands.

Hence, it was a conception of national economy proper that governed the mercantilists, and in national economy lay the roots from which it sprang. The seventeenth century demanded more gold for the same reason for which it demanded more men: because there was a deficiency! A natural economy with little circulation should be transformed into an exchange economy with much circulation; thus, more means of circulation had to be procured, and these means of circulation had to fulfill their mission—to circulate. Therefore, an expansion of the mass of money was a condition of the transition to a higher stage of economic development.

One could object to this argumentation—as Adam Smith (1904: 412 et seq.) seems to do by implication—that an increase in the mass of money is not necessary to an intensification of exchange, and that the existing mass of money (even supposing that on account of traditionalistic hindrances the velocity of circulation remains constant) could equally well perform an increased number of exchanges. This is true in the abstract. But an increase of exchanges on the side of the commodities would, if the mass of money and the velocity of

---

Belloni, Gerolamo, *Dissertazione sopre il commercio*, 1750, vol. 2: 4; English translation: *A Dissertation on Commerce*, 1752: 27 et seq.

Verri, Pietro, *Meditazioni sull' Economia Politica*, 1771, V, XIII, XXI, *Scrittori Classici Italiani di Economia Politica*, vol 15, 1804: 52 et seq., 119 et seq., 189.

Melon, Jean François, *Essai Politique sur le Commerce*, 1736: 6 et seq.

Hornigk, Philipp Wilhelm von, *Oesterreich über alles, wann es nur will*, [1684] 1708: 30 ("Cameralalphabet," Point 4).

circulation were unaltered, cause a fall of prices, and such a development every growing economy seeks to avoid. The seventeenth century needed rising prices to stimulate production and therefore needed more money.

3. But whence should come the gold that was indispensable for the transition to market and exchange economy? Whence could it come, if not from an active foreign trade? Neither France nor England, neither Germany nor Holland possessed mines of any importance, and so a favorable balance of trade was for them the only way of obtaining means of exchange. Hence, Hornigk's strange assertion that "it would be better, however extraordinary this may seem to the uninstructed, to pay for an article of merchandize 2 thalers which remain in the country than only one which leaves it" (cited in Mombert 1927: 169). Again we see the precedence of the interests of national before those of private economy. The individual is expected to make sacrifices so that the necessary means of circulation need not be withdrawn from society.

But once we have understood that the mercantilists appreciated foreign trade because in attracting gold it provided domestic economy with the technical conditions of the transition to a higher form of economy, we can also understand and acknowledge the truth of the view, which for two centuries has been incessantly decried as untenable and wrong, that in international commerce "one can never lose what the other would not gain" (Monchrétien 1889: 161). The problem was to divide the scanty stock of money in the international economy among the different countries, and if four children wish to eat a cake, one can have more than a quarter only if something is taken from the share of the others.

4. From natural to exchange economy—this is the fundamental idea of all mercantilism. Therefore, the different branches of economic life were assessed according to the state of their development. Commerce, which was relatively free, was most highly valued. Industry, which was just beginning to throw off the fetters of the guild regulations, stood somewhat lower in general esteem. On the lowest step, however, stood agriculture, still governed as it was by feudalism and traditionalism. This opinion had the deeper roots as it seemed true even from the viewpoint of private economy; the transition from natural to exchange economy was at the same time the transition from

subsistence to profit economy. "There is much more to be gained by Manufacture than Husbandry, and by Merchandize than Manufacture," said Sir William Petty (1899: 256), and he was right.

5.   Viewed geographically and politically, exchange economy presupposes a larger and also more uniform economic territory than natural economy, which may exist even in the smallest area. Hence the importance of the state for the economic life of the seventeenth century: if it was to flourish, the political disunity of the Middle Ages had to be overcome! As it was, the government, as the will-center of the state which represented the national economy, seemed indispensable. To mention only one point; if the activity of the balance of trade that attracted the life-spending metal should be secured, it was imperative to impede as far as possible the import of expensive manufactured commodities and to support their export, and at the same time to prevent the export of the cheap raw materials still to be processed and to favor their import. For this purpose the state was needed to direct by a competent trade policy the stream of goods as was desired.

All these ideas, however, were proper to a time of transition and necessarily became senseless as soon as the development of national economy had reached the first stage of equilibrium. As soon as the population in its growth overstepped the optimum, the populationist thesis of mercantilism became obsolete and—as Malthus was soon to show—the opposite was correct. The same is true of the increase of the quantity of money: it could only remain the aim of economic policy as long as the markets suffered from a lack of the medium of circulation. As soon as this changed, as soon as people became acquainted with the possibilities of paper circulation (Law), the old theory was out-of-date. In Boisguillebert (*Détail de la France*, 1697) this is first consciously expressed. He says that money (which can as well be represented by copper, leather, shells, and paper as by gold and silver) is not a value in itself and its abundance does not add to the welfare in a country—under this condition, however, there is enough of it to keep the prices of the essential commodities intact. The new situation changed the doctrine: Petty, North, and Steuart declare that the quantity of money in a national economy must neither be too small nor too great, and they endeavor to find the factors that determine its normal amount. Thus developed, on the one hand, the

quantity theory of money (e.g., Locke), and on the other, the analysis
of the process of inflation (e.g., Hume).

With the central thesis of mercantilism fell necessarily all its other
postulates: if no more metal was needed, it was no longer necessary
to insist on a constant activity of the balance of trade; and if the
constant activity of the balance of trade was no longer the end, one
could do without the help of the state, which in the meantime had
formed the home market into a great unit. The valuation of the
branches of economic life, however, changed as soon as industry and
agriculture, too, were conquered by exchange economy and had
become capitalistic. If Werner Sombart, who, following Bidermann's
admirable book (*Ueber das Merkantilsystem*, 1870), has contributed
much toward the clarification of the problems under discussion, called
mercantilism the "Political Economy of Early Capitalism" (1928, 2:
2) he has strikingly summed up the essence of this much abused
doctrine.

That the theories constituting the mercantile system can and must be
conceived as the products of a time in which Europe changed from
natural to exchange economy is also shown by the consideration of the
only important theoretician of the nineteenth century who worked
under similar conditions: the American, Henry Carey.[2] Held has
spoken of "Carey's relapse into the mercantile system"[3] and thus
described his propinquity to that doctrine—a propinquity that is simply
explained by the fact that in the time of Carey (who was born in 1793)
the American economy stood at the turning point to the modern
economic system as the Italian economy had in the time of Genovesi
to whom he is said to show a special similarity. In both cases the
same belief in the benefit of a growing population, the same will to
the increase of the monetary circulation and of the velocity of this
circulation, in both cases the same strict protectionism—in other
words, there was agreement in the principles of economic policy for
the unfolding of exchange economy, which is by the way also

---

2. Cf. also E. H. Everett, D. Raymond, and other American economists of this
period.

3. Adolf Held, *Carey's Sozialwissenschaft und das Merkantil-system*, 1866; cf. also
Eisenhart 1881: 189.

symbolically expressed in Carey's predilection for Colbert.

In England mercantilism was immediately followed by classicism: between Steuart's *Inquiry* and Smith's *Wealth of Nations* lie only ten short years. In France, however, a school inserted itself between them which though it hardly flourished for a single generation and though its basic thesis was hardly accepted anywhere outside its own country nevertheless deeply influenced the course of development: the *physiocratic school* of François Quesnay.

"The soil is the only source of wealth"—in this terse sentence Quesnay (1888: 351) expressed the fundamental idea of this teachings, the assertion that has been so incomprehensible to posterity that trade and industry are incapable of producing a net profit beyond their outlay.

> The products of agriculture reimburse the costs, pay the manual work of the cultivation, procure gains to the laborers and, in addition, produce the revenues of the estates. Those who buy the products of industry pay for the costs, the manual work, and the merchants' gain; but these products do not produce any revenue beyond that. (233)

Turgot, who is usually represented as an independent thinker, holds exactly the same doctrine; he says of the agriculturist: "What his labor causes the land to produce beyond his personal wants is the only fund for the wages which all the other members of society receive" (Turgot 1844: 9 et seq.). And although he rejects the description of the industrialists as *classe stérile*—wisely foreseeing that this nomenclature will occasion an endless chain of misunderstanding—he still shares the judgment contained in that word, for he himself speaks of the *classe des cultivateurs* as the *classe productive*, of the *classe des artisans* as the *classe stipendiée*.

The doctrine of distribution laid down by Quesnay in his *Tableau Economique* is nothing more than an application of this idea of the exclusive productivity of agriculture and the barrenness of trade and industry. The scheme rests indeed on the assumption that the productive class of a country, and that means its whole national economy, produces in one year goods to the amount of 5 milliards of francs, and suggests: 2 milliards are consumed by this class itself, a further 2 milliards go as farm rents to the landlords called *classe des propriétaires*, and 1 milliard, the last one, to the *classe stérile*, the artisans, in exchange for industrial products. Hence, all income originates in agriculture. The landlords divide their 2 milliards into halves; they return 1 milliard directly to agriculture buying food for it. The second milliard goes first to the artisans for industrial products. Thus, every year 2 milliards are accumulated by the *classe stérile*—one that they receive from the peasants and one that they receive from the nobility for their merchandise. But they must hand back this whole amount to the *classe productive* without the provisions and materials of which they can neither live nor work. The circle is closed and may begin anew.

It has often been said that this conception is based on a confusion of value and matter, on the erroneous assumption that the primary production, because it alone creates new matter, must be regarded as the sole creator of values. But this is at best to give the (supposed) error a different form. How it may have arisen Adam Smith has tried to show, and posterity has faithfully repeated his words. Smith thinks that physiocracy must be conceived as a reaction of mercantilism, Quesnay as the opponent of Colbert.

> If the rod be bent too much one way, says the proverb, in order to make it straight you must bend it as much the other. The French philosophers, who have proposed the system which represents agriculture as the sole source of the revenue and wealth of every country, [does not Smith wrong Quesnay in this point? Quesnay speaks only of a *Royaume Agricole*[4]] seem to have adopted this proverbial maxim; and as in the plan of Mr. Colbert the industry of the town was certainly over-valued in comparison with that of the country; so in their system it seems to be as certainly under-valued (Smith 1904, 2: 162 [1976b: 664])

Even these words of Adam Smith, however, do not exculpate the wrongdoers who have spread false doctrines; they plead only extenuating circumstances. But we must strive to fully understand their concept. A sentence from Smith's criticism of physiocracy

---

4. He sometimes considers also a *Royaume commerçant*; its welfare, however, he regards as problematic. "Without the products of agriculture, a nation cannot have any other resources than manufacture and commerce; but both can only exist by the riches of foreign countries; such resources are moreover very limited and little secure and can suffice only for small states" (Quesnay 1888: 220). Quesnay is obviously thinking of Holland. Cf. also 236 et seq., 343, 355.

shows us the right way: "[I]t seems . . . altogether improper to consider artificers, manufacturers and merchants, in the same light as menial servants" (1904: 173 [1976b: 675]). If they were in fact menial servants they would belong "among the barren and unproductive."

Now what was false in the English society of 1760 could well be true in the contemporary French society. For it rested on a different social system—on a social system that is truly reflected in the *Tableau Economique*. We need only turn the description a little to perceive this; we need only put the *classe des propriétaires* into the foreground and not the *classe productive*. If we do so the picture presents itself as follows: society is so constituted that all wealth that is created falls to one class, the *classe des propriétaires*, while all the other ranks gain only their subsistence. Turgot (1898: 15 et seq.; see also Quesnay 1888: 233) writes:

> The two classes of the Cultivators and the Artisans . . . have this in common, that they get nothing but the price of their labor and of their advances, and this price is nearly the same in the two classes. The Proprietor bargaining with those who cultivate the land to yield to them as small a part of the produce as possible in the same way as he chaffers with his shoemaker to buy his shoes as cheaply as possible.

However, he continues:

> although neither the Cultivator nor the Artisan gains more than the recompense of his labor, the Cultivator causes, over and above that recompense the revenue of the Proprietor to come into existence.

Hence, all riches accumulate in the hands of the *classe des propriétaires,* that is, the nobility. They draw it from their peasants, the *cultivateurs*, and to this extent the *cultivateurs* are productive. The craftsmen furnish them with all sorts of things that render life agreeable, and to this extent they are indeed useful. But they do not add to the wealth of the privileged class; they do not pay rents but help only in spending the rents, and to this extent they are unproductive, a *classe stipendiée*, or, as Quesnay somewhat unhappily expressed it, a *classe stérile*.

Have we not here before us the France of the *Ancien Régime* viewed from Versailles and fixed in a tableau?! In the service of a small upper class stand the unfree masses of the rural population who produce revenues; in their pay, however, stand the trading inhabitants of the towns who—like the lackeys—serve their luxury. For—and this is decisive—the French industry of 1760 was in its character a luxury industry for the ruling few, and this explains the singularly dependent position occupied by it in the system of physiocracy. Manufactures in France, said Adam Müller as late as the beginning of the nineteenth century,

> remained in the deplorably limited state in which we find them even now, because the great mass of the nation was far too poor to have artificial demands. The French luxury goods—mirrors, porcelain, fine cloths, fine silken materials, gold and silver articles, fancy ware—still far surpass the similar products of all other nations, even the English; there are, however, hardly any products of a moderate kind, which may be the national need of a whole people. (Müller 1936: 370).

The fact that the land owners in prerevolutionary France absorbed nearly the whole industrial output so that the industrial entrepreneurs appeared more or less as employees of the nobility, is most clearly reflected in Cantillon's *Essai*. The prototype of an industrialist is to him a hatter! As they work almost exclusively for the upper classes, Cantillon believes that all tradesmen are in the service of the *noblesse*. "[A]ll the Individuals are supported not only by the produce of the Land which is cultivated for the benefit of the Owners but also at the expense of these same owners from whose property they derive all that they have" (Cantillon 1931: 43). These words not only represent the historical root of physiocracy—they convey also its historical explanation. Towns, Cantillon believes, rise where landlords settle who draw merchants and craftsmen after them; their greatness depends on the nobility residing there. "[T]he size of a City is naturally proportioned to the number of Landlords who live there" (17). They govern the market, they give to production and commerce their task and direction: "It is always the inspiration of the Proprietors of Land which encourages or discourages the different occupations of the People and the different kinds of Labor which they invent" (93). Hence his physiocratic concept, which the school has only more clearly formulated, one might almost say, made into a slogan: "I will . . . lay it down as a principle that the Proprietors of Land alone are naturally independent in a State: that all the other Classes are dependent whether Undertakers or hired" (57).

François Quesnay was at one with Richard Cantillon as is shown not only by the fact that he quotes him with approval (1888: 218; cf. also 189, 236), but also by his own words.

> Without the produce of our soil without the revenues and expenses of the proprietors and cultivators, whence would the profit of commerce and the wages of labor arise? . . . All the costs of industrial production are only drawn from ground-rents; for the works which produce no rents can only exist by the riches of those who pay them. . . . All entrepreneurs gain fortunes only because others make expenses. . . . *The land-owners . . . pay the works of industry*; and thus their revenues become common to all men. (216, 233 et seq.)

And in one passage the roots of the view that industry is sterile lie bare:

> *The manufacturers of linens and of common materials can much increase the value of hemp, flax and wool*, and procure the subsistence to many men who would be occupied in these *very advantageous activities*. But one perceives today that the production and the commerce of the greater part of these goods is almost annihilated in France. For a long time the manufactures of *luxury* have seduced the nation;[5] we have given ourselves to an industry which was foreign to us. (193 [emphasis added])

Hence, industry, so taught Quesnay in 1757, at a time when his living doctrine had not yet turned into a dead dogma, can be productive, if like agriculture it is a *"production des matières de premier besoin;"*[6]

---

5. For the outstanding importance of luxury in prerevolutionary France cf. also Necker's writings: "Sur la législation et le commerce des grains," 1755, and "De l'administration des finances de la France," 1785.

6. Limits of space prevent my following the thesis of the text further. Cf., however, the interesting *Questions sur la Population, l'Agriculture et le Commerce*. There Quesnay speaks of the "advantages of the manufactures which process the materials of the [home] soil over those which process foreign materials" (silk, imported wool, cotton, cf. 344) into luxury goods, and in this connection we read: "Are not the proceeds of the commerce of the latter [hence not of all!] after the value of the raw materials brought from abroad has been deducted restricted to the restitution of the costs of labor and to the special gain of the merchants?" (Quesnay 1888: 287). Important also are the suggestive questions under VI, (302 et seq.).

but it is unproductive if it serves the condemned *luxe de décoration* as in Quesnay's country and time. The tradesmen, who, for the pleasure of the fashionable society of Versailles, produced coaches, wigs, knicknacks, brocades, mirrors, tapestries, powder and snuff boxes, and the like, appeared to the physician of Madame Pompadour as servants of the luxury of the nobility like chambermaids, stable grooms, lackeys, and kitchen hands—they were (in his eyes and in reality) menial servants; *they belonged to the sphere of consumption and not to that of production.* "The production of merchandize of handicraft and industry for the use of the nation are only an object of expense and not a source of income" (1888: 343)—"The sterile class . . . works only for consumption" (391). As productive he regarded only the husbandman who with his hard labor had to pay for the whole extravagance, the husbandman who, as things were, maintained in fact not only himself but also the nobility with their whole throng of servants in household, commerce, and industry.

This explanation of Quesnay's theory of distribution from the reality of his time provides us also with the key to his doctrine of taxation. The traditional formula is: as the physiocrats regarded only agriculture as productive, they wished to tax only agricultural production. But it is more correct to say: as the physiocrats saw all riches streaming into the pockets of the nobles, they wished to tax only the income of the nobles. For this was their program! (1888: 332). As under existing conditions *classe productive* and *classe stérile* worked only for the *propriétaires* and were themselves held down to the subsistence level, it seems senseless to tap any other source: to burden the classe stérile would have made the luxury goods more expensive, to burden the classe productive would have lowered the revenues—hence, in the end it would still have been the nobility who was forced to restrict their expenditure for the sake of the state, and they were the only ones who could do this.

The fact that Condillac's view as to the productivity of commerce and industry differed from that of Quesnay, is no argument against the interpretation here suggested. Condillac has been represented as an adversary of the physiocrats—wrongly so, for even he says: "It is the soil alone which produces all . . . things. It is . . . the only source of all wealth" (*Le Commerce et le Gouvernement*, 1776: 51). And if he continues: "But it becomes an abundant source only if it is made fertile by the work of men," he is merely expressing an idea that Quesnay, too, shared. ("Revenues are the products of the soil and men. Without the work of men, the soil has no value," [Quesnay 1888: 220]). He has also been accused of inconsistency because in spite of this fundamental agreement with Quesnay he still in the end reached the conclusion that "industry, too, is in the last analysis a source of riches" (1776: 65). But this judgment is not less unjust. One must understand the difference between the politically minded social reformers on the one side and the sensationalist philosopher on the other, which led them, although at one in principle, to different results. Quesnay had said: "The one group [the agriculturists] gives rise to riches by cultivation; the other [traders and artificers] prepares them for enjoyment; those who enjoy them pay both" (1888: 234; cf. further 381-82; see also Condillac 1776: 63). Now while Du Pont and Le Mercier developed the first aspect of this thesis, Condillac followed the second; while the politically minded social reformers thought in objective and social categories, the sensationalist philosopher must be understood from the standpoint of subjectivism and individualism. Then the two are seen to be complementary rather than antagonistic. The former think of riches as a stock of property, as a source of income, the latter of riches as a fund of consumption, as a source of enjoyment. The former say: in our society only agriculture produces rents; the latter say: for consumption all commodities of the first order are important. We have before us not contradictory solutions of one problem, but independent solutions of different problems. In a deeper stratum of their thought even Condillac and Le Trosne are at one; this is manifest in such doctrines as their theories of taxation.

It is manifest above all in the dogma that so deeply influenced the further course of the history of economic doctrine: the dogma of the *ordre naturel* as the "order . . . evidently the most advantageous to the human race" (Quesnay 1888: 375). In the interpretation of these ideas the thesis "physiocracy is the counterstroke against Colbertism" is in part applicable—but only in part, since a deeper analysis leads to the realization that there existed an outspoken unity of purpose between the mercantile and agricultural systems. Nevertheless; Quesnay based his program of agrarian reform on the assertion that national welfare flourishes only under free trade and declines by intervention.

A great state must not leave the plough to become a carter. It is impossible

to forget that a minister of the last century, blinded by the trade of the
Dutch and the splendor of the manufactures of luxury, has thrown his
country into such folly, that people spoke only of commerce and money. .
. . This minister . . . upset the whole economic order of an agricultural
nation. The foreign trade in corn was stopped to enable the workman to
live cheaply; the sale of wheat within the kingdom was handed over to an
arbitrary police which severed the commerce between the provinces. The
protectors of industry . . . by a miscalculation ruined their towns and their
provinces through senselessly degrading the cultivation of their soil: all
tended towards destruction. (343)

To what had Colbert led France? Fénélon as early as 1699 had
expressed it unmistakably: "A great city densely populated with
artisans occupied in softening manners by the joys of life, if it is
surrounded by a poor and badly cultivated kingdom, resembles a
monster whose head is of enormous size but whose body, exhausted
and deprived of nourishment, has no proportion to the head" (1699:
131). In such circumstances it naturally appeared most important for
the assistance of agriculture to secure a *bon prix* for the agricultural
products, and the suitable way was the abolition of the measures that
had been expressly introduced with the object of keeping the grain
cheap. "It is by no means necessary," said Boisguillebert fifty years
before Quesnay,[7] "to work miracles, but only to stop continually
offering violence to nature . . . *laissez faire la nature et la liberté*!"
Natural liberty will order all for the best; thought Boisguillebert, and
Quesnay expected from it on the one hand an increase of harvests by
the transformation of production,[8] on the other an increase of prices
by the transformation of the market. Rich harvests and good prices,
however, make up the welfare of the rural population. Hence

---

7. Cf. on this point Oncken, *Geschichte der Nationalökonomie*, 1902: 251; Gonnard
1930: 162 et seq.

8. It is impossible to give here even a short outline of the physiocratic program that
is aptly described by Gonnard who bases his account on Weulerasse's great work (218
et seq.). It contained as a matter of course the demand for the abolition of serfdom.
"The soil cannot become fruitful but by the hands of free men" - "serfdom is repellent
to the law of nature" (234). Above all, however, Quesnay wished to replace the
feudal *métayer* by the capitalistic *fermier*, the *petite culture* with oxen by the *grande
culture* with horses. Agriculture should be provided with capital: "*It is less men than
riches which it is necessary to attract to the country*" (Quesnay 1888: 333).

Quesnay's enigmatic sentence: "*Cheapness with abundance is by no means riches; dearness with scarcity is misery; abundance with dearness is opulence*" (1888: 246).

This liberalism of the physiocrats appears at first sight as a complete contradiction to the interventionism of the mercantilists. Hence the general interpretation of the younger system as an antithesis of the older doctrine. But in reality Quesnay was only the executor of Colbert's testament. For the goal of the seventeenth century, the unfolding of exchange economy, had been reached in France only partially, only in respect of trade and industry. Agriculture, however, had remained feudal. What the eighteenth century aimed at, what confronts us on almost every page of the physiocratic literature, is the assimilation of agricultural production to capitalism, hence the fulfillment of the historical mission of mercantilism. Quesnay wished to entrust agriculture to capitalist entrepreneurs: "The advantages of agriculture depend . . . on the amassing of land in great farms, brought to their highest value by rich farmers. . . . We do not envisage the rich farmer as a laborer who works the soil himself; he is an entrepreneur who commands" (1888: 219). But such a production had profitable prices for its presupposition, and these could only be brought about by the fall of interventionism. Thus, in changed conditions and with new means men still strove toward the old end.

Freedom of production and freedom of the market: from these two sober postulates of agrarian policy arose the sublime pathos of the physiocratic doctrine of the *ordre naturel*. The word of the older Mirabeau that laws that conform to nature are unnecessary, laws that contradict it impracticable, forms the transition from the concrete and political program to the abstract and philosophical system.[9] The idea of system and the system of ideas of the *ordre naturel*, however, are not Quesnay's exclusive property—they are the common basis of classical economics. They found their purest expression in Adam Smith's *Inquiry into the Nature and Causes of the Wealth of Nations*.

9. "Quesnay regards this liberty . . . above all as a device for facilitating the sale of goods, increasing the net product of the soil and bettering the position of the cultivator. But with Mercier de la Rivière it is certainly a strict principle" (Rambaud 1902: 164).

The basic thesis of Smith's work, the bible of an optimistic century, is the belief that there operates in economic life a secret but sovereign law, according to which men—perfect liberty assumed—although they only wish to serve their own interests at the same time promote the common weal, nay, that the common weal cannot be better fostered than by men serving exclusively their own interests. "The uniform, constant, and uninterrupted effort of every man to better his condition" is to Smith "the principle from which publick and national, as well as private opulence is originally derived" (Smith 1904, 1: 325 [1976b: 343]).

> Every individual is continually exerting himself to find out the most advantageous employment for whatever capital he can command. It is his own advantage, indeed, and not that of the society which he has in view. But the study of his own advantage naturally, or rather necessarily leads him to prefer that employment which is most advantageous to the society." (419 [454])

And: "The natural effort of every individual to better his own condition, when suffered to exert itself with freedom and security, is so powerful a principle, that it is alone, and without any assistance . . . capable of carrying on the society to wealth and prosperity." (1904, 2: 43 [1976b: 540]). Le Mercier de la Rivière had written to the same effect ten years before: "The desire to enjoy and the liberty to do so, incessantly provoking the multiplication of productions and the enlargement of industry impose on the whole society a movement which becomes a perpetual tendency towards its best possible state" (*L'ordre naturel et essentiel des sociétés politiques*, 1846: 617). And Ricardo said thirty-five years later: "Where there is free competition, the interest of the individual and that of the community are never at variance" (Ricardo 1846: 265).

The socialism of the nineteenth century—acting justly for its own time—relegated this thesis to the realm of errors. But as Smith, by his criticism of Quesnay, so Lassalle, by his criticism of Smith, has given posterity a hint as to how the relative truth of the idea decried as absolute error can be found: "The ethical idea of the bourgeoisie," he says in the *Arbeiterprogram* (1874: 31 et seq.), "is this, that absolutely nothing but the unhempered use of his forces should be granted to everybody. If we were all equally strong, equally clever, equally educated, and equally rich, this idea could be regarded as sufficient and moral" (cf. also Sismondi 1819, 1: 379). In an egalitarian social order the free operation of self-interest would in fact lead toward the common best.

In these words Lassalle has touched upon two problems: the question of the natural and the question of the socioeconomic equality of men. As regards the former, the question whether men are equally strong and equally clever, the answer depends on the philosophical conviction of the individual rather than on science. Smith in any case answered it in the affirmative. "The difference of natural talents in different men," he says (1904: 17 [1976b: 28-29]), "is, in reality, much less than we are aware of. . . . The difference between . . . a philosopher and a common street porter . . . seems to arise not so much from nature, as from habit, custom, and education. When they came into the world . . . they were, perhaps, very much alike." What is, however, the salient point in the social consideration, is the question whether men can be regarded as equally educated and equally rich, that is, whether society is in fact so constituted that all are equally well armed for the struggle for existence, and hence only he has subjective success who objectively achieves something—and on this point a man of 1760 and a man of 1860 could not agree.

The socialists of 1860 saw society torn by class struggles. It was the private property in the means of production that stood between capitalist and proletarian and made them irreconcilable opponents. The liberals of 1760 knew nothing of this concept and necessarily so—the laborer and the means of labor were not yet separated! In Adam Smith's time the estates of feudalism were already dissolved, the classes of capitalism not yet formed—never was society nearer to the ideal of perfect equality.[10] It was the happy epoch in which one could rightly say: "The property which every man has in his own labour . . . is the original foundation of all other property" (1904: 123 [1976b: 138]).

---

10. In religious life this state of social equilibrium found its expression in Puritanism. Its basic idea was the equality of the believers (universal priesthood) and the equality of the church functionaries (Presbyterianism). The connection between religious and social history is here manifest: "The typical puritan was the small master, who owned his land or his tools" (John Buchan, *Oliver Cromwell*, 1934: 28).

For how does Adam Smith describe the relation of entrepreneur and worker? "In all arts and manufactures" he says (1904: 67 [1976b: 83]), "the greater part of the workmen stand in need of a master to advance them the materials of their work, and their wages and maintenance till it be completed." On this passage Edwin Cannan observes (67 note 5): "The provision of tools to work with and buildings to work in is forgotten." A classical example of how the past must not be handled! It was not Smith who forgot something but Cannan: the author whom he criticizes published his book in 1776 and not in 1904. In 1776, the means of production were not yet in the possession of the entrepreneur, but still in that of the worker—the factory system had not yet ousted the domestic industry. Crompton's spinning mule and Cartwright's power loom still belonged to the future. Of the branch of production that Smith himself described as leading, H. T. Wood who has subjected this time to an intense special study, says: "Even in those places where weaving was carried on as an industry, it was still a domestic industry. The weaver worked at home, using yarn which had been collected from the farmhouses and cottages, where it was spun in single threads by the women" (Wood 1910: 42). The laborer and the means of labor were not yet separated.

But quite apart from the property in the means of production the worker of 1760 cannot be compared with his unhappy descendant of 1860; he had in the labor force itself a valuable capital. Rightly Smith emphasizes (1904: 265 [1976b: 282]): "The improved dexterity of a workman may be considered in the same light as a machine . . . which, though it costs a certain expense, repays that expense with a profit." The workman of this time could not yet be replaced by women and children as after the industrial revolution—"skill, dexterity and judgment" were still of decisive importance, and "the dexterity of hand . . . even in common trades, cannot be acquired without much practice and experience" (5; 125). Andrew Ure aptly described how great the contrast between the eighteenth and the nineteenth centuries in this respect really was, in his *Philosophy of Manufactures* (1861: 19-21):

> When Adam Smith wrote his immortal elements of economics, automatic machinery being hardly known, he was properly led to regard the division of labour as the grand principle of manufacturing improvement. . . . But

what was in Dr. Smith's time a topic of useful illustration, cannot now be used . . . as to the right principle of manufacturing industry. In fact, the division, or rather adaptation of labour to the different talents of men, is little thought of in factory employment. On the contrary, wherever a process requires peculiar dexterity and steadiness of hand, it is withdrawn as soon as possible from the *cunning* workman who is prone to irregularities of many kinds [does not Ure simply think of the social struggle?] and it is placed in charge of a peculiar mechanism, so self-regulating, that a child may superintend it. . . . The principle of the factory system then is, to substitute mechanical science for hand skill, and the partition of a process into its essential constituents, for the division and graduation of labour among artisans. On the handicraft plan, labour more or less skilled, was usually the most expensive element of production—*materiem superabat opus*; but on the automatic plan, skilled labour gets progressively superseded, and will, eventually, be replaced by mere overlookers of machines. . . . Mr. Antony Strutt, who conducts the mechanical department of the great cotton factories of Belper and Milford, has so thoroughly departed from the old routine . . . that he will employ no man who has learnt his craft by regular apprenticeship; but in contempt, as it were, of the division of labour principle, he sets a ploughboy to turn a shaft of perhaps several tons weight, and never has reason to repent his preference.

The workman of the eighteenth century was the free master of his own tools, the worker of the nineteenth century the unfree servant of another man's factory.

But what was perhaps the most important fact, the rise from workman to master, was in Adam Smith's time not yet impossible. This is manifest not only in numerous individual examples, but was quite generally true. "In years of plenty," says Smith (1904: 85 [1976b: 101]), we should say in a spell of prosperity, "servants frequently leave their masters, and trust their subsistence to what they can make by their own industry," an advancement of which the proletarian in Lassalle's environment, at once without property and without skill, could not even dream.

Hence, if the optimistic doctrine of Adam Smith is according to Lassalle's words applicable to a society, the members of which are equally strong and equally clever, equally educated and equally rich, it was true in 1760 and false in 1860. The industrial revolution, which separated the worker from the means of production and degraded him to a servant of the machine so that he was robbed of all hopes of rising, put the doctrine of class struggle in the place of the belief in the harmony of interests—and both creeds were no more than expressions of the contrasting conditions under which they arose.

Adam Smith lived before the industrial revolution. This fact explains his social philosophy. It must also be capable of explaining his theory of value that has served as the foundation to Ricardo's work, the doctrine that it is labor which in the end determines the exchange-value of all goods.

As is generally known, Adam Smith reached perfect clarity neither in the theory of value nor in the theory of price. He propounds two different explanations: the one has the "early and rude state of society" as its object, the other the "improved and civilized society." In the former, labor alone is decisive of the value-in-exchange; in the latter (after the formation of capital and the appropriation of land) wages, profits, and rents enter into the price. What had Smith in mind when he conceived these ideas?

The much quoted first sentence of his work has as a rule prevented the right interpretation of the Smithian doctrine because it seems—especially in comparison with and in contrast to the physiocratic thesis—to assign to labor an exceptional position. "The annual labour of every nation is the fund which originally supplies it with all the necessaries and conveniences of life which it annually consumes." But this utterance can only be really comprehended if it is viewed in the light of the third chapter in the second book, in the light of the chapter that discusses the cooperation of the factors of production. Here the yearly national income is consistently described as the "annual produce of the land and labour" (e.g., 315)—and the famous passage of the introduction, too, rests, without doubt, on this idea of *two* factors of production, for all work presupposes something to work at, the raw material offered by the earth. If the soil is not expressly mentioned in this connection this is so only because its cooperation is simply a matter of course.

He, however, who has clearly understood that "the real wealth and revenue of a country" consists for Smith "in the value of the annual produce of its *land and labour*" (1904: 323 [1976b: 340, emphasis added]) has also found the right approach to his doctrine of value. This is nothing but a slip from the root of the fundamental concept expressed by Sir William Petty: "Labour is the Father and active principles of Wealth as Lands are the Mother" (1899: 68, 377). Men must wrest all goods from the earth—the more difficult it is to obtain them, the greater the labor, which their gain occasions, the higher their value.[11] "At all times and places that is dear which it is difficult to come at or which it costs much labour to acquire; and that cheap which is to be had easily, or with very little labour. Labour, . . . therefore . . . is alone the ultimate and real standard by which the value of all commodities can at all times and places be estimated and compared" (1904: 35 [1976b: 50-1]). Objective costs and subjective disutility of labor are harmoniously combined in this conception. "Equal quantities of labour, at all times and places, may be said to be of equal value *to the labourer.* In his ordinary state of health, strength and spirits; in the ordinary degree of his skill and dexterity, he must always lay down the same portion of his ease, his liberty, and his happiness" (35 [50, emphasis added]). Hence, it is but "natural that what is usually the produce of two days or two hours of labour, should be worth double of what is usually the produce of one day's or one hour's labour" (49 [65]).

This inference, however, is not applicable to the present.

> [Alone in] that early and rude state of society which precedes both the accumulation of stock and the appropriation of land, the proportion between the quantities of labour necessary for acquiring different objects seems to be the only circumstance which can afford any rule for exchanging them for one another. . . . [I]n every improved society, all the three [i.e., the wages of labour, the profits of stock, the rent of land] enter more or less, as component parts, into the price. (1904: 49, 52, 65 [1976b: 65, 68])

Smith to be sure holds fast to his basic principle in so far as he describes the shares of capital and land as deductions from the produce of labor.

From these ideal elements, which in Adam Smith are not yet perfectly coordinated, David Ricardo later built his classical theory of value. He starts from all three factors of production but still arrives at a pure labor doctrine of value by neutralizing capital and land. In

---

11. The right application of this doctrine, not its development, as is usually maintained, is to be found with Carey, who asserts that men "measure the value of the articles that they desire in exchange, by the difficulty that exists in the way of their obtaining them" (Carey 1837: 11).

order to understand in what way he procures this effect it is now necessary to regard the works of master and disciple as well as their historical background from this point of view.   Above all it is imperative to understand what position was occupied by capital and land in the economic system of the time.

In his theory of value, which might be called the more primitive one, resting entirely on Petty's dictum, Adam Smith, as we have seen, wholly excluded capital and assumed only two factors of production, an active and a passive one.   This is not due to the fact that he was perhaps of the opinion that the production was ever carried on without produced means of production.   He says expressly:

> In that rude state of society . . . in which every man provides every thing for himself, it is not necessary that any stock should be accumulated. . . . Every man endeavours to supply by his own industry his own occasional wants as they occur.   When he is hungry, he goes to the forest to hunt; when his coat is worn out, he cloaths himself with the skin of the first large animal he kills: and when his hut begins to go to ruin, he repairs it, as well as he can, with the trees and the turf that are nearest it. (1904: 258 [1976b: 276])

Now one can only hunt with bow or spear, prepare a coat only with scissors and buckles, build a house with hammer and nails.   But these things are to Smith—just as the spinning wheel and the weaving loom of the domestic worker—not capital but merely an accessory to the labor force.   Capital is to him essentially a fund for the payment of laborers and the purchase of material, and *not* machinery.   Only he who fully grasps this truth and comprehends it from the setting of its time will be capable of rightly understanding the labor theory of value and all connected therewith.

Let us hear how Smith describes the function of what he calls stock. Stock is used by the employers "in setting to work industrious people, whom they will supply with materials and subsistence" (1904: 50 [1976b: 66]), "to advance the wages and furnish the materials of labour" (51), "to purchase materials and to maintain the manufacturer till he can carry his work to market" (55), "to put into motion . . . useful labour" (249).   Everywhere the produced means of production are not included, those produced means of production that theory today simply identifies with capital—for they belonged in that time to the laborer, and what is still more important in this connection, they were not an independent means of production but subject to the labor force and not beside or above it.

It is the division of labor that is the perfection of the labor force, not the perfection of the labor tools, to which Adam Smith relates the welfare of society, increased as it is in comparison with the times passed. And he describes its operation (1904: 9 [1976b: 17]) as follows: "This great increase of the quantity of work, which, in consequence of the division of labour, the same number of people are capable of performing, is owing to three different circumstances": (1) improved dexterity; (2) saving of time; and (3) application of machinery. For this third point the *Wealth of Nations* furnishes no illustration. But in the *Lectures* (Smith 1896: 167), which on this point holds exactly the same view, two examples are brought forward: plow and mill, the ancient helpers of the rural folk![12] And even the new inventions, which Smith had occasion to see introduced in the flourishing manufactures of his environment, were only helpers of the individual worker. "Whoever has been much accustomed to visit manufactures, must frequently have been shewn very pretty machines, which were the inventions of . . . workmen, in order to facilitate and quicken *their own particular part of work*" (1904: 11 [1976b: 20, emphasis added]). We see that an independent productivity of the produced means of production could not become perceptible—the laborers and the means of labor were connected not only legally but

---

12. We must not assume that Smith consciously chose the most primitive examples—all his examples would in retrospect appear equally primitive. As "complicated machines" he describes "the ship of the sailor, the mill of the fuller, the loom of the weaver" (1896: 13)—all of them not much younger than the plow. Most instructive is the passage where he speaks at some length on the progress of machinery in the woolen industry (245) because there a leading branch of production is under consideration (136). "The three capital improvements are: 1) The exchange of the rock and spindle for the spinning wheel"—but only "spinning wheels of immemorial fashion" were at that time in use (Wood 1910: 42); "2) the use of several very ingenious machines which facilitate and abridge . . . the winding of the worsted and woollen yarn, or the proper arrangement of the warp and woof before they are put into the loom" (this example is not quite clear but in any case only improvements of the hand loom can be meant); and "3) The employment of the fulling mill for thickening the cloth, instead of treading it in water." But this machinery "had been in operation from time immemorial in the subsidiary operations of the woollen trade" (Cunningham 1917: 620).

also technically and functionally; they were an aggregate not further dissoluble.

And as the capital represented by the produced means of production so the capital representing money devoted to gain (money as stock in the sense of Adam Smith) could not then claim to be promoted to the same rank as nature and man, that is, soil and labor. The fund of raw materials and wages never became operative and visible as a unit, but always only in the hand of the individual worker who drew the wage and processed the material. That capital, as Smith conceived it, stood always in relation to the labor force and could only move through industry together with the labor force is the best proof that it occupied in that time an essentially subservient position. "The number of useful and productive labourers," says Smith (1904: 2 [1976b: 11]), "is every where in proportion to the quantity of capital stock which is employed in setting them to work." And, "[w]hatever obstructs the free circulation of labour from one employment to another, obstructs that of stock likewise; the quantity of stock which can be employed in any branch of business depending very much upon that of the labour which can be employed in it" (137 [152]).

The industrial revolution utterly transformed the relation of capital and labor. In the same year in which Smith's *Wealth of Nations* appeared, 1776, James Watt succeeded in setting his first steam engine in motion, and at the end of the century already a considerable proportion of English industry worked with mechanical motion. Capital—now mainly fixed capital—was no longer the serving accessory of the independent worker, but rather the dependent worker was the serving accessory of capital. Lauderdale's *Inquiry into the Nature and Origin of Public Wealth* (1804) clearly reflects the great change: it is the fundamental idea of this work that capital must be acknowledged as an independent factor of production. It not only increases the productivity of the hands but it is itself productive. "It is a strange confusion of ideas," Lauderdale observes (1804: 185), "that has led Dr Smith to describe the operation of capital as increasing the productive powers of labour. The same process of reasoning would lead a man to describe the effect of shortening a circuitous road between any two given places, from ten miles to five miles, *as doubling the velocity of the walker*." Not by supporting the laborer, but by replacing him, capital becomes a source of value: "[I]n every instance where capital is so employed as to produce a profit, it uniformly arises, either—*from its supplanting a portion of labour, which would otherwise be performed by the hand of man; or—from its performing a portion of labour, which is beyond the reach of the personal exertion of man to accomplish*" (161).

On the basis of this new fact of life and of this new perception Say then expressed the conviction that the creation of value cannot be reduced to labor alone. Adam Smith, he held, erred in this respect. A more correct analysis, he contended, shows that value springs from the cooperation of labor with capital (and nature). "His ignorance of this principle," he says of his master (cited in Ricardo 1846: 172 [1951: 285]), "prevented him from establishing the true theory of the influence of machinery in the production of riches."

As things were, it was impossible to overlook the fact that "the principle that the quantity of labour bestowed on the production of commodities regulates their relative value" must be regarded as "considerably modified by the employment of machinery and other fixed and durable capital" (1846: 20 [1951: 30]). Did, however, the appearance of machinery as Say suggested compel the entire abandonment of the labor theory of value, or was it not sufficient to expand it? Ricardo was prone to prove the latter.

> In contradiction to the opinion of Adam Smith, M. Say . . . speaks of the value which is given to commodities by natural agents, such as the sun, the air, the pressure of the atmosphere, &c., which are sometimes substituted for the labour of man, and sometimes concur with him in producing. But these natural agents, [which, as we have to insert in explanation, represent the technique in industrial production, for "the powers of wind and water, which move our machinery, and assist navigation nothing? The pressure of the atmosphere and the elasticity of stream, which enable us to work the most stupendous engines—are they not the gifts of nature?" (40 [76])!] though they add greatly to *value in use*, never add exchangeable value, of which M. Say is speaking, to a commodity: as soon as by the aid of machinery . . . you oblige natural agents to do the work which was before done by man, the exchangeable value of such work falls accordingly. If ten men turned a corn mill, and it be discovered that by the assistance of wind, or of water, the labour of these ten men may be spared, the flour which is the produce partly of the work performed by the mill, would immediately fall in value, in proportion to the quantity of labour saved. (172 [285-86])

It is obvious what Ricardo had in mind: a reconciliation of the old perception of the technical and functional concatenation of labor and the means of labor with the new perception of their mutual replacement. And this view, too, is a reflection of its time, for it was an everyday experience that the machines made the commodities cheaper in freeing workmen and increasing productivity at the same time. Ricardo stood in the transition from manufacture to the factory system; the machines were to him as to Lauderdale above all a "means of abridging labour" (17, cf. also 42 [25]).

Machines save labor (i.e., costs) and thus lower the exchange value (i.e., price) of the products; this is Ricardo's argument against Say who has the increase of their use value in mind. But does the exchange value sink for the whole amount of the released labor? Obviously not! For into the place of the dismissed workmen steps the newly introduced machinery as a new (if more modest) element of costs. How can the increase of value caused by capital be built into the theory without making it a dualist explanation? Ricardo solves this problem from his basic conception of the character of capital—and that now means of machinery. Into the place of the freed enters, to a certain part, stored-up labor, and the decrease of value is the difference between the two. Thus, Ricardo preserves the concept of an indissoluble aggregate of labor and the means of labor—this is most manifest in the theory of distribution where a uniform income is assumed for capitalists and wage earners that only after its formation is further divided between them so that high wages mean low profits and vice versa—and he believes that he has saved the doctrine that the commodities are exchanged according to the labor necessary to their production (or rather according to the aggregate of stored-up and actual labor necessary). "Not only the labour applied immediately to commodities affect their value, but the labour also which is bestowed on the implements, tools, and buildings, with which such labour is assisted" (1846: 16 [1951: 22])—the old doctrine and the new facts seem reconciled.

However, one contradiction between dogma and life remained. Ricardo had made Smith's thesis, that labor regulates the value-in-exchange, more exact by emphasizing that it is the amount and not the reward of labor to which this effect must be ascribed. The rate of wages is under competitive conditions equal in all branches of industry—hence it cannot influence the relations of exchange. The amount of labor to be spent in the production of the exchangeable commodities, however, is different, and therefore it determines the exchange relations. If a piece of cloth is exchanged in the market for two pieces of linen, twice as much labor is necessary for producing the same quantity of cloth as the same quantity of linen. But just this improvement of the doctrine brought its problematic character to light. If the workers could produce cloth and linen without capital, or if, like the wages, the quantities of capital cooperating in production were equal per head of the worker, nothing could upset the dogma that cloth and linen are exchanged according to the mass of labor applied. But where stored-up and actual labor take part in production in different combination, it is otherwise; as soon as machinery makes its appearance, differing in extent in different industries, a change of wages no longer influences the exchange values or prices equally, for it is only the actual labor that is still to be paid that it makes more expensive, not the stored-up labor that was paid in the past. It then influences productions with much actual and little stored-up labor more than such with little actual and much stored-up labor, and thus the exchange relations are altered. It became obvious that it was not sufficient to combine capital and labor as stored-up and actual labor to an aggregate to save the doctrine that the commodities on the market are exchanged according to the labor-time necessary to their production. But rather, the assumption had to be added that capital and labor are combined in all branches of production in the same proportion—not only an aggregate, but an aggregate everywhere homogeneous.

Ricardo's keen intellect saw this quite clearly:

> It appears . . . that the division of capital into different proportions of fixed and circulating capital, employed in different trades, introduces a considerable modification to the rule . . . that commodities never vary in value, unless a greater or less quantity of labour be bestowed on their production. . . . If men employed no machinery in production but labour only . . . the exchangeable value of their goods would be precisely in proportion to the quantity of labour employed. If they employed fixed capital of the same value and of the same durability, then, too, the value of commodities produced would be the same, and they would vary with the greater or less quantity of labour employed on their production. But although commodities produced under the same circumstances, would not vary with respect to each other, from any cause but an addition or

diminution of the quantity of labour necessary to produce one or other of them, yet compared with others not produced with the same proportionate quantity of fixed capital, they would vary from . . . a rise in the value of labour, although neither more or less labour were employed in the production of either of them. . . . The degree of alteration in the relative value of goods, on account of a rise or fall of labour, would depend on the proportion which the fixed capital bore to the whole capital employed. All commodities which are produced by very valuable machinery . . . would fall in relative value, while all those which were chiefly produced by labour . . . would rise in relative value. . . . [H]owever . . . this cause of the variation of commodities is comparatively slight in its effects. . . . In estimating, then, the causes of variations in the value of commodities, although it would be wrong wholly to omit the consideration of the effect produced by a rise or fall of labour, it would be equally incorrect to attach much importance to it; and consequently . . . I shall consider all the great variations which take place in the relative value of commodities to be produced by the greater or less quantity of labour which may be required from time to time to produce them. (1846: 22 et seq. [1951: 37-38, 35-36, 36-37])

Hence, Ricardo consciously presupposes for his investigation that capital (as produced means of production) and labor are everywhere combined in the same relation, in other words: that the capital equipment of each individual laborer is equal in all branches of industry. Thus, he saves the inner logic and truth of the labor theory of value. What is to be said of this attempt? Before the industrial revolution the assumption just described was on the whole right, for the produced means of production were only tools that belonged to the individual workmen, and were thus uniformly distributed. After the industrial revolution it was on the whole wrong, for the produced means of production had become machines that had mechanized one section more than the other. This transformation, however, took place roughly between 1780 and 1850, and Ricardo lived in its midst. To him such an assumption, although no longer quite correct, naturally appeared not yet quite wrong. His definition of capital (in the chapter devoted to the theory of wages!) is characteristic: "Capital is that part of the wealth of a country which is employed in production, and consists of food, clothing, tools, raw materials, machinery &c., necessary to give effect to labour" (1846: 51 [1951: 95]). Fixed capital had not yet relegated the circulating capital to the second rank, and this is the historical explanation of the form that the labor theory of value assumed in his work.

The further time proceeded, however, the more untenable became the assumption that arose from the conditions of the past, and the stronger became Ricardo's conviction that he was wrong in postulating it. In his famous letter to McCulloch of 2 May 1820 [Ricardo 1952: 180], he finally expressed himself in favor of the idea "that there are *two* causes which occasion variations in the relative value of commodities—1 the relative quantity of labour required to produce them 2dly the relative times that must elapse before the result of such labour can be brought to market. All the questions of fixed capital come under the second rule." Thus, yielding to the victorious march of mechanization, the transition from the labor theory of value to a theory of the costs of production is achieved and the basis laid for Nassau Senior's doctrine.[13]

What Ricardo's treatment of the cooperation of labor and capital in the formation of value and price is able to prove is this: that times of transition are not called upon to leave theories of lasting value. The relation of labor to capital changed in that period from day to day. It was different with the third factor of production, land, which, like capital, had to be neutralized for the theory of value if the labor theory was to become logically unassailable. Here Ricardo had a more stable tendency before him; here he has created a more stable doctrine. And here, too, he built on Adam Smith.

In opposition to capital, Smith of course had to acknowledge the soil as an original and independent factor of production. But to the decisive question as to whether the rent must be regarded as a determining factor of the price, or whether it is itself determined by

---

13. F.B.W. Hermann, too, deserves to be mentioned in this connection. "A commodity even somewhat suited to be the measure of value must contain both elementary factors, labor and capital usings, in order that it may vary directly with either in the price." "Even if a machine itself contains labor, this is entirely different from the labor . . . passing into the product; on the whole the labor and usings combined in it leave the sphere of action, are merely the basis of a (new) using which becomes an element of the work (product)." "If we neglect . . . this second element of the products and take the capital usings in two products for equal, it will indeed be the labor which determines their exchange-value: but what is hereby gained if in reality these usings are hardly equal in any two products?" (*Staatswirthschaftliche Untersuchungen*, 1832: 129 et seq.).

the price, Smith gave two contradictory answers. In one passage he says: "High or low wages and profit, are the causes of high or low price; high or low rent is the effect of it" (1904: 147 [1976b: 162]) —here the rent is conceived as differential rent which does not enter into the price. In another place, however, we read: "In estates above ground . . . the value . . . of their rent is in proportion to their absolute, and not to their relative fertility"—hence, here rent is regarded as absolute rent and one of the determining factors of the price. Either—or! Smith came to no decision.

It was not these ideas, however, that influenced Ricardo; he built on other utterances of Smith that are generally overlooked: "As the price both of the precious metals and of the precious stones is regulated all over the world by their price at the most fertile mine in it,[14] the rent which a mine of either can afford to its proprietor is in proportion, not to its absolute, but to what may be called its relative fertility, or to its superiority over other mines of the same kind" (1904: 173 [1976b: 191]). In these words the differential principle is most clearly expressed.

What induced Smith to describe the mining rent in silver production as a differential rent is the fact that silver possessed a uniform market and a uniform price. Grain market and grain price, however, were in Smith's time only in the making. Where Smith conceives the rent as absolute, he has a state of the natural consumption of the agricultural products in mind: "The land which produces a certain quantity of food, cloaths, and lodging, can always feed, cloath and lodge a certain number of people; and whatever may be the proportion of the landlord, it will always give him a proportionable command of the labour of those people, and of the commodities with which that labour can supply him" (1904: 174 [1976b: 192]). In the context, however, where the rent is regarded as a differential rent appears "rent, considered as the price paid for the use of land" (145 [160]), hence in connection with a commercial utilization of the grain; it depends then upon the market situation:

---

14. Smith in fact regards this as the marginal mine. Such a view is problematic but this does not matter for the argumentation of the text. Cf. on this point Ricardo, *Works*, 1846: 197 et seq.

Such parts only of the produce of land can commonly be brought to market of which the ordinary price is sufficient to replace the stock which must be employed in bringing them thither, together with its ordinary profit. If the ordinary price is more than this, the surplus part of it will naturally go to the rent of the land. . . . Whether the price is, or is not more, depends upon the demand. (146 [161-62]).

In the first case, which corresponds to the conditions of a feudal world, the differential idea is of course inapplicable; in the second case, however, in the case of capitalistic market production, where precisely the same circumstances pertain as in silver production, the differential idea is true and very useful for the exclusion of the land factor of production from the process of price formation.

It is clear that Smith still wavered between the two pictures of life and thought, but Ricardo could waver no longer. To him the grain market offered the same view as the silver market to Smith, and thus he reached an internally and externally uniform theory of rent, the theory of the differential rent (cf. 1846: 198). But it was not so much the state as the development of the grain market between 1750 and 1850 that taught English political economists that the land rent in their country was to be regarded as a differential rent.

Since the middle of the eighteenth century Great Britain's population increased rapidly (cf. Clapham 1926, 1: 53 et seq.):

Year	Approximate Population
1751	7,250,000
1781	9,250,000
1801	12,597,000
1821	14,392,000

There was a parallel increase in the price of wheat (cf. Cannan 1917: 117):

Years	Price
1770-79	45s- the quarter,
1780-89	45s9d
1790-99	55s11d
1800-09	82s2d
1810-13	106s2d

This seemed, however, only the normal state of things: increasing demand-increasing prices. But what differed from the rule was the fact that even the increase of the supply did not apparently make for a cheapening. From year to year cultivation was improved and enlarged. Vast areas of common ground and heath land came under the plow—and the prices remained high and climbed higher. What was the reason for this phenomenon? A landowner from Wiltshire, questioned by a committee of the House of Lords during the corn law debates, expressed it on the basis of his experience in simple words: "The expenses are greater on inferior soils." Thus, the basic idea of the law of diminishing returns offered itself to science in reality. Malthus had behind him the knowledge of practice when he wrote in the second edition of his essay (1803: 7): "It must be evident to those who have the slightest acquaintance with agricultural subjects that in proportion as cultivation is extended, the additions that could yearly be made to the former average produce must be gradually and regularly diminishing."

This important perception—"[w]ere the law different," said Mill in 1848 (1909: 177), "nearly all the phenomena of the production and distribution of wealth would be other than they are"—was achieved in two stages. First, the increase of production took the form of a more extensive tillage (expansion of the area under cultivation); poorer and poorer soils came under the plow, the working of which, as things were, was just remunerative, and it was distinctly realized that the owners of richer lands could pocket a rent because they produced with less cost. This was apparently first noted by James Anderson who, in his *Observations on the National Industry of Scotland* (1779, 2: 208 et seq.) described the rent as a premium for the cultivation of more fertile acres. His *Inquiry into the Nature of the Corn Laws* of 1777 is the cradle of Ricardo's theory of rent.

By the end of the century and especially since the war against Napoléon the extensive increase of grain production was, however, no longer sufficient, and in order to meet the high demand it became necessary to resort to an intensification of tillage (expansion of the capital of cultivation). More and more labor and capital were applied to the old soils and it was soon realized that the returns did not increase in proportion to the outlay, but that their accretions progressively fell off after a certain point. Malthus, West, Ricardo, and Torrens almost at the same time made theoretical use of this observation. They taught that as the same land last taken into cultivation only replaces the cost, so does the capital last applied. Rent arises from the difference between the higher productivity of better classes of soil, or earlier investments, and the marginal production.

On the basis of this perception Ricardo came to the conclusion that the rent does not cooperate in the creation of value. The price is formed on the marginal soil free from rent. The rent is its effect, not its cause. It is no element of cost, but the difference between cost and market price. The price is determined by the aggregate of capital and labor alone. The cooperation of land in production does not annul the truth of the labor theory of value. "[R]ent invariably proceeds from the employment of an additional quantity of labour with a proportionally less return. . . . [T]hat corn which is produced by the greatest quantity of labour is the regulator of the price of corn; and rent does not and cannot enter in the least degree as a component part of its price" (1846: 37, 40 [1951: 72, 77]).

Thus, by the proof that nature does not take part in the formation of prices, and by the assumption that there is a fixed parallelism between the application of capital and labor, the labor theory of value was formed by the classicists into a logically unassailable dogma. The basis for a theory of distribution was thereby created at the same time. The income of the landlords was simply identical with the rent. Capitalists and workmen had to divide between them the return of the goods produced by them in collaboration. "Neither the farmer who cultivates that quantity of land, which regulates price, nor the manufacturer, who manufactures goods, sacrifices any portion of the produce for rent. The whole value of their commodities is divided into two portions . . . one constitutes the profits of stock, the other the wages of labour" (1846: 60 [1951: 110]). If it is possible theoretically to explain the formation of wages, the profit results *pari passu*: it is simply the residuum, the difference between the price and the wages.

It is traditional to distinguish in the classical world of ideas two wage theories: on the one hand the theory of the wages-fund, on the other the "iron law of wages." But in reality there is only one doctrine. "Population" says Ricardo (1846: 41 [1951: 78]), meaning the working class,[15] "regulates itself by the funds which are to employ it, and therefore always increases or diminishes with the increase or diminution of capital." In the first half of this sentence we have the basic idea of the wages fund theory, in the second the fundamental idea of the iron law of wages. The one doctrine has in view the demand for labor, the other its supply, and only their combination gives us the true conception of the classicists.

The wages fund theory is characteristic of the stage of development in which the circulating capital still far outweighed the fixed capital. At a time when the worker himself possessed the spinning wheel and weaving loom, the capital of the employer was in fact a fund for the purchase of materials and the payment of wages. The individual wage then resulted from the division of that part of the stock that remained after the material to be processed had been secured by the number of hands to be set to work. It is obvious that under such primitive conditions the demand for laborers depended upon the amount of the "wages fund." When the factory system spread, the capital had to be split into three parts: fixed capital, capital for the purchase of materials, and capital destined for the payment of wages. But it was no wonder that the conception remained that there was a wages fund that determined the demand for workmen.

The wages fund theory explained how many laborers could find employment. The iron law of wages—the term is unfortunate —endeavored to show how many workers sought employment. It rested on the simple fact that the idea and above all the technique of birth control was foreign to that age, allowing the population to rapidly increase, especially since at the same time the mortality of children greatly diminished. Families with more than ten members were no rarity then, and it is clear what this meant for the nation as a whole: "[T]he number of births everywhere increased by leaps and bounds" (Webb 1922, 4: 405). But the possibilities of employment could not become correspondingly numerous. The result was that the workers—men, women, and children—being without property by their competition reduced themselves to the very level of subsistence.

---

15. The use of the words *population* or *peuple* in this narrow sense is frequent at that time. Cf. for example Louis Blanc, *Histoire de la Révolution française*, 1847: passim.

Indeed, sometimes wages fell even below this limit; but then the weakest died out, until an equilibrium of offer and demand established itself at the margin between life and death. In Ricardo's time the means of bettering the standard of the masses—limitation of supply by birth control and trade unions—still belonged to the future.

> The natural price of labour is that price which is necessary to enable the labourers, one with another, to subsist and to perpetuate their race. . . . [B]y the encouragement which high wages give to the increase of population, the number of labourers is increased, wages . . . fall to their natural price, and indeed from a re-action sometimes fall below it. . . . It is only after their privations have reduced their number, or the demand for labour has increased, that the market price of labour will rise to its natural price, and that the labourer will have the moderate comforts which the natural rate of wages will afford. (1846: 50 et seq. [1951: 93-94])

This is less a theory of wages than a description of life. Everywhere reality presented the same picture: "The amount of wages," says Quesnay (1888: 706; in the same sense Turgot 1844, 1: 10), "and consequently the enjoyment which the wage earners can procure themselves are fixed and reduced to their lowest by the extreme competition which exists between them." "In reality," we read in Thünen (1863, 2: 2), "the wages of labor are regulated by the competition of the laborers, for . . . as experience teaches, the propagation of the workers is in the end checked only by the deficiency of the means of subsistence."

The tendency of the population to increase because of the fall of mortality and the tendency of agricultural production to fall because of the increase of costs,[16] together gave rise also to the *Malthusian*

---

16. Carey denied both tendencies. He maintained against Ricardo that cultivation progresses from inferior to superior soils. Now, he is certainly right in saying that (in a country still to be made arable) the poorer land is occupied first, because it is more easily cleared of the original growth—but England was by 1800 in a different position from the United States. Here indeed only soil previously disdained was free, meager heath land, not rich valleys, as in the golden West. Against Malthus, Carey set the thesis that the power of generation decreases with increasing culture. Now it is true that highly cultured men rarely produce large families—Shakespeare, Bacon, Milton, Newton, Wesley, Locke, Bentham, and John Stuart Mill had among them only six children—but Malthus did not think of the summit of the nation, but of its depth, and there people were nearer to animals than to supermen. The discussion of

theory of population. In the last edition of the *Essay*, which the author himself published, he formulated his thesis as follows:

> The rate according to which the productions of the earth may be supposed to increase, it will not be . . . easy to determine. Of this, however, we may be perfectly certain, that the ratio of their increase in a limited territory must be of a totally different nature from the ratio of the increase of population. A thousand millions are just as easily doubled every twenty-five years by the power of population as a thousand. But the food to support the increase of the greater number will by no means be obtained with the same facility. Man is necessarily confined in room. When acre has been added to acre till all the fertile land is occupied, the yearly increase of food must depend upon the melioration of the land already in possession. This is a fund, which, from the nature of all soils, instead of increasing, must be gradually diminishing. But population, could it be supplied with food, would go on with unexhausted vigour; and the increase of one period would furnish the power of a greater increase the next, and this without any limit. (Malthus 1890: 4 et seq.)

After all that has been said on the classical theories of rent and wages it is perhaps unnecessary to repeat the facts that, like those doctrines, have evoked Malthus' inquiry into the nature and causes of the *poverty* of nations (James Bonar).

Our analysis of classicism would, however, be incomplete if we did not glance briefly at its most important disciple: Karl Marx. Marx derived his theory of value from Ricardo as Ricardo had derived it from Smith. The only progress consisted in the fact that Smith saw the determining cause of exchange-value in the reward and quantity of labor, Ricardo only in the quantity of labor, and Marx lastly, being more exact, in the socially necessary quantity of labor. Even the Marxian theory of profits, the theory of surplus value, is only a conclusion from Ricardian premises: like all other commodities labor power has its value, and like all other values this has its measure and cause in the quantity of labor necessary to its production.

> But the past labor that is embodied in the labor power, and the living labor that it can call into action; the daily cost of maintaining it, and its daily

---

the doctrines of Ricardo and Malthus by Carey and of the doctrines of Carey by Mill proves how fruitless it is to form from local and temporary tendencies absolute dogmas, and how senseless to praise or reject them as "absolutely right" or "absolutely wrong."

expenditure in work, are two totally different things. . . . The fact that half a day's labor is necessary to keep the laborer alive during 24 hours does not in any way prevent him from working a whole day. . . . This difference of the two values was what the capitalist had in view when he was purchasing the labor power.

In the process of production then "the laborer during one portion of the labor process produces only the value of his labor power that is the value of his means of subsistence." When he has done so, he must continue to work; for he has sold the use-value of his power, not only its exchange-value. "During the second period of the labor process that in which his labor is no longer necessary labor, the workman, it is true, labors, expends labor power; but he creates no value for himself. He creates surplus-value," the visible token of exploitation, profits (Marx 1867: 159, 183 et seq.).

How closely this doctrine is connected with the kernel of classicism may be proved by a quotation from John Stuart Mill's *Principles*.

The cause of profit is, that labour produces more than is required for its support. . . . [T]he reason why capital yields a profit, is because food, clothing, materials, and tools, last longer than the time which was required to produce them; so that if a capitalist supplies a party of labourers with these things, on condition of receiving all they produce, they will, in addition to reproducing their own necessaries and instruments, have a portion of their time remaining, to work for the capitalist. . . . If the labourers of the country collectively produce twenty percent more than their wages, profits will be twenty percent. (1909: 416-17)

Marx's connection with classicism, however, is most clearly manifest in the fact that his theory encounters the same difficulties as that of Ricardo. If all capital were wage capital, variable capital as Marx calls it, or if at least the combination of constant and variable capital were equal in all branches of industry, the "organic composition of capital" uniform, his deduction of profits could be regarded as in harmony with reality. But if we start from the fact that there are industries with much machinery and little labor, and industries with little machinery and much labor, the theory of surplus value leads to an illogical consequence: for—as only the labor force is acknowledged as the source of surplus-value—the greater profit is made by that factory which applies little mechanical and much human power, in other words, that factory which is backward in development. Can this be maintained? Is the law that Marx formulated true: "The masses of value and surplus-value produced by different capitals . . . vary directly as the amount of the variable constituents of these capitals, that is as their constituents transformed into living labor power"? This cannot be maintained and was not maintained by Marx. He says with unsurpassable frankness: "This law clearly contradicts all experience based on appearance. Every one knows that a cotton spinner who, reckoning the percentage on the whole of his applied capital, employs much constant and little variable capital, does not, on account of this, pocket less profit or surplus-value than a baker who relatively sets in motion much variable and little constant capital" (Marx 1867: 285).

How can this contradiction be resolved? Ricardo in a similar situation had resorted to the assumption that the proportion of fixed and circulating capital, that is, of machinery and wages, capital was everywhere the same. But what was still possible in 1817 was no longer possible in 1867. Reality showed unmistakably that the organic composition of capital was totally different in different branches of industry.

In view of this fact Marx attempts a different solution. He conceives the idea that the whole surplus-value of a national economy, gathering from the various sources, flows into a great pool from which it is uniformly divided out to the individual capitalists so that an equal average rate of profit arises. "Since the capitals invested in the various lines of production are of a different organic composition," he says in the third volume of *Das Kapital* (Marx 1894: 136), "the rates of profit prevailing in the various lines of production are originally very different. These different rates of profit are equalized by means of competition into a general rate of profit which is the average of all these special rates of profit." Hence, it follows that what is decisive for the exchange relations is not value and surplus-value but costs and average profit—in other words, some commodities exchange over and some under their value as determined by labor time, or, value and price do not coincide.

> The prices which arise by drawing the average of the various rates of profit in the different spheres of production and adding this average to the cost-prices of the different spheres of production, are the prices of production. . . . The price of production of a commodity, then, is equal to its cost-price

plus a percentage of profit apportioned according to the average rate of profit, or, in other words, equal to its cost-price plus the average profit. (135 et seq.)

Value shrinks in this way to an altogether meaningless category. The labor theory of value is in fact abandoned and replaced by a theory of the cost of production.

That this argumentation does not save the theory of exploitation (because the equalization of profits according to Marx's description does not occur within the capitalist class but takes place in the market so that all consumers participate in it) was shown by Heimann in his ingenious book *Mehrwert und Gemeinwirtschaft* (1922). Here we are interested not in the logical but in the historical aspect of the doctrine: the contradiction between the first volume of *Das Kapital* with its labor theory of value and the third volume, which builds on a theory of the costs of production, shows impressively how facts assert themselves against theories, or rather how new facts assert themselves against antiquated theories, whether man wishes it or not.   The Marxian doctrine of surplus-value was a strictly logical development of the Smithian doctrine of value. But although the logical connection between the two dogmas is unassailable Smith was right and Marx—as far as the contents of the first volume of his great work are concerned—wrong. For in Smith's time capital was still in fixed proportion to the labor power applied; in Marx's time, however, this was no longer the case—and thus the basis on which the labor theory of value had arisen was destroyed. The new economic reality governed by constant capital, the productivity of which became every day more obvious, forced Marx in spite of himself to change from the labor theory of value to a theory of the costs of production, to acknowledge as the determining cause of price instead of the quantity of labor costs and average profits.

It is not, however, as a disciple of classicism but as a master of historicism that Marx finds his place in the history of political economy. In his work it is most clearly manifest that the one doctrine belonged to the past, the other to the future, although the two are nowhere more intimately connected than here.

The essence of historicism, which would more aptly be termed the sociological and descriptive school,[17] can best be recognized if it is viewed against the background of late classicism in opposition to which it arose. To Nassau Senior political economy was a purely deductive science.. "[T]he general facts on which the Science of Political Economy rests," he said in his *Outline* (1939: 26), "are comprised in a few general Propositions," and he regards the sentence "[t]hat every man desires to obtain additional Wealth with as little sacrifice as possible" as the first and foremost postulate. This assumption, he declares, "is in Political Economy what gravitation is in Physics: . . . the ultimate fact beyond which reasoning cannot go, and of which almost every other proposition is merely an illustration." Self-interest, however, was conceived at that time as an instinct of nature that governed all men alike, and hence it followed cogently that all the laws that are logically deduced from its operation can claim absolute validity. This conception, which narrowed political economy down to a "natural science of egotism" (Hildebrand), was fought by Sismondi, Roscher, Comte, and Knies. Against the universality and perpetualism of the old school they set the assertion that all knowledge is limited by space and time.

Already external circumstances make it clear that classicism and historicism have sprung from totally different conditions of life, for Senior's doctrine remained dominant in England,[18] while Roscher's doctrine became prevalent in Germany. These two countries stood at the time in marked contrast which was perhaps most strikingly manifest in ethics. A thesis like that of Mandeville—*Private Vices Public Benefits*—could be successful only in England where puritanism had filled life with the spirit of Calvin, that is, the spirit of a creed

---

17. It must be emphasized that the epoch-making element in the thought of Sismondi, List, Comte, and Marx is the discovery of evolution, but that the positive teaching of this school centered round society and sociology rather than history, that it aimed at an inductive comprehension of the present rather than at the investigation of the past. The Schmoller who studied the guilds of Strassburg is of little interest to the historian of political economy; but the Schmoller who conceived economics as a sociological discipline (cf. his *Grundriss*) deserves this interest—however the present time may think of the character and scope of economic science.

18. The apostles of historicism in England, Cliffe Leslie and John Ingram, were—Irishmen. This is certainly no mere chance!

that made secular success the sign of eternal salvation—even if it took the form of gain drawn from the slave trade. In Germany, however, the morals of altruism remained dominant whether it appeared in a Catholic or a Lutheran guise—the observation that consistent pursuit of self-interest fosters the public weal, or is at least capable of doing so, had not yet been made in that country.

Adam Müller explained the contrast between England and Germany by the fact that the insular economy was governed by trade and industry, while on the continent agriculture prevailed. This statement contains a good deal of truth but the argument must be given a historical turn to fully interpret the facts. England was by that time thoroughly capitalistic. The striving for gain was the mainspring of economic life, and so it seemed only correct to deduce the economic theory from its operation. Germany, however, was still deeply entangled in feudalism. *Quiota non movere* was the principle that was followed here. While the capitalistic (i.e., rationalistic) man pursues the aim of the highest material welfare even if he has constantly to revolutionize his life, the feudal (i.e., traditionalistic) man shuns all change even if he has to purchase the ideal of constancy by a sacrifice in his well-being. If Lionel Robbins's definition of political economy is correct—"Economics is the science which studies *human behaviour* as a relationship between ends and scarce means" (Robbins 1937: 16 [emphasis added])—it is clear that the two different types of man necessarily created two different types of science.

To give only one illustration of the great contrast between the environment of Nassau Senior and that of Wilhelm Roscher it may be recalled that the English agriculture of 1840 was carried on by capitalistic farmers, and the German by unfree serfs. And the German peasant was not only bound to numerous feudal dues, which made the free pursuit of his self-interest impossible, but he stood also in a sentimental relation to his inherited soil and he inherited methods, which a deep awe prevented him from giving up, however much material considerations might advocate such action. Is it then surprising that the economists of a country, two-thirds of whose inhabitants were engaged in agriculture (Sombart 1928: 627), in a feudal and traditionalistic agriculture, were not willing to accept a theory that started from the free operation of self-interest? "The light weight which would suffice to turn the scale with a calculating people," says Sismondi (1819, 1: 433), "does not suffice if it has become rusty by prejudices and long habits." And tradition must be acknowledged beside the pursuit of gain as an active factor: "Habits are a moral force which is not subject to calculation, and the writers of Political Economy have too often forgotten that they have to do with men and not machines" (312).

The German economic theoreticians of 1840 could not acknowledge the English science as correct, deduced as it was from the principle of self-interest, simply because this principle did not then prevail in their country. Thus nothing was more natural than the postulate that first by an investigation and clarification of the special character of the individual national economies the foundation should be created, on which the science had to build. "Our aim is the description of what the peoples have thought, willed, and felt with regard to economic life, what they have intended and achieved, why they have intended and achieved it," said Roscher (cited in Mombert 1927: 466 et seq.), and this aim of realistic description involved not only the transition from the isolating and abstract to the inductive and synthetic conception but still more the extension of the narrowly limited catallactics to a comprehensive science of culture. "Economics is today only a science insofar as it expands into a sociology" Schmoller proclaimed (cited in Brinkmann 1937: 126). "Its observations must be investigations into the social forms of economic life."

This economic concept, based on induction and comparison, contained from the outset the historical element. It is the perception that the contrast of economic life between the countries were due not only to geography but also to different phases of development. "The country that is more developed industrially," says Karl Marx in *Das Kapital* (1867: ix), "only shows, to the less developed, the image of its own future." Friedrich List's *Nationales System der Politischen Oekonomie* rests entirely on this idea. But it was a deeper experience that made the sociological the sociohistorical school: the experience of the dynamic process of the formation of classes, which evolved before the eyes of this generation.

The eighteenth century had been of the belief that the establishment of perfect liberty in economic life would carry with it an ideal order of society, an order of perfect equality in which everybody provided with his own labor tools would have the chance of drawing, by higher achievements for the community, higher rewards from the community. But this "democracy of petty producers" (Heimann) had to give way before the dictatorship of the great industrialists. It was possible only as long as small-scale production prevailed in which labor was dominant. It became impossible as soon as large-scale production in which capital dictated, had conquered the field. In the place of a thousand weavers who in 1770 labored with their own implements in their cottages stood by 1830 the factory. The bourgeoisie was split into capitalists and proletarians, and to the ascendancy of the few was opposed the fall of the many. "Instead of the expected equality of the classes," Lorenz von Stein lamented (cited in Spann 1932: 151), "competition has evoked an ever increasing inequality between them!" Obviously the victory of the new age was not the breakthrough of a timeless reason, but only the beginning of a new period. Into the place of the old estates stepped the new classes—into the place of the old struggles stepped new conflicts. The dream of the *ordre naturel* with its unchangeable harmony was frustrated by the reality of the *ordre positif* with its dynamic contrast. To no generation was it more impressively demonstrated that there is no standing still in this world. "Change is the only thing eternal," wrote Heinrich Heine, filled with the sentiment of his time, "nothing constant, only death."

Thus, the great industrial revolution that destroyed not only a social system but also a social ideal explains the predominance of the idea of evolution in the first half of the nineteenth century. And it explains not only the historical but also the ethical thesis of the new school. The ideal order—it was now clear—would not develop spontaneously but would have to be consciously created. It is not a law of nature but a task of man. The socialism of the revolutionaries and the social policy of the conservatives have their roots here.[19] "We persist in the belief," says Sismondi (1819, 2: 4), "that Political Economy should be the investigation and application of the great law of

---

19. Especially interesting is the attitude of the liberals in the camp of historicism. They, too, believed that the ideal order is still to be created, not however by the destruction or transformation of capitalism, but by the consistent realization of its principles, the principles of free exchange economy, which, as they believed, were not yet fully in operation (because of such facts as the continued existence of the monopoly of the soil). Cf. for example Lujo Brentano's original theory of trade unionism: Stark, *Sozialpolitik*, 1936: 47 et seq.

benevolence and charity which God has given to the human societies."
He does not, however, preach passivity but active interference: "The
true problem for the statesman is to find that combination and
proportion of population and riches (of labor and capital) which will
guarantee the greatest happiness to the human race on a given
territory" (1819, 1: v et seq.). Instead of liberalism, social reform is
now the dominant principle of economic policy.

The preponderance of the sociological and descriptive tendency that
adopted this interventionism was, however, only of short duration.
Even in Central Europe it lasted hardly for a generation. The reason
was that the conditions that had given birth to it and on which it rested
were swept away in a few decades by rapid development. In Prussia
the spirit of the east-Elbian Junkers might continue to dominate;
Austria was by 1870 already fully industrialized and thus an economic
science germane to the English could arise there. By this time,
moreover, Western Europe had overcome the shock that had been
caused by the breakdown of the ideal of harmony in the age of the
industrial revolution, and so here too the way was prepared for a new
Political Economy as the "Mechanics of Self-interest" (Jevons 1931:
xvii et seq.).

The new classicism that now developed could not, however, start
like the old, from the picture of a society in which every man, with
his labor had to contend in freedom and equality for his share in
production in the struggle of competition. Freedom and equality of
the producers had been destroyed by the splitting of the third estate
into antagonistic classes. Not, however, freedom and equality of the
consumers. The endeavor to reach the greatest possible effect with the
given means could now fully develop only on the market of the
consumers' goods and thus it was this aspect of economic life that was
chosen as the starting point for economic theory.

To Carl Menger national economy was an agglomeration of
individuals competing for scarce commodities. About the origins of
human economy, he writes (1934: 59):

> The endeavor of the individual members of a society to command to the
> exclusion of all the other members the right quantities of goods, has . . . its
> origin in the fact, that the quantity of certain goods at the disposal of society
> is smaller than the demand, and that therefore, as under such conditions the
> complete satisfaction of the demand of all individuals is impossible, each

individual has the incentive to provide for his demand by the exclusion of all the other economic subjects. But in view of the competition of all members of society for a quantity of goods which under no circumstances suffices completely to satisfy all needs of the individuals . . . a practical solution of the conflict of interests here obtaining is conceivable only by delivering the individual partial quantities of the entire quantity at the disposal of society into the possession of individual economic subjects and protecting the latter in their possession by society, simultaneously excluding all the other economic subjects.

This passage is very illuminating. It exposes the fundamental idea of the utility theory of value as well as its historical roots. The fundamental idea consists in basing the theory of value and price on the individual man and the individual psyche. "Menger," Wieser once said (1924: 120), "sees . . . in all social formations of economic life nothing more than unintended social resultants of teleological endeavors of individuals." This is true.[20] "He who wishes to understand theoretically the phenomena of national economy . . . must go back . . . to its true elements, the single economies in the nation," says Menger (1933: 87), "and try to fathom the laws according to which the former arise from the latter." For the national economy is only a *Complication von Singularwirtschaften* [collection of individual economies]. In the same sense Jevons writes, "Economics must be founded upon a full and accurate investigation of the conditions of utility; and, to understand this element, we must necessarily examine the wants and desires of man," that is, of the isolated individual (Jevons 1931: 39). Hence, the endeavor to view man first of all outside the bonds of society, to choose the individual not as a social but as a natural being for the starting point of economic theory. "The needs spring from our instincts, and these have their roots in our nature," says Menger (1934: 32), and he exemplifies his doctrine by the "inhabitant of a primeval forest," by an "individual cast ashore on a desert island," and by an "economic subject living in isolation which inhabits a rocky island in the sea" (82, 95, 100). In short he tries to deduce the laws of the social occurrences in the market from the laws of the presocial psyche of the individual. "The value of goods," we

---

20. Cf. especially Menger's *Untersuchungen über die Methode der Sozialwissenschaften*, 1883: 182 et seq.

read in the *Grundsätze* (80), "is . . . independent . . . of the existence of society." And it becomes a social category simply by the fact that every nation is but "an aggregate of individuals" (Jevons 1931: 15). "[I]n reality, it is a law operating in the case of multitudes of individuals which gives rise to the aggregate represented in the transactions of a nation" (Menger 1934: 80).

These laws of the presocial psyche of the individual, and, indeed, their importance for economic theory were by no means unknown to the age of the classicists.[21] Still the classical doctrine remained social. What gave birth to the atomistic conception of society as the consequence of which the attempt to advance from individual psychology to market analysis must be understood?[22]

It is easy to find the answer to this question. Never was society

---

21. Hobbes had already said in *Leviathan* (cited in Boucke 1921: 43 et seq.): "The value of all things contracted for, is measured by the appetite of the contractors"—as pure subjectivism as can be conceived. And F. W. Lloyd as early as 1834 combined subjectivism and the marginal principle. Value, we read in his *Lecture on the Notion of Value* (Lloyd 1837: 16), "in its ultimate sense undoubtedly signifies a feeling of the mind which shows itself always at the margin of separation between satisfied and unsatisfied wants."

22. The only attempt hitherto undertaken historically to interpret the theory of marginal utility was made by Bukharin; he describes it, as the title of his book suggests, as the *Economic Theory of the Leisure Class*. His argumentation is roughly this: in the course of evolution the bourgeoisie become more and more a class of people living on their money rents. "As a result of the development of the various forms of credit, the accumulated surplus flows into the pockets of persons having no relation whatever to production; the number of these persons is constantly increasing and constitutes a whole class of society—that of the rentier" (1927: 24). These men are interested exclusively in consumption. "The psychology of the *consumer* is characteristic of the rentier" (27), hence the doctrine of the Austrians, especially the basing of the doctrine of value and price on the idea of use-value. "[W]e here find . . . a consistent carrying out of the point of view of consumption. . . . It was the international *rentier* who found his learned spokesman in Böhm-Bawerk" (29, 34). Bukharin finally sums up his deductions in the following words (31): "We consider the Austrian theory as the ideology of the bourgeois who has already been eliminated from the process of production." Apart from all other considerations this interpretation is untenable if only for the one reason that the time of the origin of the marginal utility doctrine, the years 1854-74, mark the climax of capitalistic development, in which the bourgeois conceived and felt himself as an entrepreneur and not as a rentier!

nearer to the state of perfect competition than in the years in which the utility theory of value arose—never, in fact, was it more a sum of independent individuals. There were as yet few protective tariffs for the peasants, few cartels for the entrepreneurs, and few trade unions for the workmen. All these limitations of the freedom of economic life developed only after 1871—this year, however, marks in economy and science the climax in the evolution of individualism. Even Menger only brought reality into words when he described the essence of the economic system as "the competition of all members of society for scarce quantities of goods" and moved "the individuals who endeavour completely to satisfy their needs" into the center of theory.

This causal concatenation between atomistic market system and atomistic market theory is no less strikingly apparent in Walras's works both externally and internally: externally, because the will to prove "that free competition procures the maximum of utility" (1936: 466), was the starting point and end of his theoretical endeavors; and internally, because his whole system is nothing but an exact description of an ideal market with unhampered competition in the state of equilibrium.[23] Walras, too, conceives national economy as a system of competing individuals who aim at realizing the greatest possible satisfaction of their needs.

> The world may be considered as a vast general market composed of different special markets where social riches are bought and sold, and we should recognize the laws according to which this buying and selling tends spontaneously to take place. For this purpose we suppose always a market perfectly organized with regard to competition, as in pure mechanics machines without friction are supposed. (1938: 57)

Vienna and Lausanne have the same reality in view: an equilibrium system of man-atoms who strive after the maximum realization of pleasure (cf. Edgeworth, *Mathematical Psychics*, 1881, part 1). The only difference is that in Vienna the man-atom, in Lausanne the

---

23. Even the decisive idea of the doctrine of Walras and Pareto was known to the classicists, as Bousquet (1927: 62) has rightly emphasized: "The whole of the advantages and disadvantages of the different employments of labor and stock," says Smith (1904, 1: 100 [1976b: 116]), "must, in the same neighbourhood be either perfectly equal or continually tending to equality."

equilibrium system, was made the pivot of the theory. The historical background is in both cases the struggle of all against all, as it had been realized through the principle of competition then at the height of its power.

This doctrine of Menger, Jevons, and Walras is today the dominant dogma, although the discussion of the problems of imperfect competition and economic planning has recently made it manifest that even in the present day, economy and science grapple with the same problems. Edgeworth's and Pareto's disciples consider the theory of marginal utility and equilibrium as a piece of eternal truth, which mankind may regard as its secure possession just as Ricardo's disciples had regarded classicism and Schmoller's disciples historicism. But even this new doctrine is only the expression of a transient epoch in the change of history,[24] yesterday not yet dreamed of, today in full splendor, tomorrow abandoned and forgotten. Alfred Marshall, humanly perhaps the greatest in this circle, knew this: "Though economic analysis and general reasoning are of wide application," he states (1936: 37), "yet every age and country has its own problems; and every change in social conditions is likely to require a new development of economic doctrines." And Keynes says: "Economists

---

24. In his introduction to the *Collected Works of Carl Menger* (Menger 1934) F. A. Von Hayek says (xi): "Wieser reports that Menger once told him that it was one of his duties to write surveys of the state of the markets for an official newspaper, the Wiener Zeitung, and that it was in studying the market reports that he was struck by the glaring contrast between the traditional theories of price and the facts which experienced practical men considered as decisive for the determination of prices." Today the study of the market reports must arouse similar impressions: the leading international markets for raw materials—rubber and tin may serve as representative examples—show no price formation in the sense of Menger and Böhm-Bawerk, in other words, no price formation by the cooperation of subjective valuations of isolated and competing individual sellers and buyers. But rather price formation is through sellers' cartels and by the regulation of supplies according to the total demand; in other words, it is determined by the relation of objective quantities—of social demands and social supplies conceived as units. Thus, a new reality is given which demands a fundamentally new theory and will bring it forth. If J. R. Hicks says: "It has to be recognized that a general abandonment of the assumption of perfect competition . . . must have very destructive consequences for economic theory" (Hicks 1939: 83), he only shows that any orthodoxy must one day come into conflict with facts and succumb.

. . . write always sub specie temporis, and achieve immortality by accident, if at all" (1933: 212).

The awareness that we are not capable of unveiling eternal truths may well give a somber coloring to our work. But to be ephemeral is the destiny of all that is human, and we must reckon with this fact. It is not given to us to bid the stars stand still, as did Joshua over the vale of Aijalon. We must strive each day anew to win truth as we strive to win our bread, and in this task too science and learning are but the mirror of life.

References

Adler, Max. 1921. *Marx als Denker.* 2d ed. Vienna: Wiener Volks Buchlandlung.

Albrecht, Gerhard. 1925. *Zeitschrift fuer Sozialwissenschaft.* Jena, Germany: G. Fischer.

Anderson, James. 1777. *Inquiry into the Nature of the Corn Laws.* Edinburgh: Mundell.

———. 1779. *Observations on the National Industry of Scotland.* Edinburgh: Mundell.

Ashley, William James. 1888. *An Introduction to English Economic History and Theory.* London: Longmans & Company.

Bagehot, Walter. 1880. *Economic Studies.* Edited by Richard Holt Hutton, London: Longmans, Green & Company.

Barthélemy, Edouard. 1876. *Etude sur Jean Bodin.* Paris: Sandoz & Fishbacker.

Bastiat, Claude Frederic. 1851 [1850]. *Les Harmonies Economiques.* 2d ed. Paris: Guillaumin.

Baudrillart, Henri. 1853. *Bodin et son temps.* Paris: Guillaumin.

Belloni, Gerolamo. 1752. *A Dissertation on Commerce.* London: R. Manly.

Bentham, Jeremy. 1789. *Introduction to the Principles of Morals and Legislation.* London: T. Payne.

———. 1793. Manual of Political Economy. In *Jeremy Bentham's Economic Writings,* vol. 1, edited by Werner Stark. London: George Allen & Unwin, 1952.

Bidermann, Hermann. 1870. *Ueber das Merkantilsystem.* Innsbruck: Wagner.

Blanqui, Jérôme-Adolphe. 1837-38. *Histoire de l'Economie Politique en Europe.* Paris: Guillaumin.

Bodin, Jean. 1568. *Réponse à M. de Malestroit touchant le fait des monnaies et l'enchérissement de toutes choses.* Paris.

———. 1593 [1576]. *Les Six livres de la République,* Paris: Libraire lure, a la Samaritane.

Boisguillebert, Pierre le Pesent. 1697. *Le Detail de la France.* Querard, France.

Boucke, Fred Oswald. 1921. *The Development of Economics 1750-1900.* New York: The Macmillan Company.

———. 1922. *A Critique of Economics, Doctrinal and Methodological.* New York: The Macmillan Company.

———. 1925. *Principles of Economics.* New York: The Macmillan Company.

Bouglé, C. 1932. L'Historien Des Doctrines. *Revue d'Economie Politique* 46:1719-24.

Bousquet, G. H. 1926. Un Grand Économiste Italien Francesco Ferrara. *Revue d'histoire économique et sociale* 14:344-77.

———. 1927. *Essai sur l'Evolution de la Pensée Economique.* Paris: Marcel Giard.

———. 1928a. *Cours d'économie pure.* Paris: Libraire Des Sciences Politiques and Social.

279

————. 1928b. *Vilfredo Pareto, sa vie et son oeuvre*. Paris: Payot.

Brentano, Franz. 1874. *Psychologie vom empirischen Standpunkt*. Leipzig: Duncker and Humblot.

Brinkmann, Carl. 1937. *Gustav Schmoller und die Volkswirtschaftslehre*. Stuttgart: Kohlhammer.

Buchan, John. 1934. *Oliver Cromwell*. London: Hodder & Stoughton.

Bücher, Karl. 1922. *Beiträge zur Wirtschaftsgeschichte*. Tubingen, Germany: Laupp.

Bukharin, Nikolai. 1927. *The Economic Theory of the Leisure Class*. New York: International Publishers.

Cairnes, John Elliott. 1875 [1857]. *The Character and Logical Method of Political Economy*. 2d ed. London: Macmillan.

Cannon, Edwin. 1917 [1893]. *A History of the Theories of Production and Distribution in English Political Economy from 1776 to 1848*. London: Percival & Co.

Cantillon, Richard. 1931 [1755]. *Essai sur la Nature du Commerce en General*. Edited with an English translation by Henry Higgs. London: Macmillan.

Carey, Henry Charles. 1837. *Principles of Political Economy*. Philadelphia: Carey, Lea & Blanchard.

————. 1848. *The Past, the Present and the Future*. Philadelphia: Carey & Hart; London: Longmans, Brown, and Longmans.

————. 1852. *The Harmony of Interests, Agricultural, Manufacturing and Commercial*. 2d ed. New York: M. Finch.

Clapham, John H. 1926. *An Economic History of Modern Britain*. Cambridge: Cambridge University Press.

Cohen, Hermann. 1871. *Kants Theorie der Erfahrung*. Berlin: Dummler.

Comte, Auguste. 1875-77. *System of Positive Polity, Social Dynamics*. Edited by Edward Spencer Beesly. London: Longmans, Green and Co.

Condillac, Etienne Bonnot de. 1776. *Le Commerce et le Gouvernment*. Paris: Jombert & Cellot.

Condorcet, Marquis de. 1795. *Esquisse d'un tableau historique des progrès de l'esprit humain*. Paris: Agasse.

Cossa, Luigi. 1875. *Primi elementi di economia politica*. Milan: Hoepli.

————. 1878. *Saggi di economia politica*. Milan.

————. 1880. *Guide to the Study of Political Economy*. London: Macmillan.

————. 1893. *An Introduction to the Study of Political Economy*. Translated by Louis Dyer. London: Macmillan and Co.

Cunningham, William. 1917. *The Growth of English Industry*. Cambridge: Cambridge University Press.

Dandé-Bauell, A. 1932. Charles Gide. L'Homme: Sa Vie, Sa Personnalité. *Revue d'Economie Politique* 46: 1681-89.

Dühring, Eugen. 1865. *Natürliche Dialektik*. Berlin: Vergriften.

————. 1866. *Kritische Grundlegung der Volkswirtschaftslehre*. Berlin: Eichhoff.

————. 1869. *Kritische Geschichte der Philosophie*. Leipzig: O.R. Reisland.

————. 1873a. *Kritische Geschichte der allgemeinen Principien der Mechanik*. Leipzig: O.R. Reisland.

————. 1873b. *Cursus der National-und Sozialökonomie*. Berlin: T. Grieben.

————. 1875. *Kursus der Philosophie als streng wissenschaftlicher Weltanschauung*. Leipzig: E. Koschny.

————. 1894a. *Wirklichkeitsphilosophie*. Leipzig: O.R. Reisland.

————. 1894b. *Der Werth des Lebens*. Leipzig: O.R. Reisland.

————. 1897. *Der Ersatz der Religion durch Vollkommeneres*. Berlin: E. Keil.

————. 1900 [1871]. *Kritische Geschichte der Nationalökonomie und des Sozialismus*. Leipzig: Druck und Verlag Von C. G. Naumann.

Edgeworth, Francis Y. 1881. *Mathematical Psychics*. London: C. Kegan Paul & Co.

Eisenhart, Hugo. 1843. *Philosophie des Staats oder Allgemeine Socialtheorie*. Leipzig: F. A. Brockhaus.

————. 1844. *Positives System der Volkswirtschaft*. Leipzig: F. A. Brockhaus.

————. 1856. *Die gegenwaertige Staatenwelt in ihrer natuerlichen Gliederung*. Leipzig: F. Fleischer.

————. 1881. *Geschichte der Nationaloekonomik*, Jena, Germany: Berlag von Gustav Fischer.

Ely, Richard. 1891. *Introduction to the Study of Political Economy*. New York: Chautauqua Press.

————. 1938. *Ground Under Our Feet*. New York: Macmillan.

Espinas, Alfred. 1877. *Des Sociétés Animales*. Paris: G. Baillière.

————. 1891. *Histoire des Doctrines Economiques*. Paris: Armand Colin et Cie.

————. 1898. *La Philosophie Sociale du XVIIIe siècle et la révolution*. Paris: F. Alcan.

————. 1901. Etre ou ne pas etre, ou du Postulat de la Sociologie. *Revue philosophique de la rance et de L'Étranger*. 51:449-80.

————. 1925. *Études su l'Histoire de la philosophie de l'Action; Descartes et la morale*. Paris: Éditions Bossard.

Fechner, Gustav Theodor. 1860. *Elemente der Psycho-Physik*. Leipzig: Breitkopt und Hartel.

Fenelon, François. 1699. *Telemaque*. Edited by Didot.

Ferrara, Franscesco. 1889-91. *Esame storico-critico di economisti e dottrine economiche del secolo XVIII e prima meta del XIX*. Turin, Italy.

————.1938. *Oeuvres économiques choisies*. Edited by G. H. Bousquet and J. Crisafulli. Paris: Riviére.

Gide, Charles. 1884. *Principles D'Économie Politique*. Paris: Larose et Forcel. 26th ed. 1931.

————. 1909. *Cours D'Économie Politique*. Paris: Larose et Forcel.

Gide, Charles, and Rist, Charles. 1909. *Histoire des Doctrines Economiques depuis les Physiocrates*. Paris: Librairie de la Societe du Recueil Sirey.

Gonnard, René. 1898. *La Dépopulation en France*. Lyon, France: Storck.

————. 1904a. Les Idées Economiques d'Aristophane. *Revue d'Economie Politique* 14:53-67.

————. 1904b. Un Précurseur de Malthus, Giammaria Ortes. *Revue d'Economie Politique* 14:638-66.

————. 1907. *L'Emigration Européenne au 19e siècle*. Paris: A. Colin.

————. 1908. *La Hongrie au 20e siècle*. Paris: A. Colin.

————. 1911. *Entre Drave et Save*. Paris: L. Larose et L. Tenin.

————. 1923a. *Histoire des Doctrines de la Population*. Paris: Nouvelle Libraire National.

————. 1923b. Stuart Mill et Sa Théorie de L'État Stationnaire. *Questions Pratiques*: 12-20.

————. 1927a. *Essai sur l'Histoire de l'Emigration*. Paris: Libraire Valois.

————. 1927b. Les Progrès de la Pologne. *Revue Economique Internationale*.

————. 1930 [1921-22]. *Histoire des Doctrines Economiques*. Paris: Libraire Valois.

————. 1935-36. *Histoire des Doctrines Monétaires dans ses Rapports avec l'Histoire des Monnaies*. Paris: Librairie du Recueil Sirey.

Graslin, Jean Joseph Louis. 1767. *Essai analytique sur la richesse et sur l'impôt, où l'on refute la nouvelle doctrine économique*. Paris: Londres.

Haney, Lewis H. 1908-10. *A Congressional History of Railways in the United States*. Madison, Wis: Democrat Printing Company.

————. 1913. *Business Organization and Combination*. New York: Macmillan.

————. 1914. The Social Point of View in Economics. *The Quarterly Journal of Economics* 28:115-39; 292-321.

————. 1931. *Business Forecasting*. Boston and New York: Ginn and Company.

————. 1936 [1911] *History of Economic Thought*. 3d ed. New York: The Macmillan Company.

Hartley, David. 1748. *Observations on Man*. London and Bath: J. Leake and W. Frederick.

Heckscher, Eli Filip. 1935. *Mercantilism*. Translated by Mendal Shapiro. London: G. Allen & Unwin.

Held, Adolf. 1866. *Carey's Sozialwissenschaft und Merkantil-system*. Würzburg: F.E. Thein.

Heimann, Eduard. 1922. *Mehrwert und Gemeinwirtschaft*. Berlin: H.R. Engelmann.

Hermann, F. B. W. 1832. *Staatswirthschaftliche Untersuchungen*. Munchen: A. Weber.

Hicks, John R. 1939. *Value and Capital*. London: Oxford University Press.

Hornigk, Philipp Wilhelm von. 1708 [1684]. *Oesterreich über alles, wann es nur will*. Regenspurg: J.Z. Seidel.

Ingram, John Kells. 1878. *The Present Position and Prospects of Political Economy*. London: Longmans.

————. 1900. *Outlines of the History of Religion*. London: A. & C. Black.

————. 1904. *Practical Morals; A Treatise on Universal Education*. London: A. & C. Black.

————. 1915 [1888]. *History of Political Economy*. Edinburgh: A. & C. Black.

Izoulet, Jean. 1895. *La Cité moderne: metaphysique de la sociologie*. Paris: F. Alcan.

Jevons, William Stanley. 1931. *The Theory of Political Economy*. London: Macmillan.

Kautz, Julius. 1860. *Die Geschichtliche Entwickelung der National-Oekonomie und ihrer Literatur*. Vienna: C. Gerold.

Keynes, John Maynard. 1933. *Essays in Biography*. London: Macmillan.

Knies, Karl Gustav Adolf. 1853. *Die Politische Oekonomie vom Standpunkt der geschichtlichen Methode*. Braunschweig: Schwetschke.

Lassalle, Ferdinand. 1874. *Arbeiterprogram*. Berlin: C. Thringmachf.

Laskine, Edmond. 1920. *Le socialisme suivant les peuples*. Paris: E. Flammarion.

Lauderdale, James Maitland. 1804. *An Inquiry into the Nature and Origin of Public Wealth*. Edinburgh: Archibald Constable Company.

Lemberger, J. 1923. Review of *A Critique of Economics* by O. Fred Boucke. *The Economic Journal*. 33:556-58.

Leslie, T. E. Cliffe. 1969 [1888]. *Essays in Political Economy*. 2d ed. New York: Augustus M. Kelley.

List, Friedrich. 1841. *Das Nationales System der Politischen Oekonomie*. Stuttgart and Tübingen, Germany: J. G. Cotta.

Lloyd, William Foster. 1837. *Lecture on the Notion of Value*. London: Roake and Varty.

Longe, Francis D. 1866. *A Refutation on the Wage-Fund Theory of Modern Political Economy as Enunciated by Mr. Mill, M.P. and Mr. Fawcett*, M.P. London: Longmans, Green.

Malthus, Thomas Robert. 1890 [1803]. *Essay on Population*. 2d ed. London: J.M. Dent & Sons.

Marshall, Alfred. 1936 [1890]. *Principles of Economics*. 8th ed. London: Macmillan.

Karl Marx. 1847. *Misère de la Philosophie*. Paris: A. Frank.

————. 1867. *Das Kapital, Volume I*. Humburg: O. Meissner.

————. 1894. *Das Kapital, Volume III*. Humburg: O. Meissner.

————. 1904. *Theorien ueber den Mehrwert*. Edited by Karl Kautsky. Berlin: J.H.W. Dietz.

Mastrofini, Marco. 1831. *Le Usure*. Roma: Vincenzo Poggiolo.

Melon, Jean François. 1736. *Essai Politique Sur le Commerce*. Amsterdam: Chez P. Changuion.

Menger, Carl. 1933 [1883]. *Untersuchungen über die Methode der Sozialwissenschaften*. Reprints of Scarce Works in Economics and Political Science, London School of Economics.

————. 1934 [1871]. *Grundsätze der Volkswirtschaftslehre*, Reprints of Scarce Works in Economics and Political Science, London School of Economics.

Le Mercier de la Rivière. 1846. *L'ordre naturel et essentiel des sociétés politiques*. In *Physiocrates*. Edited by Eugène Daire. Paris: Librairie de Guillaumin.

Meyer, Eduard. 1895. *Die wirtschaftliche Entwicklung des Altertums*. Frankfurt: Jena G. Fischer.

Mill, John Stuart. 1909 [1848]. *Principle of Political Economy*. Edited by William Ashley. London: Longmans, Green & Co.

Miyajima, Tsunao. 1934. *Souvenirs sur Charles Gide*. Paris: Librairie du Recueil.

Moeser, Justus. 1774. *Patriotische Phantasien*. Berlin: F. Nicolai.

Mombert, Paul. 1927. *Geschichte Der Nationalönonomie*. Jena, Germany: Verlag von Gustav Fischer.

Monchrétien, Antoyne. 1889 [1615]. *Traicté de l'oeconomie politique*. Edited by T. Funck-Brentano. Paris: M. Riviére.

Müller, Adam. 1936 [1808-9]. *Die Elemente der Staatskunst*. Edited by Hendel-Verlag. Berlin: Haude & Spenersche Verlagsbuchhandlung.

Oncken, August. 1902. *Geschichte der Nationalökonomie*. Leipzig: C.L. Hirschfeld.

Oresme, Nicole. 1360. *Tractatus de origine et natura, jure et mutationibus monetarum*.

Paley, William. 1785. *Principles of Moral and Political Philosophy*. London: R. Faulder.

Pareto, Vilfredo. 1896. *Cours d'économie politique*. Lausanne: Libraire de l'Université.

Petty, William. 1899. *The Economic Writings of Sir William Petty*. 2 vols. Edited by C. Hull. Cambridge: The University Press.

Quesnay, François. 1888. *Œuvres Économiques et Philosophiques*. Edited by Auguste Oncken. Francfort: J. Baer.

Rambaud, Joseph. 1895. *Éléments D'Économie Politique*. Paris: Larose.

———. 1902 [1899]. *Histoire des Doctrines Economiques*. Paris and Lyons: Librairie de la société du Recueil Général Des Lois et Des Arrês et du Journal du Palais.

———. 1910. *Cours d'Economie Politique*. Paris: L. Larose et L. Tenin.

Rentsch, Hermann. 1866. *Handwörterbuch der Volkswirtschaftslehre*. Leipzig: G. Mayer.

Ricardo, David. 1846. *The Works of David Ricardo*. Edited by John Ramsay McCulloch. London: J. Murray.

———. 1951 [1817]. *On the Principles of Political Economy and Taxation*. Edited by Piero Sraffa. Cambridge: Cambridge University Press.

———. 1952. *The Works and Correspondence of David Ricardo*. vol. 8. Edited by Piero Sraffa with the collaboration of M. H. Dobb. London: Cambridge University Press.

Rist, Charles. 1921. *Les Finances de guerre de l'Allegmagne*. Paris: Payot & Co.

———. 1938. *History of Monetary and Credit Theory from John Law to the Present Day*. London: Allen and Unwin.

Robbins, Lionel. 1937 [1932]. *An Essay on the Nature and Significance of Economic Science*. 2d ed. London: Macmillan.

Roll, Erich. 1930. *An Early Experiment in Industrial Organization*. London: Longman, Green & Co.

———. 1934. *About Money*. London: Faber and Faber.

———. 1937. *Elements of Economic Theory*. London: Oxford University Press.

———. 1938. *History of Economic Thought*. London: Faber and Faber.

Roscher, Wilhelm. 1843. *Grundriss zu Vorlesungen über die Staatswirthschaft nach geschichtlicher Methode*. Göttingen: Druck und Verlag der Dieterichschen Buchhandlung.

———. 1849. *Üer das Verhältnis der National-Oekonomik zum klassischen Alterthume*. In Roscher 1861.

———. 1851. *Zur Geschichte der englischen Volkswirthschaftslehre*. Leipzig: Weidmann.

————. 1854-94. *System der Volkswirtschaft*. Stuttgart: Cotta.

————. 1874. *Geschichte der NationalÖekonomik in Deutschland*. Munich: Oldenbourg.

————. 1878 [1861]. *Apsichten der Volkswirtschaft aus dem geschichtlichen Standpunke*. 3d ed. Leipzig and Heidelberg: Winter.

Salin, Edgar. 1921. *Platon und die griechische Utopie*. München und Leipzig: Duncker & Humbolt.

————. 1923. *Geschichte der Volkswirtschaftslehre*. Berlin: Julius Springer.

————. 1926. *Civitas Dei*. Tübingen, Germany: Mohr.

Say, Jean-Baptiste. 1817. *Petit volume contenant quelques apercus des hommes et de la société*. Paris: Chez Deterville.

————. 1840. *Cours complet d'economie politique pratique*. Paris: Guillaumin.

Schaffe, Albert. 1875. *Bau und Leben des socialen Koerpers*. Tübingen, Germany: H. Laupp.

Schmoller, Gustav von. 1884. Studien ueber die wirtschaftliche Politik Friedrichs des Grossen. In *Jarhbuch für Gesetzebung* vol. 8. Leipzig.

————. 1888. *Zur Litteraturgeschichte der Staats- und Sozialwissenschaften*. Leipzig: Dunker & Humblot.

————. 1900. *Grundriss der allgemeinen Volkswirtschaftslehre*. Munich and Leipzig: Duncker & Humblot.

Schriften, Vermischte. 1817. *Prolegomena einer Kunst-Philosophie*.

Schumpeter, Joseph. 1908. *Das Wesen und der Hauptinhalt der theoretischen Nationalökonomie*. Leipzig: Duncker & Humblot.

————. 1912. *Theorie der wirtschaftlichen Entwicklung*. Leipzig: Dunker & Humblot.

————. 1914. *Epochen der Dogmen - und Methodengeschichte*. Tübingen, Germany: J.C.B. Mohr.

————. 1939. *Business Cycles*. New York: McGraw-Hill.

Scott, William Amasa. 1903. *Money and Banking*. New York: H. Holt & Co.

————. 1933. *The Development of Economics*. New York: The Century Company.

Senior, Nassau. 1939 [1836]. *An Outline of the Science of Political Economy*. London: Allen & Unwin.

Sismondi, Jean Charles Leonard Simonde de. 1819. *Nouveaux Principes d'économie politique*. Paris: Delaunay.

Smith, Adam 1861 [1759] *The Theory of Moral Sentiments*. Edited by Dugald Stewart. London: H. G. Bohn.

————. 1896. *Lectures on Justice, Police, Revenue and Arms*. Edited by Edwin Cannan. Oxford: Oxford University Press.

————. 1904 [1776]. *An Inquiry into the Nature and Causes of the Wealth of Nations*. Edited by Edwin Cannan. New York: Modern Library.

————. 1976a [1759]. *The Theory of Moral Sentiments*. Edited by D. D. Raphael and A. L. Macfie. Oxford: Clarendon Press.

————. 1976b [1776]. *An Inquiry into the Nature and Causes of the Wealth of Nations*. Edited by R. H. Cambell and A.S. Skinner. Oxford: Clarendon Press.

Sombart, Werner. 1928 [1902]. *Der Moderne Kaitalismus*. 2d ed. Leipzig: Dunker & Humblot.

Spann, Otto. 1918. *Das Fundament der Volkswirtschaftslehre*. Jena, Germany: Derlag G. Fischer.

———. 1924. *Kategorienlehre*. Jena, Germany: Derlag G. Fischer.

———. 1928. *Der Schoepfungsgang des Geistes*. Jena, Germany: Derlag G. Fischer.

———. 1930. *Gesellschaftslehre*. 3d ed. Leipzig: Derlag Quelle & Mener.

———. 1931. *Der wahre Staat*. 3d ed. Jena, Germany: Derlag G. Fischer.

———. 1932 [1911]. *Die Haupttheorien der Volkswirtschaftslehre auf dogmengeschichtlicher Grundlage*. Leipzig: Quelle & Meyer.

Spinoza, Benedictus de. 1803. *Tractatus politicus*. In *Benedicti de Spinoza Opera qvae svpersvnt omia*. Edited by H. E. G. Paulus. Ienae: Bibliopolio Academico.

Stark, Werner. 1936. *Sozialpolitik*. Brunn-Prag-Leipzig-Wien: Verlag Rudolf M. Rohrer.

Steuart, James. 1805 [1767]. *An Inquiry into the Principles of Political Economy*. In *Works Political, Metaphysical and Chronological*. Edited by Sir James Steuart, Jr. London: T. Cadell and W. Davies.

Storch, Heinrich Friedrich von. 1823. *Cours d'économie politique*. Paris: J. P. Aillaud.

Suranyi-Unger, Theo. 1931. *Economics in the Twentieth Century*. London: George Allen & Unwin Ltd.

Tautscher, A. 1940. Der Begrunder der Volkswirtschaftslehre-ein Deutscher. *Schmollers Jahrbuch für Gesetzgebung*, Vol. 60.

Temple, Sir William. 1673. *An Essay Upon the Advancement of Trade in Ireland*. Dublin.

Thorton, William T. 1869. *On Labour*. London: Macmillan.

Thünen, Johann Heinrich von. 1863. *Der isolierte Staat in Bezziehung auf Landwirtschaft und Nationalökonomie*. Rostock, Germany: Leopold.

Tucker, Abraham. 1768. *The Light of Nature Persued*. London: T. Jones.

Turgot, Anne Robert Jacques. 1844. *Oeuvres de Turgot*. Edited by Eugéne Daire and Hyppolite Dussard. Paris: Guillaumin.

———. 1898 [1770]. *Reflections on the Formation and Distribution of Riches*. New York: Macmillan.

———. 1919. *Oeuvres de Turgot et Documents le Concernant*. Paris: Alcan.

Twiss, Travers. 1847. *View of the Progress of Political Economy in Europe*. London: Longmans, Brown, Green, and Longmans.

Ure, Andrew. 1861 [1835]. *Philosophy of Manufactures*. London: Charles Knight.

Veblen, Thorstein. 1899. *Theory of the Leisure Class*. New York: Macmillan.

———. 1914. *Instinct of Workmanship*. New York: B. W. Huebsch.

Verri, Pietro. 1771. *Meditazioni sull'Economia Politica*. In *Scrittori Classici Italiani di Economia Politica*. Edited by P. Custodi, vol. 15, 1804. Milano: Nella Stamperia e Fonderia di G. G. Destefanis.

Villeneuve-Bargemont, Albert de. 1841. *Histoire de l'économie politique*. Paris.

Walker, Karl. 1895 [1884]. *Geschichte der Nationaloekonomie*. 3d ed. Leipzig.

Walras, Léon. 1936 [1898]. *Etudes d'économie politique appliquée*. Lausanne: F. Rouge.

———. 1938. *Abrégé des Eléments d'économie politique pure*. Lausanne: F. Rouge.

Webb, Beatrice, and Webb, Sidney. 1922. *English Local Government*. London: Longmans & Co.

Weulerasse, Georges. 1910. *Le Mouvement Physiocratique en France*. Paris: Félix Alcan.

Wieser, Friedrich. 1889. *Der Natürliche Werth*. Vienna: Hölder.

———. 1924 [1914]. *Theorie der gesellschaftlichen Wirtschaft*, 2d ed. Tübingen, Germany: Mohr-Siebeck.

Wood, Henry Truemann. 1910. *Industrial England in the Eighteenth Century*. London: J. Murray.

Workman, H.B. 1929. *The History of Christianity in the Light of Modern Knowledge*. London and Glasgow: Blackie & Son..

Zola, Emile. 1880. *Le Roman Experimental*. Paris: G. Charpentier.

Index

289